This study examines the literary complexities of the poetry which Ovid wrote in Tomis, his place of exile on the coast of the Black Sea after he was banished from Rome by the emperor Augustus in A.D. 8 because of the alleged salaciousness of the *Ars Amatoria* and a mysterious misdemeanour which is nowhere explained. Exile transforms Ovid into a melancholic poet of despair who claims that his creative faculties are in terminal decline. But recent research has exposed the ironic disjunction between many of the poet's claims and the latent artistry which belies them. Through a series of close readings which offer a new analytical contribution to the scholarly evaluation of the exile poetry, this book examines the nature and the extent of Ovidian irony in Tomis and demonstrates the complex literary designs which are consistently disguised under a veil of dissimulation.

Gareth Williams aims to counteract traditional scholarly antipathy to the exile poetry, which could be said to represent the last frontier in modern Ovidian studies. Scholars working in the field will welcome his insights.

CAMBRIDGE CLASSICAL STUDIES

General editors
M. F. BURNYEAT, M. K. HOPKINS,
M. D. REEVE, A. M. SNODGRASS

BANISHED VOICES

BANISHED VOICES

Readings in Ovid's exile poetry

GARETH D. WILLIAMS

Assistant Professor of Classics, Columbia University, New York

CAMBRIDGE
UNIVERSITY PRESS

Published by the Press Syndicate of the University of Cambridge
The Pitt Building, Trumpington Street, Cambridge CB2 1RP
40 West 20th Street, New York, NY 10011-4211, USA
10 Stamford Road, Oakleigh, Melbourne 3166, Australia

© Faculty of Classics, University of Cambridge 1994

First published 1994

Printed in Great Britain at the University Press, Cambridge

A catalogue record for this book is available from the British Library

Library of Congress cataloguing in publication data

Williams, Gareth D.
Banished voices: readings in Ovid's exile poetry / Gareth D. Williams.
p.   cm. – (Cambridge Classical Studies)
Includes index.
ISBN 0 521 45136 1 (hardback)
1. Ovid, 43 B.C. – 17 or 18 A.D. – Criticism and interpretation.   2. Epistolary
poetry, Latin – History and criticism.   3. Elegiac poetry, Latin – History and
criticism.   4. Constanta (Romania) – In literature.   5. Romans – Romania –
Constanta.   6. Exiles in literature.   7. Rome – In literature.   I. Title.   II. Series.
PA6537.W53   1994
871'.01 – dc20 93-42189 CIP

ISBN 0 521 45136 1 hardback

CONTENTS

Contents

PREFACE

This study, a revised version of a Cambridge doctoral thesis submitted in early 1990, owes many debts. Jim McKeown and Michael Reeve patiently monitored my researches, John Henderson and Robin Nisbet supplied many helpful suggestions in judging the outcome; I am indebted to Eric Handley and Stephen Hinds for showing an interest in my research which was barely deserved; Neil Hopkinson gave invaluable support at every stage. My greatest debt, however, is to Byron Harries, my superlative teacher and friend. I am grateful to the British Academy for the award of a Research Fellowship in the Humanities in 1990; I am grateful to Churchill College, Cambridge, for the award of a Research Fellowship in the same year; and my gratitude is also due to the staff of the Cambridge University Press, especially Pauline Hire and Glennis Foote, for the skill and care taken over the process of publication.

INTRODUCTION

The exile exists in a median state, neither completely at one with the new setting, nor fully disencumbered of the old; beset with half-involvements and half-detachments; nostalgic and sentimental on one level, an adept mimic or a secret outcast on another. Being skilled at survival becomes the main imperative, with the dangers of getting too comfortable and secure constituting a threat that is constantly to be guarded against.[1]

Ovid meets this threat in the *Tristia* and *Epistulae ex Ponto* by repeatedly describing his physical insecurity in war-torn Tomis, his cultural isolation in an allegedly barbaric wasteland, and his desperate yearning for the city, friends and family he has left behind. And yet how many of these poems are the work of 'an adept mimic' whose exilic voice is potentially as ambiguous as the 'median state' it describes? Ovid is 'a secret outcast' in the sense that he passes unrecognized as a *Romanus vates* in a cultural wasteland; but to what extent is he a secretive, dissimulating outcast when he invites his Roman audience to believe that he is an exiled poet in terminal decline?

Before the potential complexities of the literary persona were fully recognized, generations of modern critics saw little reason to disagree with Ovid's own judgement of his exilic verse. His monotonously plaintive tone, his seemingly tedious repetition of standard devices such as *adunata* and familiar mythical *exempla*, his constant appeals for help in verse which claimed no artistic merit or ambition – the evidence of Ovid's literary demise in exile spoke for itself. More recent critics have seen behind the mask and rightly countered traditional scholarly antipathy towards the exile poetry with expositions

---

[1] So Edward Said in the third of his 1993 Reith Lectures, a series entitled 'Representations of the Intellectual'; the extract is taken from an edited text of the lecture published by *The Independent* newspaper (London, 8 July 1993, p. 16).

of its latent quality; and yet recognition of Ovid's dissimulating voice in exile poses a set of new questions. How is that dissimulation to be understood and interpreted? Is Ovid striving to present a seemingly candid picture of his exilic condition and failing in the attempt, his sophisticated Muse unable to convey a fully persuasive impression of artistic decline? If so, Ovid's *ingenium* would indeed fail him in exile, but for the wrong reason. How is his sophisticated readership to respond to this failure? Does Ovid attempt a large-scale deception which the initiated reader cleverly sees through, or is the poet engaged in a complex experiment with literary irony for which deception is too strong a term? And is Ovid's dissimulating technique consistently applied throughout the exile poetry, or does he modify his approach according to whom he addresses and thematic variations in different elegies?

Few scholars would now argue that Ovid's exile poetry confirms the fact of his artistic demise by its alleged imperfections. But it is not enough simply to answer Ovid's harsher critics by demonstrating that his *ars* retains its creative vitality in exile. Why allow the sophisticated Muse to apply her subtle techniques if Ovid's sole aim was to win sympathy, and perhaps even a reprieve, through an unambiguous display of his artistic and personal deterioration in exile? A sense of uncertainty over the 'reality' of Ovid's physical and social environment in a desolate extremity of the Roman empire was very possibly as disconcerting for his contemporary Roman reader as it is for his modern audience. Ovid exploits this discomfort by constructing a body of verse which, on one reading, confirms every conceivable assumption about the attritional effects of Tomitan exile; on another reading, the exile poetry undermines those very assumptions. The object of this study is to monitor the progress and extent of this undermining process.

1

THE 'UNREALITY' OF OVID'S EXILE POETRY

My use of the word 'unreality' in the title of this chapter is intended to imply something other than the recently revived view that Ovid never in fact set foot in Tomis. Various scholars have argued for this possibility,[1] making capital out of obvious rhetorical exaggerations in the exile poetry and the absence of any reference to Ovid's relegation in such historians as Tacitus, Suetonius or Cassius Dio, all of whom might have been expected to mention it.[2] But to sound a note of caution over these recent claims is not necessarily to accept Ovid's relegation as a historical fact which lacks supporting evidence. Two kinds of fact must be distinguished here.

Within the context of the *Tristia*, *Ibis* and *Epistulae ex Ponto* the exile serves, along with the *carmen et error* (*Tr.* 2.207), as the one inescapable fact which transforms the nature and direction of Ovid's creative life. Until recently, little difficulty has been felt in transferring this textual fact to the wider historical framework. But the recent tendency to regard the Roman elegiac persona as emotionally self-contained and penned up within a subjective enclosure, or cleverly juggling with received topoi, has reinforced the scepticism which has been growing for other reasons. Even scholars inclined to accept the traditional view that Ovid was exiled must now draw a distinction between the certainty of the textual fact, continually reaffirmed in the poems, and the meagre external evidence which can be adduced to support the recording of this text-centered hypothesis in a historical chronology. Historically

---

[1] So, e.g., Fitton Brown (1985), 18–22. Claassen (1986), 24 surveys the history of the theory.

[2] For later testimony see Plin. *Nat.* 32.152, Stat. *Silv.* 1.2.254–5. Jerome, *Chron. Ab Abraham* 2033 and [Aur. Vic.] *Caes.* 1.24. Ovid's *error* becomes especially hard to explain as a literary conceit if he did not go into exile.

acceptable evidence is another matter, but it is in short supply both for the period and the geographical area which relate to Ovid's exile. Moreover, negative historical statements are notoriously hard to prove, and the burden of proof must lie with those who believe the historical exile, not with those who oppose it. Belief in the exile of Ovid as a historical fact can never be held, even by its defenders, with the conviction which the textual fact inspires in, and demands of, the readers of these poems.

The state of the evidence which is actually available to us does not allow a firm conclusion to be reached on the probability or improbability of Ovid's relegation as a historical fact. While indecision on this issue must inevitably leave some features of the poems unexplained, it nevertheless makes it possible to read and evaluate these poems without the insistent pressure of a question which is of overriding importance only to historical biographers. The better strategy, and the one I shall follow here, is to examine the deployment of Ovid's poetic skill in these poems, without prejudice to the extra-literary question of their status as historical documents – though my results may well have implications for that status. Critics of the exile poetry need room to manoeuvre, free from the constraints of historical preconceptions and assumptions, some of which are now seen to rest on shaky foundations. The historical features of these poems should therefore be subjected to the same critical approach as the more obvious literary features, and evaluation of the historical evidence need have no immediate relevance to the question of the historical credibility of Ovid's exile.

To examine the reliability of the *Tristia* and *Epistulae ex Ponto* as sources of testimony for the physical, geographical and ethnographical conditions in the Pontic region during the Augustan era is an equally hazardous enterprise. Even if it also turns out to be partially inconclusive, the very nature of the difficulties revealed will tell us much about the character of the poems themselves. The crucial issue is to consider how far we can determine whether it is the Ovidian eye or the Ovidian poetic *ingenium*, or a combination of both, which is at work in the descriptive sections of these poems. It remains to clarify the immediate historical background against which the evidence of the poems themselves will be measured.

Moesia, the region in which Tomis was located, was brought under firm Roman control only late in the first century B.C.; M. Terentius Varro Lucullus, consul of 73, had entered Moesia in 72 B.C. (App. *Ill.* 85–8; cf. Liv. *Per.* 97). But the Greek cities on the Pontic coast rose against the Romans under the command of C. Antonius Hybrida in 62 B.C., only to fall under the control of Burebistas, king of the Getae – who, according to Strabo (7.3.11; cf. D. Chr. 36.4), had subjugated the coastal territory from Olbia to Apollonia (and therefore Tomis as well). After his death, probably in 44 B.C., his kingdom was dissolved, and the permanent subjugation of Moesia was effected by M. Licinius Crassus in 29–28 B.C. (Dio 51.25–7).[3] The first imperial legate recorded in Moesia is A. Caecina Severus in A.D. 6 (Dio 55.29.3), and Tacitus mentions the *legatus Moesiae* for A.D. 15, stating that C. Poppaeus Sabinus' governorship of Moesia was extended (*prorogatur*) in that year (*Ann.* 1.80.1). When had it begun? At *Ann.* 6.39.3 Tacitus records his death in A.D. 35 after he had held provincial governorships for twenty-four years. On this evidence he presumably started in Moesia in A.D. 11 after his consulship in A.D. 9. It follows that Ovid does not invent his facts when, for example, he states that the Pontic area of Moesia has only recently come under Roman dominion (cf. *Tr.* 2.199–200).[4] Moreover, historical evidence corroborates

---

[3] Cn. Cornelius Lentulus led later operations in Moesia to suppress the Bastarnae, Scythians and Sarmatae, but the only sources mentioning Lentulus by name (Flor. *Epit.* 2.28.19, Tac. *Ann.* 4.44) do not specify a date; Syme (1934), 115–22 favours 6 B.C.–A.D. 4. For further references to Roman operations in the Pontic region see Nagle (1980), 134. Augustus gives a vague and exaggerated account of operations against the Dacians at *R.G.* 30–1; see Della Corte (1976), 57ff. Ovid's picture of conditions in Pontus may be designed to reverse the Augustan picture (so Claassen (1986), 220).

[4] Appian (*Ill.* 86) sets the date at the start of Tiberius' reign (coinciding with the extension of Sabinus' governorship of Moesia in the same year); so Parvan (1921), 192. But excavations in Constanza (modern Tomis) have revealed a rich supply of bronze coins, some dating from the Augustan period; see Soutzo (1881), 298. At Histria, near Tomis, a temple was dedicated Αὐτοκράτορι Καίσαρι Σεβαστῷ, suggesting that the imperial cult reached the Pontic region in Augustus' lifetime; see Pippidi (1977), 250–1.

his claim that Tomis is constantly threatened by outside attack (cf. *Tr.* 4.1.65ff., 5.2.69–72 etc.). Two inscriptions from Tomis, dated to the time between Burebistas' death and the early years of the first century A.D., mention the creation of a civic guard within the town and the panic of its inhabitants when threatened by attack.[5] A primary cause for concern is the condition of the town's defensive wall, which offers such meagre resistance to outside attack that part of the population abandons Tomis. Ovid is equally unconfident about the town's defences (cf. *Tr.* 4.1.69–70, 5.10.17–18).[6]

These initial consistencies are deceptive, however. The general picture suggests that, if not worthless, the historical value of the exile poetry is certainly limited – as the recent studies by Vulikh and Podosinov have demonstrated.[7] Take, for example, Ovid's grossly exaggerated portrayal of the barbarian threat in and around Tomis. Besides the Getae, he mentions the Bastarnae, Bessi, Bistonii, Colchi, Cizyges, Coralli, Iazyges, Odrysii, Sarmatae and Sauromatae at various points in his narrative. As Syme observes,[8] Ovid is the first Latin author to mention the Iazyges, but Tacitus, who mentions them next (*Ann.* 12.29.3), locates them differently, beyond the Carpathian range in modern Hungary. Syme puts this discrepancy down to a possible migration, undertaken later with Roman encouragement, but Ovid's geographical vagueness is a more plausible explanation. The Coralli are nowhere attested except by Ovid as inhabitants of Dobrogea; Strabo locates them with the Bessi (7.5.12). And if we accept that Ovid knows the Bessi as his immediate neighbours (*Tr.* 3.10.5, 4.1.67), we also have to accept that all or part of this tribe made a substantial move north-eastwards from their attested home; Strabo locates them in the region of Mt Haemus and the upper waters of the Hebrus in Thrace (7.5.12), while ac-

---

[5] For these inscriptions see *SIG*[3] 731; for their date see Pippidi (1971), 279 n. 73.

[6] Aricescu (1976), 85–90 argues that Ovid's description of the defensive walls around Tomis closely accords with archaeological evidence; but see *contra* Claassen (1990), 93 n. 63.

[7] Vulikh (1974), 64–79; Podosinov (1981), 174–94 and (1987), *passim*.

[8] (1978), 165.

cording to the elder Pliny they lived on the left bank of the Strymon (*Nat.* 4.40).[9] It is scarcely credible that, as Ovid claims, tribal forces from throughout the vast geographical area of Thrace, Scythia and Moesia are all active in the immediate vicinity of Tomis.[10] Nor is there any evidence to suggest that the Greek language and culture of Tomis, originating from its Milesian foundation, were barbarized by the Getic presence in and around the town (cf. *Tr.* 5.7.51–2, 5.10.27–34 etc.).[11] The enduring Hellenistic character of Tomis up to and including the era of Roman influence is beyond reasonable doubt;[12] though it is likely that the Getic and Thracian peoples had considerable involvement with the Greeks, the traditional culture of Greek/Milesian Tomis remained intact.

This evidence confirms that accuracy of geographical and social detail in these matters was not Ovid's chief concern. Though he draws on many names, incidents and features which can be paralleled individually here and there in the very wide area of which Tomis forms a part, Ovid's portrayal of the Pontic environment is primarily literary, by which I mean that the material at his disposal was freely manipulated to serve his literary intentions. Such a result might have been expected anyway: elegy was never the medium for the bland reporting of geographical surveys. The very remoteness and alien nature of Tomis, which might in other contexts have required accuracy to be a prime virtue, here ensured that very few potential readers would be able to check Ovid's details from their own experience. Rather, it was to the literary experience of his readers that Ovid primarily appealed, adapting an alien environment and culture for his special purposes.

[9] Taking *Tr.* 3.10.5 and 4.1.67 at face value, Casson (1927), 97–101 accepts that the Bessi did make such a move. Syme (1978), 164 is forced to the same expedient, referring to 'a portion ... which the Romans had transferred from their homeland in inner Thrace'.

[10] See further Videau-Delibes (1991), 162–5.

[11] See Lambrino (1958), 379–90 for the alleged corruption of Greek culture in Tomis; cf. Gandeva (1968), 106, arguing that Getic was the predominant language in Tomis.

[12] See Pippidi (1977), 250–6. But for the survival of Getic culture despite the general Romanization of Scythia, Dacia and Moesia see Scorpan (1973), 137–50 and Berciu (1978), 77.

While this point has not passed unrecognized in previous scholarship,[13] the extent to which Ovid's literary considerations outweigh his alleged commitment to factual reliability in the exile poetry bears further examination; the complexity of Ovid's artistic designs in exile has yet to be fully recognized.

Tomis and the Tomitans

Though Tomis was actually located in Moesia, Ovid states that Scythia is his destination: *Scythia est, quo mittimur* (*Tr.* 1.3.61; cf. 3.2.1). His citation of Scythia may at first sight appear to be innocent enough and typical of the licence with which Roman poets often distort geographical detail;[14] but on closer examination it proves to be no accident. Ovid stretches geographical fact for a purpose which is determined by the traditional depiction of Scythia in Roman literature.

Scythia was of course standardly portrayed as a geographical extreme, set at the very edge of the Roman world. In *C.* 2.11, for example, Horace urges Hirpinus not to concern himself with distant problems, but to enjoy his youth while he can: *quid bellicosus Cantaber et Scythes ... cogitet ... remittas quaerere* (1–4). The Cantabrians pose a threat in the extreme west of the Roman world, the Scythians in the east.[15] What Horace portrays as the eastern extremity, Virgil portrays as the northern at *G.* 1.240–1:

> mundus, ut ad Scythiam Riphaeasque arduus arces
> consurgit, premitur Libyae devexus in Austros.

The contrast between Scythia in the north and Libya in the south is developed more fully at *G.* 3.339–83. Virgil has just completed his account of the seasonal management of live-

---

[13] Cf. Podosinov (1981), 194: 'In using Ovid's work of the Tomis period, we must take into account that much of it is written for the educated reader, and therefore corresponds to established notions about these places, and composed in a style thick with the literary clichés and rhetorical rules of his day.'

[14] For illustration see Thomson (1951), 433–8 and Syme (1987), 49ff. with Videau Delibes (1991), 168–9.

[15] Cf. *C.* 3.8.18–24, 4.5.25–8 and 4.14.41–4, where Scythia represents the same extreme.

stock in winter (295–321) and summer (322–38). Italy's balanced climate, with its clearly defined winter and summer, is
contrasted with Libya's unremitting heat in the south (339–
48) and Scythia's permanent winter to the north (349–83).[16]

These contrasts had long formed part of the way in which
writers conceived the limits of the inhabited world. Whether
Scythia's function was to provide the uniform background of
a remote wilderness in the *Prometheus Vinctus*, or to support
the more complex Herodotean symmetry which required a
counterpart to the climate and civilization of Egypt in the
south, the need for a coherent conceptual picture tended, at
least in literary texts, to take little account of those inconve-
nient inconsistencies which unprejudiced research, had it tak-
en place, might have brought to light.[17] The earlier literary
pictures already reflect the fact that the solitude and harsh
climate of Scythia were proverbial. The same must be true
of Horace and Virgil, though the picture in Greek writers
is sometimes less uniform and monotonously bleak. Virgil,
for instance, exaggerates when he claims that the winter in
Scythia is permanent; a different picture emerges from the
Hippocratic *De aeribus, locis, aquis* (19 Heiberg), Strabo
(7.3.18) and Herodotus (4.28), though the latter in particular
had his own structural reasons for wanting to complicate and
systematize the conventional picture. Indeed, the resulting
symmetry between the second and fourth books of the *His-
tories* only intensifies suspicion that Herodotus never actually
visited the Black Sea region, despite his claims to that effect.[18]

A good example of the difficulties faced in establishing an
accurate picture of the Scythian climate is provided by ancient
reports of how the streams in the Pontic region, and even

---

[16] Martin (1966), 301 claims that the Scythian passage was partly based on information retrieved from an expedition to Moesia in 29. But the details of Virgil's
account – and so Ovid's parallel version in *Tr.* 3.10 – are traditional; see Richter
(1957), 304–5.

[17] On the function of Scythia in earlier literature see Hartog (1988), 12–33. This
paragraph draws heavily on Hartog's analysis of the Herodotean picture and on
supporting citations in Thomas (1982), 66 n. 70.

[18] Cf. Kimball Armayor (1978), 62: 'If we cannot believe that he [Herodotus] saw the
Pontus that he talks about, we can hardly be sure that he went to the Pontus at
all.'

whole stretches of the sea, freeze over so solidly that men and waggons can cross the ice. Herodotus (4.28), Strabo (7.3.18) and the elder Pliny (*Nat.* 4.87) all report the phenomenon, but even in antiquity such claims were sometimes met with scepticism.[19] Reliable or not, the phenomenon became an indispensable feature of Scythia in poetry.[20] Plutarch offers a telling insight into the proverbiality of the Scythian climate; in the preface to his life of Theseus (1.1), he notes the free licence which geographers allow themselves in plotting on their maps parts of the earth of which they have no first-hand knowledge and to which they append such vague explanatory comments as Σκυθικὸν κρύος. This proverbial picture was reproduced by several Greek poets (e.g. [Aesch.] *Pr.* 2, 417–19, Ar. *Ach.* 704), for whom Scythia was a cold, barren, deserted region with no favourable features.

Roman poets generally continue to portray Scythia as a uniformly frozen desert, ignoring the modifications to this picture which appear in Herodotus and Strabo.[21] Virgil's account in *Georgics* 3 for the most part clearly provides the model for Ovid's depiction of Pontus in *Tr.* 3.10 – despite Ovid's insistence that his narrative is based on personal observation (cf. 35–40). His dependence on Virgil has been well documented,[22] though different reasons are given why he chose to follow a model so closely. One suggestion is that Ovid pays homage to the accuracy of Virgil's Scythian description by alluding to *Georgics* 3 in his own account of climatic conditions in Pontus;[23] another is that Ovid's use of

---

[19] See, e.g., Plutarch on Theseus' campaign against the Amazonian women: εἰ μὲν οὖν, ὡς Ἑλλάνικος ἱστόρηκε, τῷ Κιμμερικῷ Βοσπόρῳ παγέντι διαβᾶσαι περιῆλθον, ἔργον ἐστι πιστεῦσαι (*Thes.* 27.2; *FGrH* 323a fr. 17). Cf. Gellius' depiction of the philosopher Taurus debating the question of why rivers freeze but not the sea (17.8.16); Taurus dismisses as highly unorthodox Herodotus' claim that the Black Sea does in fact freeze (*contra omnium ferme, qui haec quaesiverunt, opinionem*).

[20] So, e.g., Virg. *G.* 3.360–2, Ov. *Tr.* 3.10.27–34, *P.* 4.7.9–10, Luc. 5.436–41, V. Fl. 6.328–9; see further Hornstein (1957), 154–61.

[21] So, e.g., Prop. 4.3.47–8, Sen. *Her. F.* 533ff. Cf. Ov. *M.* 2.224, where even Scythia's cold melts before the global fire which Phaethon precipitates (*nec prosunt Scythiae sua frigora*).

[22] See Martin (1966), 295ff., Besslich (1972), 177ff., Evans (1975), 1ff., Gahan (1978), 198ff.

[23] Martin (1966), 295–6.

Virgilian material exemplifies his practice of describing his personal experience (cf. *vidimus*, 37) through standard literary devices.[24] Neither interpretation is fully satisfactory, however, because neither takes into account the relation between Scythia and Italy which makes so significant a contribution to the structuring of *Georgics* 3.

In Virgil's structure Italy is located between the climatic extremes of north and south, Scythia and Libya. Scythia, like Libya, lacks the balanced climate which complements Italy's central location. For Ovid, too, the contrast between the edge of the world and the Roman centre is a dominant idea. The epistolary mode is itself a device which keeps this contrast continually active, and its ramifications go far beyond distinctions of climate to cover social and ethnographical differences and the significance which these differences hold for personal relationships and literary culture. There is, however, a shift in polarities. In *Georgics* 3 Rome is the balanced centre between the polarized extremes of Scythia and Libya; in Ovid Rome itself is in effect portrayed as a polarized social and cultural antithesis to the untamed barbarism of Tomis. In this respect, then, the Ovidian picture is simpler, but its sharper intensity is due to the invidious consequences which the polarization has for the poet himself. The reason Ovid is not, like Virgil and his Greek predecessors, constructing a balanced centre between polarized opposites is, of course, that he views the world from its edge and not from its centre. His vision of these two distinct and contrasted geographical locations does not relate them to each other by a common distance from a medial point – though such a medial point is sometimes vainly broached in the form of a *mitius exilium pauloque propinquius* (*Tr.* 4.4.51; cf. 2.185); rather, it is the poet's personal involvement which gives these disparate places a point of convergence in his own awareness of the Roman past and the Pontic present, of his former literary fame and his now 'declining' Muse.

The balanced structure of *Georgics* 3 is therefore considerably modified in the exile poetry, though the latter draws free-

[24] Evans (1975), 5.

ly on Virgil's descriptive account of Scythia. By borrowing from Virgil, Ovid immediately characterizes the Pontic region not only as a climatic extreme, but an extreme which shares the remoteness from Italy which is a fundamental element in the Virgilian structure. The impression he conveys is one of radical dislocation, not harmonious balance, and the personal consequences of this deracination add a dimension of extreme suffering to the environmental consequences with which they run in parallel. Ovid loses the fine balance of his constitution – he falls ill in Tomis (*Tr.* 3.3.13, 3.8.23–4), unable to endure either the weather (*Tr.* 3.3.7, *P.* 1.7.11) or the local food and water (*Tr.* 3.3.7–9, 3.8.28, *P.* 1.10.7–10). Italy is safe under the protection of Augustus (cf. *Tr.* 2.157); but, after his relegation, Ovid's physical safety is threatened in the war-torn environment of Tomis (*Tr.* 3.14.41–2, 4.1.69–70 etc.). The contrast between the environments of Pontus and Italy is at least implicitly present throughout the exile poetry. More notably in *Tr.* 3.10, however, Ovid's partial derivation of his picture of the Tomitan environment from Virgil's Scythia serves to recall the latter's function as a foil to Italy's ordered seasons and temperate climate.

When, therefore, Ovid states that Scythia is his destination (cf. *Tr.* 1.3.61), he subscribes more to Roman literary convention than to strict geographical fact. That he simply uses geographical terms loosely is unlikely, especially as literary tradition visibly determines his portrayal of the Pontic region in so many other ways. One of these – his depiction of the region as if it were the underworld – is already well known. He often equates relegation with death (e.g. *Tr.* 5.9.19, *P.* 1.8.27, 4.9.74); on the eve of his departure from Rome, his family and friends are mourners at a funeral (*Tr.* 1.3.22–3); in *Tr.* 3.3, urging his wife not to mourn for him when he dies in Tomis, he makes his first death, his exile, the more grievous loss (53–4).[25] Such a death is a prelude to the Stygian torments which

---

[25] Exile was commonly portrayed as living death in antiquity; had Quintus visited Cicero in exile, he would have found *non eum quem noras ... sed quandam effigiem spirantis mortui* (*Q. Fr.* 1.3.1). On the motif see Nagle (1980), 35, Wistrand (1968), 6–26 and Doblhofer (1987), 166ff.

await him, for the physical characteristics of the Tomitan environment are also those of the underworld. The cold of Pontus (*P.* 1.7.11–12, 4.12.33–4 etc.) is as unbearable and unrelenting as that of the underworld (cf. *pallor hiemsque tenent late loca senta*, *M.* 4.436). On the coast of the Black Sea only wormwood grows (*P.* 3.1.23–4, 3.8.15; cf. Plaut. *Trin.* 934–5, Cato *Agr.* 159); in all other respects the soil is barren (*Tr.* 3.10.71–6, *P.* 1.3.51–2) in accordance with both the Virgilian portrayal of Scythia (*G.* 3.352–5) and the familiar poetic vision of Hades (cf. *non seges est infra, non vinea culta*, Tib. 1.10.35) which was to be vividly recreated by Seneca in the *Hercules Furens* (698–702).

But the subtlety of Ovidian diction can suggest the same comparison without the need of direct cross-reference:

> sive locum specto, locus est inamabilis, et quo
> esse nihil toto tristius orbe potest.
> (*Tr.* 5.7.43–4)

Although *inamabilis* occurs rarely in Roman poetry, it is applied on a number of occasions to the underworld.[26] The two instances in Virgil, the first writer to apply the adjective to a place, both describe the marshy waters (*palus*) of the underworld (*G.* 4.479, *Aen.* 6.438). Ovid himself twice describes the underworld as *inamabile regnum* (*M.* 4.477, 14.590), appropriating Virgil's language in a way which strongly suggests that his use of the same vocabulary to describe his place of exile at *Tr.* 5.7.43 is no accident. An additional point is that at *Tr.* 5.7.43–4 Ovid uses *inamabilis* in close proximity to *tristis*, a common poetic adjective for the underworld (cf. Virg. *Aen.* 4.243, Hor. *C.* 3.4.46, Sen. *Med.* 11). Virgil in fact uses the combination of *inamabilis* and *tristis* together for the same descriptive purpose at *Aen.* 6.438: *tristis ... palus inamabilis undae*. This Virgilian usage again suggests that at *Tr.* 5.7.44 *tristius* reinforces the reference implicit in *inamabilis* and confirms Ovid's deliberate association of the Pontic world with the underworld.

Stygian bleakness is only one of the disadvantages of Ovid's

---

[26] See Borzsak (1952), 461.

Pontus, however; he also casts the region as the antithesis of the idealized Golden or Saturnian Age. Necessary material was provided for this portrait by the familiar notion of the degeneration of the Golden Age into succeeding ages of moral imperfection. Already at *M*. 1.89–150 Ovid had adapted the mythical age-cycles of Hesiod (*Op*. 109–201) and Aratus (114–36), portraying their evolution from the Golden to the Silver, Bronze and Iron Ages/Races. This amplification depended on a reversion by Ovid to the general outline of the earlier Greek picture; more recent Roman modifications were set aside. Virgil's own inconsistencies – he omits the Silver and Bronze Ages in *Eclogue* 4 and contrasts only two ages, the Saturnian and the post-Saturnian, at *G*. 1.118–46 – may have facilitated Ovid's return to the familiar Greek patterns.

Ovid's portrayal of the Pontic region contains all the worst features of the post-Saturnian ages. There was no war in the Golden Age (Ov. *M*. 1.98–100, Tib. 1.3.47–8); Tomis is wartorn (*Tr*. 3.10.55ff., 3.11.11–14 etc.). The Golden Age needed no defensive walls around cities (*M*. 1.97, *Am*. 3.8.47); Tomis is defended by walls which are inadequate for the purpose which they are meant to serve (cf. *Tr*. 5.10.17–18). The earth in the Golden Age abounded with natural produce which grew wild and uncultivated (cf. Virg. *Ecl*. 4.18–20, 23, 27–30, Ov. *M*. 1.101–6, *Am*. 3.8.39–40); in Tomis there is little natural vegetation apart from wormwood (*P*. 3.1.19–24). Warring was as prevalent in the Iron Age as it is in Tomis (cf. *M*. 1.142–3); men lived by plunder (*vivitur ex rapto, M*. 1.144), as do the local peoples around Tomis (*gentes ... sibi non rapto vivere turpe putant, Tr*. 5.10.15–16). The Iron Age was proverbially hard (cf. [*Iuppiter*] *ferro duravit saecula*, Hor. *Epod*. 16.65); and Ovid endures his own *tempora dura* (*Tr*. 5.10.12) among peoples whose character corresponds to the age (cf. *duros ... Getas, P*. 1.5.12, 3.2.102) and in a region which, lacking the permanent springtime of the Golden Age, is eternally hard and frozen (cf. *Tr*. 5.10.2, *P*. 4.10.38).

The harsh conditions of life in Tomis are not to be equated with the ethos of the post-Saturnian Age, an ethos which teaches man the need for honest *labor* in order to survive.

Such is the theme of *G*. 1.118–46: 'The spontaneously benefi-
cent world of the Fourth Eclogue has gone, replaced by the
reality of toil and by the possibility of failure, and it is that
reality which concerns Virgil throughout the *Georgics*, one
which he unequivocally establishes early in the poem.'[27]
Ovid's portrayal of the hardness of life in Tomis is more com-
patible with his own depiction of the Iron Age at *M*.1.127–50
– an era whose hardness is characterized by corruption and
violence, not by honest toil. And yet certain aspects of the
Tomitan environment seem to share common features with
the Golden Age. Both lack an ordered system of agriculture;
there was, of course, none in the Golden Age (Tib. 1.3.45,
Virg. *G*. 1.125–8 etc.), and there is none in the region of Tomis
(*Tr*. 3.10.67ff.). The Golden Age saw no mining for mineral
resources (Ov. *Am*. 3.8.35–8; cf. *M*. 1.137–40), and there is
none in the Pontic area (*P*. 3.8.5–6). The Golden Age had no
formal system of justice (*M*. 1.91–3; cf.Virg. *G*. 2.501–2), and
there is none in Tomis either (*Tr*. 5.7.47–8; cf. 5.10.43–4).

But these ostensible parallels with the Golden Age are of
course deceptive. The absence of agriculture in Pontus is
hardly the result of the liberal bounty of nature: the harsh
climate of Ovid's environment and the constant fighting
which takes place there are the two reasons why there is no
crop-cultivation in the region of Tomis. There is no formal
system of law and order not because it is unnecessary, but
because force is the crude instrument of justice (cf. *cedit
viribus aequum*, *Tr*. 5.7.47). There is no mining not because the
Pontic region's mineral resources are left unexploited in an era
of innocence about mineral wealth, but as a result of the constant hostilities which make such exploitation of the land impossible (cf. *P*. 3.8.5–6). Clearly, such correspondences as
there are between the Pontic region and the Saturnian era are
only a paradoxical way of reinforcing the vast divergences
between them. In creating a new context in the exile poetry
for some of the traditional features of the Golden Age, Ovid
makes those features serve the ironic purpose of showing

---

[27] Thomas (1988), I 87.

how different their new context in Tomis is to that idealized world.

An alternative underworld, a negation of the Golden Age and a recreation of familiar Scythian extremes: in three different ways Ovid creates a literary landscape in exile which is anything but a simple record of reliable first-hand observation. Predictably, he also matches the peoples of Tomis and its surrounding regions to the character of the literary landscape they inhabit. As rugged and coarse as their physical environment, the Getae are said to be *crudi* (*Tr.* 5.3.8), *duri* (*P.* 3.2.102), *feri* (*P.* 3.9.32) and *saevi* (*P.* 4.8.84). Their crude appearance further corresponds to their crudeness of character, for they are *intonsi* (*P.* 4.2.2) and *hirsuti* (*P.* 1.5.74) and they have full, shaggy beards (*non coma, non ulla barba resecta manu*, *Tr.* 5.7.18), whereas in the Rome of Ovid's day a small, neatly trimmed beard was the fashion (cf. *sit coma, sit trita barba resecta manu*, *A.A.* 1.518);[28] in this latter instance, as in so many others, the difference between Rome and Tomis is made all too apparent.[29]

This correspondence between the Tomitans and their physical environment has its own literary background which Ovid typically adapts to his own special purposes. The relation between a people's character and environment was a well-worn theme in antiquity.[30] The Hippocratic *De aeribus*, for example, describes at length the physical effects which weather-patterns have on the Scythians, though these effects are rather different from those envisaged by Ovid: the constant cold weather and the barrenness of the region they inhabit stunt their growth; the people differ little from one another in physique; the lack of seasonal change means that their bodies are not hardened by exposure to different climatic conditions; the effect of living in a cold, moist environment is that mind and body are both sluggish (19–20 Heiberg). The Scythians are a convenient illustration of the thesis that εὑρήσεις ... ἐπὶ τὸ

---

[28] See Hollis (1977), 120 on 518. For beards and long hair associated with foreigners and barbarians in Ovid's Rome see Balsdon (1979), 215–16.

[29] See further Videau-Delibes (1991), 139ff.

[30] See Johnson (1960), 465–80 with Froesch (1976), 61–2.

πλῆθος τῆς χωρῆς τῇ φύσει ἀκολουθέοντα καὶ τὰ εἴδεα τῶν ἀνθρώπων καὶ τοὺς τρόπους (24 Heiberg).

Transferred to a Roman context, the thesis identified the climatic conditions of central Italy as the norm by which all other areas were to be judged.[31] An extension of Italy's temperate climate was the temperate character of her peoples as opposed to that of peoples living to the far north and south. Lucretius, for example, has Pontus represent the northeastern extremity of his world (6.1108), and relates the appearance and characteristic ailments of the peoples at each extremity of the earth to their geographical location (1110–13). Vitruvius portrays the peoples of southern countries as intelligent because of the warm atmosphere in which they live, but cowardly because the heat drains their strength; northern peoples are unintelligent because of the damp, thick air of their environment, and reckless in their courage (6.1.9–10). Since Italy occupies the mean between these climatic extremities, its peoples are strong in both mind and body, lacking both northern and southern deficiencies (6.1.11). This is the reason for Rome's world domination; *ita divina mens civitatem populi Romani egregia temperataque regione conlocavit, uti orbis terrarum imperii potiretur (ibid.).*

The elder Pliny represents a similar picture. The Ethiopians are a tall, dark race of acute intelligence, while northern peoples have a fair complexion, a fierce temperament and an equally tall stature. Between these climatic extremes men are of medium bodily stature, their complexion is a mixture of fair and dark, and they also possess a temperate, measured character which the other races lack: *ritus molles, sensus liquidos, ingenia fecunda (Nat. 2.190).* Manilius gives this theory an astrological dimension by placing Italy and the founding of Rome under the sign of Libra, or Balance, in his zodiacal geography (4.773–4). Since Tiberius was born under the same sign (776), his character exemplifies the same balanced

---

[31] On the prevalence of *laudes Italiae* in antiquity see Canter (1938), 457ff. with Thomas (1982), 39. But Virgil's *laudes* in *Georgic* 2 (and elsewhere) may not convey an entirely favourable picture of the so-called *Saturnia tellus*; see Thomas (1982), 39ff.

restraint which Rome exhibits on a universal scale in its dominion over crude and intemperate peoples.[32]

Ovid's depiction of the Getae accords well with this theory of the relation of a people's character to its climatic conditions, a theory which had already contributed to the ethnography of the *Georgics*. The Getae are as intemperate in character as their habitat is in climate; they lack the equipoise and harmonious social culture enjoyed by the Romans living in temperate Italy. To emphasize the cultural difference between Rome and the local peoples of Tomis, Ovid applies the full pejorative force of *barbarus*, locating himself *in media ... barbaria* (*Tr.* 3.10.4).[33] The connotation of *inhumanus* (cf. *P.* 1.5.66, 4.13.22) is equally damning: the cultural ideal of *humanitas* which Ovid attributes to his Roman correspondent, Graecinus, at *P.* 1.6.5–10 is quite alien to the *inhumani Getae*.[34] And yet an elegy such as *P.* 3.2 may at first seem to be an exception to the general rule. Here Ovid depicts the Getae and Sauromatae as recognizing the value and commitment of Roman friendship (cf. *nos quoque amicitiae nomen, bone, novimus, hospes*, 43). He does so, however, for a specific purpose in this instance; his aim is to illustrate how the Roman friends who disown him after his fall (cf. *P.* 3.2.7ff.) are morally inferior even to the Getae.[35] The amicable disposition here attributed to the latter merely serves the rhetorical purpose of *amplificatio*.

Yet in one respect Ovid's depiction of the Getae as *barbari* is paradoxical. Though he pictures them as crude and unso-

---

[32] For fuller discussion of Italian balance as portrayed by Vitruvius, Pliny and Manilius see Dauge (1981), 168–70. For the ancient significance of the astral sign of Rome's foundation in Manilius see Housman (1937),103 on *Astron.* 4.773.

[33] Cf. Sinor (1957), 47: '... in its primary and principle meaning the term [*barbarus*] is the antonym of "civilized" and is, therefore, for all practical purposes synonymous with "uncivilized"; it has a distinctly pejorative flavour'. For brief analysis of the range of senses in which *barbarus* was used in antiquity see Haarhoff (1948), 216–21; for the characteristics conventionally attributed to the *barbarus* see Dauge (1981), 413–49.

[34] On *humanitas* as a Roman cultural ideal see Herescu (1961), 65–82. Elsewhere ((1960), 258–77) Herescu argues (implausibly) that Roman imperial power was based not just on military might, but on the civilizing constraints of *humanitas*.

[35] Cf. Evans (1983), 118: 'The moral is obvious: if the Getae honor friendship, he expects at least as much from fellow Romans.'

phisticated, the picture itself is a highly sophisticated literary production which regularly alludes to literary models. For the life-pattern, appearance and equipment of the Pontic tribesmen, Ovid drew on the Virgilian portrayal of the Italian tribes in the second half of the *Aeneid*; his debt is clearest in *Tr.* 5.7 and 5.10.

Ovid's systematic allusions to Virgil can assume a variety of forms, from the straightforward reminiscence of Virgilian vocabulary to complex cross-references which add a new literary dimension to Ovid's unlettered tribesmen. Take, for example, at the most basic level, the simple matter of fighting equipment. In *Tr.* 5.7 a dense mass of Sarmatian and Getic tribesmen pack the streets of Tomis on horseback (13–14), each man carrying *coryton et arcum|telaque* (15–16). The rare Homeric γωρυτός or quiver makes its first appearance in Roman literature in the *Aeneid*, later to be repeated by Virgilian imitators like Statius and Silius.[36] At *Aen.* 10.168–9 a thousand men follow the Etruscan chief Massicus, *quis tela sagittae|gorytique leves umeris et letifer arcus*. This is very likely the source of the combination of weapons carried by Ovid's Pontic tribesmen, and the only known Roman source for Ovid's use of *corytos*. Moreover, the Pontic tribesmen carry arrows dipped in poison (*Tr.* 5.7.16), the *telum immedicabile* of the Parthians and Cydonians at *Aen.* 12.857–8 (cf. *felle*, 857 with *Tr.* 5.7.16). And if *verissima Martis imago* is read in line 17, Ovid echoes *Aen.* 8.557 (*it timor et maior Martis iam apparet imago*).[37] There, the spectre of war against Turnus looms large for the Etruscans; at *Tr.* 5.7.17 Ovid intensifies the threatening aspect of the Virgilian *imago* by portraying the Sarmatian and Getic peoples as a living likeness of the god of war.

---

[36] Stat. *Theb.* 4.269, Sil. 2.106, 7.443, 15.773; cf. Sen. *Her. F.* 1127. The Scythian *corytos* (or *gorytos*) was in fact a combination of bow-case and quiver; see Talbot Rice (1957), 75.

[37] *Martis* is generally preferred to *mortis* by modern editors, though it is attested only in the second hand of a single ms; the Virgilian echo supports the reading. Housman (1890), 342 = (1972), 134–5 rejected *Martis*, conjecturing *mentis*, but his argument – that Mars makes an inappropriate appearance in a Pontic context – takes no account of (e.g.) *Tr.* 5.2.69.

It is misguided, however, to attempt to form a coherent picture out of these Virgilian allusions, for a complication is added to this same section of *Tr.* 5.7 by what appear to be allusions to the *Ars Amatoria*. As we saw earlier, line 18 is a reversal of *A.A.* 1.518: the dishevelled, coarse appearance of the Pontic tribesmen is contrasted with that of the neatly trimmed, fashionable Romans. These tribesmen carry knives at their side as weapons (19–20), a descriptive point which is possibly an elaboration of line 18. The *culter* was generally not a weapon of war for the Romans; it was a tool chiefly used for non-military purposes such as trimming beards or hair. This latter function is widely attested from Plautus to Apuleius,[38] but Ovid may well be referring ironically in lines 19–20 to the fact that this basic domestic function of the *culter* was unknown to the uncouth Getae (cf. 18). Finally, Ovid depicts himself as *lusorum oblitus amorum* (21). The claim that he has forgotten his youthful love poetry is itself a playful reference to the fact that when he quotes *A.A.* 1.518 at *Tr.* 5.7.18, he reverses the sense of the line from a positive instruction to a negative statement. Despite his claim, his love poetry is only too well remembered here, even to the extent that the weapons steeped in poison (16) may recall his depiction at *A.A.* 2.520 of the weapons which inflict the pains of love (*quae patimur, multo spicula felle madent*).[39]

The *Aeneid* and the *Ars Amatoria* make a curious combination as the joint sources of influence on *Tr.* 5.7.15–20. The skilful blending of such disparate reminiscences is a display of sophisticated artistry wholly at odds with the nature of the subject-matter. The tone of Ovid's poetic diction here exhibits an ambivalence which it owes to the fundamental incoherence in the source material. And the way in which these lines are read has consequences for our reading of the remainder of the poem (25ff.), which Luck designates as a separate elegy

[38] See *TLL* 4.1317.31ff. with Courtney (1980), 580 on Juv. 14.216–17.
[39] See Nagle (1980), 57 on the parallel between *Amor pharetratus* and *Getes pharetratus*.

because he finds the transition between lines 24 and 25 too ⨉ abrupt.[40]

Luck's division is misguided because the ironic effects just noted from Ovid's amalgamation of sources in lines 15–20 gather cumulative force as the elegy proceeds. This is the poem in which Ovid announces his decline as a poet, his loss of Latin (55ff.) and his abandonment of *fama* as a motive for writing (cf. 37–40). Everything we see in this and other poems runs contrary to the likelihood that these claims are true, or even sincerely intended. As I shall argue when I turn to this pose of poetic decline in the next chapter, the difficulties in reconciling the statements in the poetic narrative with the evident skill of the narrator strongly suggest that a tone of self-deprecating irony is intended here. Luck's division is therefore unnecessary because a consistent and ironic tone unites what he considers to be the two parts of this poem.

The formative influence of the *Aeneid* on the depiction of the Pontic tribes is more in evidence in *Tr.* 5.10, a poem which proves to be no more reliable than 5.7 as an authentic account of social conditions at Tomis. In lines 15–28 Ovid constructs a picture of the town and its inhabitants which is once more rich in Virgilian reminiscences. War is threatened by *innumerae . . . gentes* (15), the phrase used by Virgil at *Aen.* 6.706 to depict the souls of the dead fluttering on the banks of the river Lethe. Evocation of Virgil's underworld here complements Ovid's portrayal of Tomis as an alternative Hades (cf. *Tr.* 5.9.19). Virgil's ghostly *gentes* are compared to swarms of bees in a summer meadow (707–9), a Homeric/Apollonian simile whose pathos is intensified by the anticipatory *volabant* (706). Ovid's gloomy picture makes no such attempt to achieve pathos by introducing contrasting scenes from the idyllic, pastoral world. Indeed, far from providing something like the Virgilian contrast, the pastoral world at Tomis is under threat itself (cf. *Tr.* 5.10.23–6) and merges with the grim

---

[40] See Luck (1977), II 305 and the introduction to what he cites as 7(a); he follows Heinsius and one ms, though all other mss give a single elegy of 68 lines. Evans (1983), 188 n. 5 rightly rejects the division.

horror of war (cf. *sub galea pastor*, 25) instead of providing relief from it. The simile which Ovid introduces in line 19 to describe the fluttering of his own *innumerae gentes* has the same un-Virgilian effect as the 'pastoral' section which follows in 23–6; the swarming enemy forces (*densissimus hostis*) are compared to vulture-like birds of prey which intensify the overall impression of unremitting terror and insecurity. Virgil's summer bees, which ironically carry out their tasks like a military operation (*insidunt*, 708, and *funduntur*, 709, may suggest the attacking force), are replaced by Ovid with something very like the Virgilian Harpies. Both groups of birds fly to the attack suddenly and snatch their prey like booty (*Tr.* 5.10.19–20; cf. *Aen.* 3.225–7, 233). It is difficult to imagine a more radical departure from Virgil's idyllic scene.

Living by plunder (16), Ovid's *gentes* share the lifestyle of two Virgilian peoples. The words *rapto vivere* appear twice in the *Aeneid*, first at 7.749, where the Aequi are described as a people whom *convectare iuvat praedas et vivere rapto*. More significantly, the same line is repeated, with one change, at 9.613. In contrasting the hard life of the native Italian population with Trojan effeminacy (598–620), Numanus Remulus states that the Rutulians live by plunder: *comportare iuvat praedas et vivere rapto*.[41] Numanus' speech yields further points of association with *Tr.* 5.10, for his description of the rough, hardy life of the Rutulians is a major source for Ovid's depiction of the Pontic tribes. Numanus boasts that his people's children are toughened by exposure to freezing water (603–4) and accustomed to the use of bows and arrows (606); the hardy Rutulians also plough the soil with weapons ready in their hands (*versaque iuvencum|terga fatigamus hasta*, 609–10; i.e. the spear acts as a goad to spur on the oxen). As with the Rutulians, bows and arrows are everyday objects for the peoples in and around Tomis (cf. 22); these peoples, too, are accustomed to the severe cold which freezes the waters of the

[41] Living by plunder is a common attribute of barbarian peoples in ancient ethnographical description; see Horsfall (1971), 1113.

Danube and the Black Sea (cf. 1–2), and they carry arms as they cultivate the soil (*hac arat . . . hac tenet arma manu*, 24).[42]

While Ovid artfully creates his picture of the Tomitan *barbari* by reverting in part to Virgil's depiction of the hard and partially barbaric Rutulians,[43] these parallels, however suggestive, should not be taken further than Ovid himself takes them. It does not follow, for example, that Ovid envisages himself as an Aeneas besieged by hordes of quasi-Rutulians on the Pontic coast. His central concern continues to be literary artifice, and has not become a subjective, dream-like exercise in self-projection. A more legitimate inference, however, is that Ovid's debt to Virgil in *Tr.* 5.10 strongly suggests a correspondence between the war-like environment of Tomis and a familiar aspect of martial epic.[44] Sensitivity to the tone and nuance of poetic diction, combined with a subtle, allusive technique, emerges as a continuing feature of Ovidian poetics, and the creative involvement with the *Aeneid* is pursued with the same emphasis on supplying a new context for the Virgilian text which had characterized Ovid's method in the *Metamorphoses*.[45] This sophisticated use of language, with its subtle reminiscences and echoes, confirms the cultural divide between the poet and the peoples he describes within the poem. This, of course, is not in itself an unusual situation, but what gives the great divide between the poet and his material its significance here is the fact that the whole drift of a poem like *Tr.* 5.7 is in the direction of identifying the poet as now being at one with the Pontic peoples he describes. But if the distinguishing mark of belonging to a people is the ability to com-

[42] Virgil's depiction of the Rutulians carrying arms as they work the soil seems to be an innovation in an otherwise conventional ethnographical description; see Horsfall (1971), 1109. By repeating this innovation, Ovid signals his explicit debt to Virgil.

[43] Cf. Horsfall (1971), 1109: 'The Rutuli have clearly much in common with the stereotype picture of early Roman or honest countrymen, as also with ethnographical notices of barbarian peoples.'

[44] Cf. Hinds (1987a), 23 on *Tr.* 5.3: 'When Ovid describes Pontus in line 11 as a place clashing with arms, the programmatic hint in *armis* offers a literary analogy for his exile (the world of the Getae is like the world of strident epic).'

[45] For a subtle appreciation of Ovid's earlier creative involvement with the *Aeneid* see Due (1974), 36–42.

municate, then Ovid as *vates* and *artifex* is much more remote
from his Pontic tribesmen than (he complains) he is from
Rome.

The language which the Getae share is a simple social expedient with no subtle application – as Ovid indicates when he
states that the forum, the proper arena for articulate debate,
is often the scene of fighting rather than reasoned argument
(*Tr.* 5.10.44). These unlettered tribesmen mock Ovid's *verba
Latina* (38).[46] But Ovid's skilful manipulation of his language
in this poem makes nonsense of his claim that isolation from
Rome is driving him to develop an affinity with these inarticu-
late, unsubtle and illiterate Pontic tribesmen. On the contrary,
his poetic dexterity ensures his continuing alienation from the
peoples around him (cf. 37) in a secondary form of exile.

But despite the fact that Ovid is linguistically and culturally
isolated in Tomis, he claims to live *discrimine nullo* (29) with
some local tribesmen under the same roof; there is no parti-
tion or dividing wall to separate him from them. The cohabi-
tation of Roman and barbarian is anticipated, in different
circumstances, in Virgil's use of *nullo discrimine*, as when
Dido invites the Trojans to settle at Carthage and unite with
her own people:

> Tros Tyriusque mihi nullo discrimine agetur.
> (*Aen.* 1.574)

At *Aen.* 10.108 Jupiter refuses to side with either Venus or
Juno, confusing the tribal identities of the parties they
champion:

> Tros Rutulusne fuat, nullo discrimine habebo.

In both these cases *nullo discrimine* is used with reference to
the confusion of identities which are fated to be kept apart.
The Virgilian connotation, reduced from the national to the

---

[46] See Doblhofer (1986), 100–16 on Ovid's linguistic isolation in Tomis as a typical
feature of exilic experience in any age. Hauben (1975), 61–3 further suggests that
Ovid is isolated even on the level of gesture (cf. 41–2); when he nods 'yes' (*adnuit*)
in response to what the Tomitans say, they interpret it as a 'no' (*abnuit*) and vice
versa.

individual level, underlies Ovid's use of the phrase. Though he lives under the same roof as some Pontic tribesmen, with no dividing wall (*discrimen*) to separate him from them, the suggestive force of his allusive technique establishes the poet's distinctive pre-eminence over his fellow inhabitants: the *discrimen* which divides Ovid from the Getae is cultural, not physical. Hence the irony of Ovid's portrayal of himself as a *barbarus* because he does not speak the local language and cannot make himself understood by the Getae (37–8).[47] Although the term *barbarus* is used both of Ovid and his fellow-inhabitants in this poem (28, 30, 37), it is only its application to the poet himself which is ironical.

In this poem, as previously in *Tr.* 5.7, Ovid's depiction of the Tomitans and of his relations with them constructively exploits Virgilian reminiscence. If we view the poem as 'primarily descriptive and not a literary epistle',[48] then we are no more alive to the potential of Ovid's literary language than the Getae are to his spoken language.

Ovidian 'facts'

Ovid's Pontic ethnography owes more than has generally been realized to traditional stereotypes and to the evocation of the *Aeneid* through seemingly casual reminiscence. But while ethnographical distortions in previous writers such as Virgil entitle Ovid to take similar liberties in the *Tristia* and *Epistulae ex Ponto*, a second category of exilic 'fact' would appear to leave less room for creative manoeuvre. Three conspicuous 'facts' of this sort are the following: first, Ovid's report in *P.* 1.8 of a military campaign waged in the Pontic region by an unnamed king; secondly, his account in *P.* 4.7 of the part which Vestalis, a Roman *primus pilus*, played in that (or a similar) campaign; and, thirdly, his description in *P.* 2.10 of the youthful travels he made with the poet Macer. Even for a self-

---

[47] Cf. Saddington (1961), 91: 'Essentially a barbarian was someone who could not be understood.'
[48] Evans (1983), 99.

conscious poetic artist, a fact must, it would seem, remain inescapably a fact. But this is to underestimate Ovid's response to a challenge; as the following readings of these three elegies will show, Ovid makes objective factual reporting subordinate to his controlling artistic designs.

i

I begin with *P*. 1.8, a poem to Severus[49] in which Ovid contrasts the war-torn reality of Tomis (5–24) with fond recollection of the family, friends, city and countryside he has left behind in Italy (25–48); his wish for a simple rustic existence in Tomis (49–60) is as unrealistic as his hope of returning to Italy (61–74). Within this structure, my starting-point is Ovid's depiction of Rome and Italy in lines 25–48.

The cultured city and cultivated countryside form a harmonious compact.[50] The cohesive interaction between Rome and the surrounding countryside illustrates the security and stability which *Martia ... Roma* (24) has brought to Italy. The city has all the landmarks of a sophisticated urban environment; fora, temples, theatres and porticoes (35–6) are material monuments to social harmony, while canals and water-courses and landscaped gardens create the familiar civilized scene of *rus in urbe* (37–8).[51] The balance achieved within the city between the urban and the rural, city buildings and expanses of greenery, complements the balance between Rome and the Italian countryside as a whole. Roads connect the city with its surrounding regions (44). Rome is well supplied with water (38), and so is the Paelignian countryside (42; cf. *arva per-*

---

[49] This Severus is not to be identified with Cornelius Severus, the addressee of *P*. 4.2; Ovid states that the latter has not yet been named in the exile poetry (cf. *P*. 4.2.3–4). On the distinction between the two Severi see Syme (1978), 80–1 with Froesch (1967), 103 and 179 n. 104.

[50] In the *Eclogues* 'the city represents a constant threat to Arcadian values' (Coleman (1977), 32). In the *laus Italiae* of *G*. 2.136–76 the description of the Italian cities (155–7) is at odds with the vision of Italy as an idealized *Saturnia tellus* (173); see Thomas (1988), I 185–6 on 2.155–7. But at *P*. 1.8.33–48 I find no implicit criticism of urbanization in Ovid's portrayal of the harmonious unity between urban and rural elements in Italy.

[51] See Scholte (1933), 158–9 for detail on the locations Ovid mentions in lines 35–8.

errantur Paeligna liquentibus undis, *Am.* 2.16.5). Gardens adorn the rural hillsides (43) as well as the city (37), though in the countryside they are of course crop-producing rather than ornamental. Cultivation of the countryside (cf. 45–8) is a sign of Italy's security under the guardianship of Rome; in the exile poetry Ovid shows only too vividly how a war-torn environment is far from conducive to agriculture (cf. *Tr.* 3.10.67ff.).

This idyllic portrayal of Rome and its environment is set in stark contrast to Tomis and its environment. Tomis lacks the well-ordered buildings and gardens of Rome, and the social cohesion which the integrated Roman landscape symbolizes is in any case disrupted by the constant threat of war. The surrounding area lacks the exuberant fertility of the Paelignian region, and the harsh climate is as disruptive to crop-cultivation as the constant fighting. But Ovid's recollection of *horti* (37, 43) evokes more than the picturesque world from which he is excluded in Tomis. In *Tr.* 1.11 he excuses the allegedly poor quality of his exilic verse by citing the adverse circumstances in which it was composed (27–36), and then adds *non haec in nostris, ut quondam, scripsimus hortis* (37). Since the garden was once the haven of Ovid's creative *otium*, his recollection of himself as a gardener (*P.* 1.8.45–8) should also recall the poetic associations of *horti*. The verb *colo* (45) can of course denote not only the nurturing of plants but the cultivation of literary pursuits as well,[52] and the spring-water which refreshes plants (*fontanas . . . aquas*, 46) is also a source of poetic inspiration.[53] Both literary connotations are redundant in Tomis; if the absence of gardens deprives Ovid of the opportunity for cultivation, he is also denied the idyllic surroundings so conducive to his art.

If we allow, as I think we must, these literary associations of Ovid's representation of the Italian urban and rural land-

---

[52] Cf. *P.* 4.2.11–12 (on Cornelius Severus' poetic talent): *fertile pectus habes, interque Helicona colentes|uberius nulli provenit ista seges. Cultus* also describes elegant, polished verse (e.g. *carmina culta* (of Horace), *Tr.* 4.10.50; cf. *culte Tibulle, Am.* 1.15.28).

[53] For the inspiring *fons* see Virg. *G.* 2.175, Hor. *C.* 3.4.25, Prop. 3.1.3, 3.3.5, 51, Stat. *Ach.* 1.9 etc. with Nisbet and Hubbard (1970), 305 on *C.* 1.26.6.

scape, then his attempt at an imaginative recreation of this environment in Tomis (49–60) will be seen as the doomed, futile enterprise it in fact proves to be. The Tomitan mock-idyll, whose extensive affiliations to the pastoral mode will be illustrated presently, is a pathetic daydream (cf. 49–50; *velim*, 52). Ovid imagines himself (*ipse ego*, 51, 53) imposing the familiar pattern of ordered cultivation on a hostile and un-responsive environment. The cultivation of plants, which in Italy was part of a common social effort, is now a lonely, unproductive exercise in nostalgia. What Ovid would like to do in Tomis (51–60) is only possible in the context of a secure and ordered society and of collective social action; an individ-ual cannot create a civilization in a wilderness. The horticul-tural metaphor again has implications for Ovid's literary activity. As the Italian landscape cannot be successfully trans-planted to a different climatic region, so the literary culture which is a product of the *otium* of that landscape is inextrica-bly bound to its original geographical context. Hence, of course, Ovid's strong conviction that his poetic enterprise in Tomis is doomed to failure.

The idealized picture of a peaceful rustic existence (49–60) is a world apart from what Ovid portrays as the reality in Pontus – the fighting he describes in lines 5–24. These two sections do not simply contrast the 'reality' of a warlike envi-ronment with an idealized rural world; the contrast here ex-tends to the literary modes appropriate to the two worlds, those of martial epic and pastoral. These two worlds are, as we have seen, united in Rome and Italy, where the city's mar-tial supremacy both complements and guarantees the security of the countryside's rural tranquillity. But in Ovid's depiction of the Tomitan environment, both as it is (5–24) and as he would wish it to be (49–60), that harmony has never existed. It is the contrast between the respective literary modes relat-ing to these two worlds that makes the digression on Aegisos an integral part of *P*. 1.8.[54]

---

[54] Cf. Evans (1983), 137: 'the elegy is uneven in its development; the digression on Aegissos appears out of place with that which follows'. I follow the spelling of the name which is preferred by Ovid's mss and editors. Some writers, including Syme, prefer the variant Aegissus/-os.

After describing the war-like surroundings in which he lives (5–10), Ovid depicts a campaign waged by a local king, who remains unnamed, against the Getae after they had seized the town of Aegisos (11–24). Ovid is our only source for this campaign.[55] The unnamed king is commonly identified with Cotys, a Thracian ruler and son of Rhoemetalces.[56] He is the addressee of *P.* 2.9, though in that poem Ovid does not ascribe any particular campaign to him; had Cotys led a successful campaign against Aegisos, such an achievement would surely warrant mention in an elegy like *P.* 2.9, which is clearly designed to flatter. Aegisos is also mentioned twice in *P.* 4.7 (21, 53), a poem which recounts Vestalis' military exploits in the Pontic region. Little is known of Vestalis, though it is assumed that his campaign against Aegisos is the same as that portrayed in *P.* 1.8; Syme speculatively suggests that Vestalis was involved because 'perhaps the victory of Cotys was imperfect'.[57] In the absence of any corroborating evidence for the campaign against Aegisos and the exploits of either Cotys or Vestalis, the factual reliability of *P.* 1.8.11–24 is far from self-evident. Indeed, the stylistic techniques and allusions which give form and shape to the narrative in this passage are such that Ovid may well be inventing a campaign which never in fact took place.

In lines 3–24 as a whole Ovid brings the themes, tone and diction of martial epic into elegy. The theme itself is the most hackneyed motif in the epic stereotype, *rex et proelia*. The Roman precedents which cause the theme to be equated with the epic mode were already there in *Eclogue* 6 (*reges et proelia*, 3) and in Propertius 3.3 (*reges ... et ... facta*, 3),[58] and Horace had added to them by naming the characteristic epic themes as *res gestae regumque ducumque et tristia bella* (*Ars* 73). The epic theme presupposes an artistically contrived nar-

[55] See Syme (1978), 82.
[56] See Scholte (1933), 154–5 on line 16 and Syme (1978), 81–2.
[57] (1978), 82.
[58] Callimachus supplies an obvious precedent for the Virgilian and Propertian characterizations of epic (cf. βασιλ[η ...|ἢ ...] ... ἥρωας, *Aet*. fr. 1.3–5 (Pf.)); see Wimmel (1960), 78–83 on 'Könige und Heroen' with Brink (1971), 160ff. on 'norms of diction in poetic genres'.

rative to do it justice. For present purposes, the question of whether or not a campaign actually did take place to capture Aegisos from the Getae is consequently of secondary importance; my priority is to explore the artistic function and nature of Ovid's narrative, and not to weigh historical probabilities for which no historical evidence exists.

Ovid's artistic purpose can best be appreciated by examining the extent to which the basic epic theme of *rex et proelia* is consolidated in lines 3–24 with the help of supporting detail translated into elegy from its original epic context. Take lines 3–4, where Ovid declines to recount his sufferings to Severus, who must make do with a summary of them (*summa ... nostri ... mali*, 4). It is common epic practice to give the impression that a list of sorrows or complaints is unending by cutting short the list with a summary comment. At *Aen.* 1.341–2, for example, Venus cuts short the extended narrative of Dido's *longa iniuria* with *summa sequar fastigia rerum*. But a more telling model for *P.* 1.8.3–4 is a narrative which complements Venus' portrayal of Dido's past – the account which Aeneas gives Dido of his own past in *Aeneid* 2 and 3. First, Aeneas describes the distress which comes with the opening of old wounds: *quis talia fando ... temperet a lacrimis?* (2.6–8). Yet in deference to Dido's wishes (10–11), he will proceed with a summarized account of Troy's fall (cf. *breviter*, 11). Ovid's sufferings are equally distressing (*si persequar omnia, flebis, P.* 1.8.3); but, like Aeneas, he will relate them in summary form, anticipating Severus' wish to know the worst (cf. *neve roga quid agam*, 3). These associations between *P.* 1.8.3–4 and the opening of *Aeneid* 2 prepare the way for the elevated tone and epic diction of lines 5–24; and, as in *Aeneid* 2, Ovid's theme will be the capture of a city.

That an elegist should use epic diction in contrasting his turbulent present with the *pax* and *otium* of a past recreated in nostalgia was not, of course, a new phenomenon. Tibullus (1.10.45–50) pictures a rural environment in which peace prevails and the soldier's weapons grow rusty through neglect. That world is the antithesis of the world which the invention of war reduces to turmoil (1–4). The reason for Tibullus' invective against war at the start of the poem becomes apparent in line 13: *nunc ad bella trahor*. Like Tibullus, Ovid is torn away from his formerly peaceful existence and thrust into the theatre of war; and as in Tibullus' poem, *pax* evokes a world from which he is far removed (*P.* 1.8.5; cf. Tib. 1.10.45–8). Ovid's earlier military metaphors now take on a harsh realism. No longer the soldier of love (cf. *Am.* 1.9.1) but a real soldier (*P.* 1.8.7), he is threatened not by Cupid's arrows but by those of the Getae (6).[59] Since he loses the peace of mind (cf. *pacem mentis*, *Tr.* 5.12.4) which a poet needs to write competent verse (*Tr.* 5.12.3–4), it comes as no surprise when Ovid seeks Severus' indulgence for the deficiencies of poetry which is supposedly written before the commencement of battle (9–10).[60] His use of poetic military diction (*armis*, 5; *dura ... bella*, 6; *in procinctu*, 10) also locates the Pontic region in the literary world of Horace's *tristia bella* (*Ars* 73); the adjective *dura* (6) may signal the generic affiliations of the passage which follows.[61]

Predictably, Ovid's description of the campaign against Aegisos in lines 11–24 continues to offer programmatic insights into the function of the passage. *Stat vetus urbs* (11) is an ecphrastic opening of a kind which Ovid had used before in various contexts (cf. *Am.* 3.1.1, *F.* 2.253, 4.649–50), but which was a recognized epic conceit.[62] The incentive which the unnamed king has for going to war against the Getae – the enhancement of his family's prestige (*ille memor magni generis, virtute quod auget|... adest*, 17–18) – is a familiar motive for action in the world of martial epic. Dido had been quick to perceive such a spirit in the Trojans, declaring their *genus* to be famous for its *virtus* (*Aen.* 1.565–6). The Etruscan Valerus acted in accordance with *virtus avita* when he brought

---

[59] See again Nagle, (1980), 57.

[60] *In procinctu* does not mean that Ovid writes his poetry on the battlefield, as Wheeler (1924), 305 translates. The phrase denotes a state of readiness for battle (see *OLD* s.v. *procinctus*[2] 1); for its figurative application cf. Quint. *Inst.* 12.9.21; [*oratorem*] *armatum semper ac velut in procinctu stantem*.

[61] For the epic connotation of *durus* in Augustan literary debate see Hinds (1987), 141 n. 58 with Jackson (1914), 123–5.

[62] See Scholte (1933), 154 *ad loc.* with Helzle (1989), 167 on *P.* 4.7.24.

down Agis (*Aen.* 10.751–3), and the familial piety of Ovid's heroic king emulates that displayed by the Rutulian Camers (cf. *clarum ... paternae|nomen ... virtutis, Aen.* 12.225–6). The unnamed king's success entitles him to be hailed with the elevated superlative *fortissime* (21) in recognition of his prowess; there are a number of epic parallels (cf. *Aen.* 1.96, 5.389, 8.154, 513, 10.865).

While the depiction of this war-torn place of exile (5–24) relies heavily on epic language and conceit, the rustic tranquillity imagined in lines 49–60 evokes the contrasting literary world of pastoral poetry. A Virgilian allusion in this latter section points the way in which these two generically contrasted episodes are related. Escaping from the so-called 'reality' of Tomis, Ovid presents an idyllic picture of goats perched on the rocky hillside (*pendentis ... rupe capellas*, 51). This reminiscence of *Ecl.* 1.75–6 (*non ego vos [capellas] ... dumosa pendere procul de rupe videbo*) highlights the solemn farewell with which Meliboeus leaves both his goats (74) and his poetic music (77), renouncing the delights of the countryside. The reminiscence is especially pertinent to Ovid's own situation, since Meliboeus is being driven from his home (3–4), a victim of the confiscations, and must appeal to Octavian to redress the loss.[63] Like Meliboeus, Ovid describes in lines 49–60 the rural world from which he too is excluded by force of circumstance and which he longs to recreate elsewhere. His poetic visualization of the pastoral dream combines the fateful reference to the first *Eclogue* with the Tibullan vision of rural peace, which is introduced by the allusion in line 54 to Tib. 1.10.45–6 (*pax candida primum|duxit araturos sub iuga curva boves*). As we saw earlier, the influence of Tibullan *pax* only serves to emphasize the contrast between the idyllic pastoral world of 49–60 and the prevailing martial tone in 5–24, where Ovid lives among those *expertes pacis* (5). Then there is Ovid's curious picture of himself as a shepherd *baculo ... nixus* (52), a picture which recalls his depiction in *Metamorphoses* 8 of

---

[63] Ovid may possibly have in mind that Tityrus in *Eclogue* 1 was successful in his plea to Octavian for some measure of restitution for his loss of land (cf. 44–5). *P.* 1.8 will end with Ovid's 'moderate' plea for a *terra propior* (73–4).

the shepherd who, *baculo ... innixus* (218), catches sight of
Daedalus and Icarus in full flight. In *Metamorphoses* 8 the
shepherd's pastoral simplicity is set in contrast to Daedalus'
technical sophistication. In *P.* 1.8, however, the contrast with
the pastoral world is provided not by technological advance-
ment but by the disorder and chaos caused by war.

This simple but effective contrast between war and peace
adds a new dimension to the reminiscence of the first *Eclogue*.
That poem introduced the Virgilian synthesis of the contrasting themes of pastoral simplicity and the menacing intru-
sion of war (cf. 70–2). Similarly, the reality of Ovid's circumstances in exile casts a shadow over his description of the
pastoral world, and in lines 61–2 his dream is dispelled. Only
a thin defensive wall separates Ovid from the marauding enemy outside the town, and such a slender barrier (*minimum ...
discrimen*, 61–2) makes a rural existence in and around Tomis
an impossibility. In setting the world of incessant warfare and
the world of rustic tranquillity in opposition to each other,
Ovid contrasts two sections which are clearly distinguished in
their stylistic and generic affiliations.[64] The harmonizing of
these contrasting sections in a unified and balanced picture is
a theme which re-emerges at the end of the poem. In lines
65–8 Ovid reminds Severus of the balance achieved between
urban and rural elements in Italy. The Campus, porticoes and
forum detain Severus, while the Appian Way connects the city
with the rural delights of his Alban estates and Umbria. At
the end of the poem Ovid returns to Italy's environmental
balance, which is his theme in lines 31–48; in doing so, he
drives home the point that no such balance exists between
Tomis and its surrounding environment. The poem is therefore structured in a way which polarizes the martial and pastoral sections around the central *laudes Italiae*: here alone
both sections are united in harmony.

The intricate poetic mechanism of *P.* 1.8 distinguishes and
harmonizes contrasted generic stereotypes in a way which in-

[64] This kind of contrast is sharply delineated in the opening *recusatio* of *Eclogue* 6
(1–8), the generic affiliations of which are clearly mapped out by Servius on lines
3 and 5 (p. 65 Thilo).

tegrates what has been thought to be a digression on Aegisos
(11–24) into a structured and unified whole. This does not in
itself make the Aegisos narrative a fiction; but it does entail
the narrative's subservience to a poetic structure, to the extent
that in the absence of corroborating evidence it would be un-
wise to try to fix the boundaries of Ovidian invention.

ii

The historical status of the Aegisos narrative in *P*. 1.8 has
obvious implications for Ovid's portrayal in *P*. 4.7 of Vestalis'
part in a campaign against the same town. Again, we have no
corroborating evidence. Next to nothing is otherwise known
about Vestalis and nothing at all is heard about his military
exploits in the Pontic region.[65] Ovid is our sole source for
these extraordinary achievements, a fact which should at once
arouse suspicion. A Roman legion, in which Vestalis serves as
primus pilus, supposedly sails down the Danube (27) and
mounts a ferocious assault (33ff.) on a city which is notoriously inaccessible (24) and under Getic occupation. After very
fierce fighting the Romans break in, and the ensuing battle at
close quarters ends with a virtual massacre of the Getic defenders (47–8). Whether the captured city was returned to the
Thracian king who had formerly ruled it (cf. 25), whether that
king is the Cotys of *P*.2.9 or someone else, and whether the
Romans were acting on his behalf or independently, are all
questions which the poem leaves unresolved. The lack of contemporary reference in the historians to this bold and highly
successful campaign is both surprising and perhaps revealing
about the nature of Ovid's poetic performance.

To return briefly to *Tr*. 3.10, Ovid uses two tactics to enhance the credibility of his description of the Tomitan environment, even though his account is clearly dependent on

---

[65] See Syme (1978), 82–3 and Helzle (1989), 157 for discussion of Vestalis' possible
origins and status as a minor official on the lower Danube. Helzle notes that
Vestalis' career must have been quite remarkable (or incredible?) if he was a
primus pilus while still a *iuvenis* (cf. 6) and so under 45; the usual age was about 50
(see Dobson (1974), 411).

Virgil's depiction of Scythia at *G*. 3.349–83. First, Ovid emphasizes the narrator's personal experience of the conditions he describes (*vidimus*, 37, 49; cf. *nec vidisse sat est. durum calcavimus aequor*, 39). Along with *aspiceres* (75), these are the most obvious indications that the description is an ecphrastic artifice. Secondly, he attempts to draw the fire of sceptics by claiming that he tells the truth, even though the truth defies belief:

> vix equidem credar, sed, cum sint praemia falsi
> nulla, ratam debet testis habere fidem.
>
> (35–6)

But Ovid's exaggerations, of which these protestations of trustworthiness are a sure sign, combine with his clear dependence on Virgil to undermine his credibility. In *P*. 4.7, however, he finds an ally and potential witness to his credibility. Vestalis can see for himself the conditions in which Ovid lives (*aspicis en praesens*, 3), a point driven home rather obviously by the triple *ipse vides* (7, 8, 9; cf. *aspicis*, 11). Vestalis' own observation of the scene will bear out Ovid's portrayal of the region, or so the poet claims: *accedet voci per te non irrita nostrae ... fides* (5–6). Here *voci* must refer to Ovid's account of the environmental conditions in Tomis as they are presented in the exile poetry, especially *Tr*. 3.10. It comes as no surprise to find that lines 7–12 yield a number of points of contact with the *Tristia* elegy.[66]

Now if we accept the likely proposition that Ovid's portrayal of the Pontic environment in *P*. 4.7 as well as *Tr*. 3.10 is truer to a literary model than to any external reality in Tomis, he is left with a seemingly insurmountable problem. How can he seek confirmation from Vestalis for an account of environmental conditions which is untrue to fact? The answer is that Ovid enters into something like a reciprocal arrangement with his addressee. In return for Vestalis' testimony to

---

[66] Cf. *P*. 4.7.7 and *Tr*. 3.10.37; *P*. 4.7.8 and *Tr*. 3.10.23–4; *P*. 4.7.9–10 and *Tr*. 3.10.33–4 (adding *Tr*. 3.12.29–30); *P*. 4.7.11–12 and *Tr*. 3.10.63–4; see also Gahan (1978), 198–202. For parallels between Virgil's Scythia and *P*. 4.7, cf. *P*. 4.7.7 and *G*. 3.360; *P*. 4.7.8 and *G*. 3.364; *P*. 4.7.9–10 and *G*. 3.361–2.

the truthfulness of Ovid's depiction of the Tomitan environment (cf. *nec me testis eris falsa solere queri*, 4), the poet bears witness to his addressee's military prowess (cf. *testata ... tempus in omne|sunt tua ... carmine facta meo*, 53–4). This reciprocal arrangement places Vestalis in an impossible position. If he were to deny the factual reliability of Ovid's portrayal of the region, the veracity of his own deeds as recorded by the poet would also invite scepticism. In effect, Vestalis cannot afford to challenge the poet's credibility and so damage his own claim to greatness – a claim which is founded entirely on Ovid's poetic celebration of him.

But if, on the other hand, Ovid's dependence on Virgil reduces his credibility as a reporter of environmental conditions in the Pontic region, what faith can we have in his portrayal of Vestalis' exploits, which may prove to be similarly derivative? What faith can we have in a poet who claims at *Am.* 3.12.19, admittedly when put on the defensive, *nec ... ut testes mos est audire poetas* and who then excuses himself with the assurance

> exit in immensum fecunda licentia vatum
> obligat historica nec sua verba fide?
>
> (41–2)

The reader who is familiar with such asseverations is duly cautious when confronted with *P.* 4.7, since no specific limit has been marked out for the kind of *credulitas* which Ovid warns against at *Am.* 3.12.44. Why, then, should we be reluctant to believe the scale of Vestalis' exploits as described by Ovid (15–52)? The answer lies in more than Ovid's hyperbolical tone; his diction abounds with conceits and points of allusion which turn Vestalis into the kind of hero who exists only in the unreal world of martial epic.

As at *P.* 1.8.11–24, Ovid's subject-matter at *P.* 4.7.15–52 is the staple epic theme of *reges et proelia*. Vestalis is of royal stock, or so Ovid claims when he addresses him as *Alpinis iuvenis regibus orte* (6). This periphrastic form of address, as exuberant and misleading as *progenies alti fortissima Donni* in line 29, has little to do with presenting reliable information; it

belongs to the elevated style and anticipates the epic affiliations of the martial section which follows (15ff.).[67] Anaphora
of the verb (19, 21) is, of course, a common rhetorical device
for creating emphasis and increasing tension,[68] while the per-
sonified Danube (19) and Aegisos (21) recall similar personifi-
cations in Homer (e.g. *Il.* 21.211ff. etc.) and Virgil (e.g. *Aen.*
8.728 etc.).[69] Adjectives in *-eus* such as *puniceam* (20) and
vipereo (36) are notable features of the grand style,[70] and the
theme of rivers turned red by the blood of the vanquished has
a long literary history which extends back to Homer (*Il.* 21.21)
and includes Virgil (*Aen.* 6.86–7). Not content with turning
the Danube red with blood, Vestalis makes a frontal assault
on the enemy (29–30); *impetus* (30) both conveys the urge
which drives him on and foreshadows the attack he mounts.
Gleaming in his shining arms (*conspicuus longe fulgentibus
armis*, 31) as if another Pallas (cf. *pictis conspectus in armis*,
Aen. 8.558) or Marcellus (cf. *egregium forma iuvenem et fulgentibus armis*, *Aen.* 6.861), his epic uniform is complete.

Advancing as if with the urgency of the Trojan and Italian
forces pitted against each other in *Aeneid* 12 (cf. *nec mora nec
requies*, 553), this one-man army is unstoppable and never
hesitant (cf. *nec mora*, 31). The assonance of the repeated *-que*
in lines 33–4 evokes the strident clash of arms as well as the
impact of the hail-like shower of rocks which rains down in-
cessantly on Vestalis: *saxa ... brumali grandine plura subis*
(34). Here Ovid uses a well-worn literary conceit to portray
his addressee's supposedly unique achievement. Missiles falling like a shower of hail or snow appear in Homer (cf. *Il.*
12.278–89) and recur on a number of occasions in the *Ae-*

---

[67] See Helzle (1989), 162 on 5f. with Nisbet and Hubbard (1970), 164 on *C.* 1.12.50 for examples of periphrastic address in the elevated genres. The royal pedigree attributed to Vestalis here is apparently a fiction; see Syme (1978), 82 ('The labels do not deceive').
[68] See, e.g., *Aen.* 2.483–4 with Austin (1964), 189 on 484.
[69] Quintilian (*Inst.* 8.6.11) writes of the heightened effect (*mira sublimitas*) attained by using names *quae audaci et proxime periculum tralatione tolluntur, cum rebus sensu carentibus actum quendam et animos damus*, and then cites the example at *Aen.* 8.728.
[70] See Norden (1957), 218 on *vipereum* at *Aen.* 6.281.

neid;[71] but a more immediate point of contact for Ovid's use of the motif in *P.* 4.7 is *M.* 5.158. During the fight over Andromeda between Perseus and the band led by Phineus, his rival suitor, Perseus is faced by his attackers, one against many (*omnibus unum*|*opprimere est animus*, 149–50). The weapons fly thicker than hail (*tela volant hiberna grandine plura*, 158; cf. *P.* 4.7.34), and though he parries the immediate attack (162), force of numbers soon compels him to produce Medusa's head and petrify the enemy (177ff.). Like Perseus, Vestalis is depicted as fighting the enemy almost single-handed; unlike Perseus, however, he has no need of a magical device to help him win. Relying on his own strength as he sweeps all before him, Vestalis is being turned into a figure of heroic legend in his own lifetime.

Even poisoned arrows do nothing to halt his progress (36). Ovid is in mortal danger from the arrows of the locals in and around Tomis (cf. *Tr.* 3.10.64, 4.1.77, 5.7.15–16, *P.* 1.2.16), but Vestalis simply ignores them with superhuman disdain. A literary precedent also lies behind the portrayal of the arrows which are lodged in his helmet and leave no part of his shield unscathed (37–8). In his confrontation with Aeneas, Mezentius hurls missile after missile at his opponent, but Aeneas' shield stands up to the attack (*Aen.* 10.884). As Mezentius wheels around him, Aeneas turns as well:

> ter secum Troius heros
> immanem aerato circumfert tegmine silvam.
> (886–7)

Silvam denotes the 'forest' of missiles fixed in Aeneas' shield.[72] As if a second Aeneas, Vestalis' armour is also thickly covered with missiles – though not the missiles of a single

---

[71] At *Aen.* 9.666–71 the ferocity of the fighting between the Trojans and Italians is likened to the ferocity of a heavy rainstorm (668–9) and hailstorm (669–70); after the reference to bows in 665 and missiles littering the ground in 666, the downpour of rain and hail suggests the mass of falling arrows. At *Aen.* 10.803–10 the missiles raining down on Aeneas (cf. *obrutus undique telis*, 808) are likened to a hailstorm. Cf. *Aen.* 5.458–60, where Entellus showers Dares with a series of boxing-blows which fall as heavily as hail.

[72] Cf. Luc. 6.205, Stat. *Theb.* 5.533 and Sil. 4.619, all of whom make the Virgilian picture more grotesque by lodging the 'forest' of arrows in the warrior's body.

enemy as in Aeneas' case, but those of the whole massed ranks of the Getae.

Like Sarpedon, who refuses to give way to Ajax and Teucer ἐπεί οἱ θυμὸς ἐέλπετο κῦδος ἀρέσθαι (*Il.* 12.407), Vestalis is driven on by ambition for glory (*acri laudis amore*, 40). Equipped as he is with the motivation and prowess of an epic hero, it comes as no surprise that he is explicitly compared to such a hero in lines 41–2. The simile is evidently hyperbolical, making Vestalis appear an epic hero incarnate rather than reducing him to a merely fictional construct like Ajax. But Ovid tactfully overlooks the fact that Vestalis is not confronted by enemies like Hector, Ajax's opponent at *Il.* 15.415ff.; Vestalis is able to show off his Ajax-like powers against rather less formidable opposition.

Equally hyperbolical is Ovid's claim that he finds difficulty in recounting Vestalis' exploits (45). Virgil faces a similar dilemma in portraying the number of Camilla's victims at *Aen.* 11.664–5:

> quem telo primum, quem postremum, aspera virgo,
> deicis? aut quot humi morientia corpora fundis?[73]

Only a token selection of her victims can be listed because there are so many of them (cf. 676–7). Like Camilla, Vestalis is the author of wholesale slaughter, and the epic scale of his achievement is complemented by the epic nuance of Ovid's diction in line 46. *Neci dederis* is a suitably grandiloquent phrase which Virgil also uses for Turnus' slaughter of the enemy at *Aen.* 12.341.[74] But Ovid's choice of diction may also discredit his own attempt at epic hyperbole. His language in line 46 closely resembles that at *Am.* 2.8.27–8, where he warns Cypassis that if she denies him her favours, he will tell Corinna *quo ... loco tecum fuerim quotiensque ... quotque quibusque modis*. There are grounds for suspecting that at *P.* 4.7.46 Ovid redeploys a tried and tested formula and that by converting the amatory context into a battle-scene, he gently deflates his inflated portrayal of Vestalis' deeds.

---

[73] Conington and Nettleship (1898), III 381 *ad loc.* give *Il.* 5.703 and 16.692 as precedents for this kind of epic apostrophe.

[74] For further examples see *TLL* 5.1695.26ff. with Bömer (1982), 152 on *M.* 12.459.

Vestalis' rout leaves a trail of destruction with corpses littering the battlefield (47–8). The epic affiliations of this couplet have been well documented,[75] but one possible implication seems to have passed unnoticed. The hexameter ending *victor acervos* (47) is paralleled at *Aen.* 8.562, where Evander, recalling his victory over Erulus of Praeneste, describes how he celebrated his victory by burning piles of shields captured from the enemy. At *P.* 4.7.47 Ovid applies *acervos* to heaps of corpses, and the juxtaposition with *victor* takes on a sinister significance. Evander's action anticipated and provided a model for the heroic Roman ritual of shield-burning after a victory. Vestalis, however, is not satisfied with the triumphal ceremony performed by Evander or, for example, by Claudius Marcellus after Nola (Liv. 23.46.5). He unceremoniously sweeps aside both precedent and propriety, heaping up not the enemy's shields but their bodies, and trampling on top of the pile (48). The Virgilian echo here suggests the extent of Vestalis' departure from the heroic model; it must also cast in an ironic light the celebration of Vestalis' *virtus* in 51–2. How appropriate can it be to apply to Vestalis the manly courage and moral sensibility which are fundamental characteristics of an epic hero?

Through Ovid's allusive use of diction in lines 15–54, Vestalis' exploits are given a highly stylized epic dimension which, as the closing couplet informs us, is as decisive in establishing Vestalis' heroic status as his contribution was to the conquest of Aegisos. Such *fama* as the poem will confer clearly answers the addressee's own expectations (cf. 32, 40) and will presumably be sufficient to elicit his support as a witness to Ovid's veracity. Yet the epic allusions which underpin this poetic construction must also call into question whether what we read is even a moderately accurate historical report. And the construction itself is not monotonously uniform in its effect; cross-currents from other than epic sources (e.g. *Am.* 2.8) introduce nuances which run counter to what is superficially the declared purpose of the piece. Above all, Ovid's eulogy simply

---

[75] See Helzle (1989), 173 with references to *Il.* 5.886, *Aen.* 10.509 etc.

goes too far. The kind of epic hero which Vestalis becomes in
P. 4.7 simply does not exist outside the world of literary invention. Literary cliché, stylized vocabulary, gross exaggera-
tion – all combine to form a picture of military heroism which
is surely stretched beyond the bounds of belief.

This point needs to be stressed because recent criticism has
inclined towards taking Ovid's eulogy at face value. Wilkinson, for example, shows not the slightest hint of scepticism
when he states that *P.* 4.7 'is a citation of his [Vestalis'] act of
gallantry in leading the assault on the apparently impregnable
site, regardless of the steepness and the hail of stones and
poisoned arrows'.[76] Reactions of this sort seem to overlook
both the extensive use of hyperbole in Ovid's eulogy and the
possibility that, in the absence of any corroborating evidence,
his portrayal of the campaign against Aegisos may be either a
creation of his own which accords Vestalis an ironically inflated status as an epic hero, or at least liberally embellished
fact. The consequence of this uncritical acceptance of Ovid's
eulogy is that he has again imposed on his readers' credulity.
If, however, we adopt a more critical approach by taking full
account of the exaggerations and literary conceits which per-
vade Ovid's account of Vestalis' heroism, our confidence in
him is diminished. And as soon as his portrayal of Vestalis is
seen to be incredible, what faith can we have in the portrayal
of his environment (5–12)?

The answer is that Ovid is simply not to be trusted on either
count, and the further consequence is that we must take *P.* 4.7
to be fundamentally ironic. Several indications in the earlier
analysis have already pointed in this direction. Ovid appeals
to Vestalis to confirm the accuracy of his portrayal of environmental conditions in Tomis. But this tactic backfires because
the eulogy he offers in exchange for Vestalis' support lacks
the very credibility which he sets out to enhance by means

---

[76] Wilkinson (1955), 362. For similarly credulous responses see Nagle (1980), 172,
Evans (1983), 159 and Claassen (1986), 214. Cf. Helzle (1989), 160: 'Ovid ... uses
encomiastic topoi and epic motifs in conjunction with more matter of fact histor-
iographical vocabulary and material in order to secure Vestalis' *amicitia* which
might prove useful to him in Tomi.'

of this elegy. Ovid, it would seem, is anything but a candid reporter.

iii

P. 2.10 is a different kind of elegy. In this instance Ovid offers descriptive detail not about his environment in exile but about his pre-exilic past. As in the case of *P.* 1.8 and *P.* 4.7, however, a close examination of the poem's diction suggests that in his account of his past he carefully structures his facts to execute an intricate artistic design.[77] The elegy is addressed to a certain Macer, an epic poet who is also presumed to be the addressee of *Am.* 2.18.[78] There, as in *P.* 2.10, generic differentiation provides the poem's central theme of comparison and contrast. While his addressee writes an epic prelude to the *Iliad* (*Am.* 2.18.1–2),[79] Ovid marks out the lighter genre of love elegy for himself: *nos ... ignava Veneris cessamus in umbra,|et tener ausuros grandia frangit Amor* (3–4). A formal *recusatio* (11) leads him away from the world of martial epic to the domestic wars he wages as a soldier of love (12).

In *P.* 2.10 these different poetic identities are reaffirmed in accordance with the earlier generic differentiation. Macer perseveres with the Trojan cycle (13–14), while Ovid pays the penalty for his ill-fated *Ars Amatoria* (15–16). This distinction is clearly marked by *diversum ... iter* in line 18, which denotes more than the different courses which the lives of Macer and Ovid have taken, with the latter's fall from favour and subsequent relegation. The phrase also embraces the contrasting poetic paths (the Callimachean κελεύθους of *Aet.* fr. 1.27 (Pf.)) which Macer and Ovid follow as practitioners of different genres,[80] while still sharing common literary interests (*com-*

---

[77] Cf. G. D. Williams (1991), 173–6; the present section expands my earlier treatment of the poem.
[78] The Macer addressed in *P.* 2.10 is generally assumed to be Pompeius Macer, son of the historian Theophanes of Mytilene and appointed director of libraries by Augustus (cf. Suet. *Iul.* 56.7); so Syme (1978), 73–4, but see now White (1992), 210–18. Schwartz (1951), 193 claims that Macer was the father of Ovid's second wife, but uncertainty remains (see Froesch (1967), 218 n. 394).
[79] Cf. *P.* 4.16.6, where Ovid refers to *Iliacus ... Macer.*
[80] For this sense of a poetic *iter* cf. *P.* 4.16.32: [*cum*] *Callimachi Proculus molle teneret iter.*

munia sacra, 17). When Ovid immediately appears to be interpreting *iter* in a concrete sense (21ff.), referring to the travels he claims to have made with Macer through Asia Minor and Sicily, the journey need not necessarily be read as authentic, undoctored autobiography. The poem has already touched on the ways in which Ovid and Macer follow different poetic paths, alluding to their contrasting *itinera* in line 18. As their joint expedition unfolds, we should expect the route they follow to reflect features of the literary path which each pursues independently, and it is no surprise to find their shared *via* (32, 35) productive of rich satisfaction to each party.

The significance of the journey will become more apparent when the generic differentiation which lines 11–16 inherit from *Am.* 2.18 is put in a wider context. Already in 17 *tamen* introduces a balancing factor: the two poets may follow different paths, but their shared interest in poetry is a bond which holds them together to their mutual advantage. What is emphasized from this point on is that the generic differences of lines 11–16 are no longer as sharply divisive as they once were (cf. *tu*, 13; *Naso*, 15), but rather complement each other by bringing variety and richness to a shared relationship. Their interaction and mutually supportive co-operation provide, of course, a close parallel to the relationship between the poets themselves. This is not surprising, since the very beginning of the poem was concerned to stress the way in which the epistle's seal is an *imago* (cf. 1) or *index* (3) of its *auctor*, enabling the personal identity of the poet to be recognized in his stamp and, more significantly, in his creation: *cognitane est nostra littera facta manu*? (4). If the 'real' poet is to be found in his work and not in his physical presence, the relationship between Ovid and Macer is not interrupted by the former's exile (45–8), and the poet's *imago* on the seal and ring (1–3) is more securely stamped on the *memori pectore* (52; cf. 19, 47); the impression made on each by the reading of each other's poetry is firmly fixed as an unmistakable poetic 'presence', even though Ovid and Macer are apart.

Essential elements in the relationship between Ovid and Macer as it unfolds in lines 35–42 are common to earlier poems on the theme of friendship between poets. Conversation characterized by witty exchanges (*iocos*, 42) and pursued to the point of exhaustion (37–8) was a feature of Catullus' relationship with Licinius Calvus (cf. 50.1–13); Ovid and Macer converse until well after sunset (37), like Callimachus and Heraclitus of Halicarnassus (cf. *Epigr.* 2.3 (Pf.)). Callimachus' epigram takes us further in providing a model for Ovid's central theme: the physical separation of friends need not affect a continuing life and 'presence' in their poetic achievement. Heraclitus is dead, but his poetry lives on (αἱ δὲ τεαὶ ζώουσιν ἀηδόνες, 5);[81] Ovid is forcibly separated from Macer, but Macer is still vividly 'present' in Ovid's cherished memory of him as both a friend (*hic es, et ignoras, et ades celeberrimus absens*, 49) and fellow poet (cf. 17–18). The way in which Ovid's portrayal of his friendship with Macer recalls these earlier poetic friendships shows in itself how such relationships enjoy a continuity which transcends the physical separation of the participants. Here again the personal identity of the poet is subsumed in the greater, more durable identity of his poetic achievement.

The harmonious poetic *convictus* which Ovid and Macer continue to share alters the complexion of the poem's generic differentiation. The latter is no longer the divisive factor of lines 13–16; each may follow his *diversum ... iter* (18), though they jointly travel along the same *via* (32, 35). Their unity in diversity is characterized in lines 33–4 by the contrasting modes of transport which, despite their differing generic affiliations, are shared jointly by both poets. *Seu rate caeruleas picta sulcavimus undas* (33): the hexameter (appropriately) recalls the 'painted ships' which Virgil took from Homer (*Aen.* 5.663, 7.431, 8.93),[82] and their metaphorical 'ploughing' of the sea seems to be a Virgilian innovation (cf. *Aen.* 5.158, 10.197) which Ovid copied in the *Metamorphoses* (cf. 4.707) and also in his extended comparison with Jason in *P.* 1.4 (cf.

---

[81] See Gow and Page (1965), II 192 *ad loc.* for ἀηδόνες denoting Heraclitus' poetry, just as its cognate term denotes Callimachus' own poetry if Housman's ἀ[ηδονίδες] is read at Call. *Aet.* fr. 1.16.

[82] On these painted ships in Homer see Kirk (1985), 221–2 on *Il.* 2.637. Ovid copies this epic motif at *M.* 2.533, 3.639 and 6.511.

35) – a comparison (23–46) which is designed to elevate the poet's exilic woes up to and even beyond (cf. 45–6) the heights of epic heroism. In contrast to the epic connotations of the hexameter, the pentameter refers to the former barbarian warchariot 'adopted as a light "gig" by the Romans':[83] *esseda nos agili sive tulere rota* (34). The *essedum* was a fashionable vehicle for pleasure-trips, carrying Cynthia to Tibur (Prop. 2.32.5) and Corinna to Sulmo (*Am.* 2.16.49). Its light, swift progress (cf. *agili rota*) offers elegiac relief to the heavy ploughing of the epic waves in the hexameter. The distinction between the two modes of travel here only suggests different areas of generic interest and does not divide the two travellers from each other. A similar balance of unity in generic diversity can be detected in the course of the poets' joint itinerary (21–30).

It is highly appropriate that Macer should be depicted as Ovid's guide on their joint travels (*te duce*, 21–2; cf. 32), for by going to Asia Minor Macer travels to his literary home, the setting for the war which supplies the themes of his poetry both here (cf. 13–14) and in *Am.* 2.18.[84] He subsequently conducts Ovid from Asia Minor to Sicily, thereby repeating the journey which Aeneas made. Ovid and Macer see Etna in its fiery splendour (23) as Aeneas and his men had before them (*Aen.* 3.554; cf. 574). At *Aen.* 3.578–80 Virgil portrays Enceladus as lying beneath Etna after being struck down by Jupiter's bolt, though according to the more common tradition in antiquity he was buried under Mt Inarime and Typhon was buried under Etna.[85] In view of Ovid's choice at *M.* 5.346–8 and *F.* 1.573–4, where Typhon is located under Etna, it is likely that he refers to Typhon when he writes *subpositus*

[83] Butler and Barber (1933), 193 on Prop. 2.1.76.
[84] But line 21 is generically complicated by a possible evocation of Catullus 46. About to leave Bithynia for Rome, Catullus writes *ad claras Asiae volemus urbes* (6); like Catullus, Ovid visits *Asiae ... urbes* (21) on a journey westward bound from Asia Minor. Does Ovid combine Macer's epic presence in line 21 with a Catullan hint of (unity in) generic diversity?
[85] For Typhon buried beneath Etna see [Aesch.] *Pr.* 365, Pi. *P.* 1.20, *O.* 4.8–9, Ov. *M.* 5.346–8, *F.* 1.573–4, 4.491–2 etc. As at *Aen.* 3.578–82, Virgil reverses the punishments of Enceladus and Typhon at 9.716 (*Inarime Iovis imperiis imposta Typhoeo*); so Luc. 6.293–5, Stat. *Theb.* 3.594–7, 11.8, 12.275 and Claud. *Rapt. Pros.* 1.153.

monti ... Gigans (24); but it is also possible that *Gigans* is left undefined as a deliberate ploy to facilitate the Virgilian association. For present purposes, however, the important point is that Ovid's reference to the Giant buried under Etna continues the associations with the scene which confronted Aeneas on approaching Sicily. It should also be recalled that in Augustan poetry references to the Gigantomachy most often occur in the standard epic *recusatio*.[86]

The use in lines 21–4 of material usually associated with an epic context is both clear and unproblematic, but the literary associations of 25–8 are more complex. Here, Ovid creates points of contact with two sources – his accounts of the rape of Persephone at *F*. 4.417–620 and *M*. 5.341–571. In all three places Sicily is styled [*terra*] *Trinacris* (*F*. 4.420, *M*. 5.347, *P*. 2.10.22), a form which seems to be an Ovidian coinage from the Greek. Ovid and Macer visit Henna (25), the scene of the rape in *Fasti* 4 (cf. 422, 455, 462), and Cyane and Anapus (26), which are also combined in one line at *F*. 4.469 as places passed by Ceres in searching for her daughter. Evocations of *Metamorphoses* 5 are more extensive and significant. Before his account of the rape Ovid sets the scene by describing Typhon's restlessness (346–58); the phrase *vomit ore Typhoeus* (353) appears in *P*. 2.10 as *vomit ore Gigans* (24).[87] In both the *Fasti* and *Metamorphoses* the scene of the rape is mentioned after reference to the buried giant. The setting in *Metamorphoses* 5 is specified as a lakeside glade at Henna (385ff.), and Pluto carries his victim *per ... lacus altos et olentia sulphure ...|stagna Palicorum rupta ferventia terra* (405–6). Ovid and Macer visit both places, *Hennaeos ... lacus et olentis stagna Palici* (25). On returning to Sicily after her fruitless search, Ceres visits Cyane (465) and finds Persephone's girdle (470); Arethusa eventually reveals her daughter's whereabouts. Ovid's narrative sequence in *P*. 2.10 is again comparable: first he mentions Cyane (26), then he refers to Arethusa with

---

[86] Examples are conveniently listed by Hardie (1986), 87 n. 6 with supporting bibliography. Add Ov. *M*. 10.149–51, and see also Nisbet and Hubbard (1978), 189–90 on *C*. 2.12.7 with Hinds (1987), 129.

[87] So Hinds (1987), 141 n. 1.

nymphe (27). The story Arethusa tells, at the end of the Persephone myth in *Metamorphoses* 5, of her pursuit and rape by
Alpheus is matched by Ovid's allusion to this same story at
the end of his account of his Sicilian travels with Macer (27–
8). The Sicilian visit turns out to have been a whistle-stop tour
of places connected with the story of Persephone's abduction,
and the sequence of these places in *P.* 2.10 repeats the sequence in which they occur in *Metamorphoses* 5.

After noting some of these verbal echoes at *P.* 2.10.21ff.,
Hinds draws a speculative conclusion: 'One might perhaps
read Ovid's insistent allusion to *Metamorphoses* 5 . . . as a hint
(which need not, of course, be taken at face value) that it was
on this early trip with Macer that he drew the main inspiration for the narrative of this part of the *Metamorphoses*.'[88]
But quite apart from the question of whether the Sicilian to-
pography of *Metamorphoses* 5 presupposes first-hand familiarity with the island's geography, we should be reluctant to
accept with Hinds that the itinerary of *P.* 2.10 is an innocent
narrative of a supposedly 'real' journey. It is not simply that
Ovid's allusive technique can make such a reading seem too
literal, but that Hinds' view does not account fully for the
contribution which the itinerary makes to the understanding
of *P.* 2.10 as a whole. In arguing my earlier point that a pervasive theme of this poem is the way in which the respective
'poetic identities' of Ovid and Macer are both stamped on the
texture of the verse, I already anticipated the integration of
the itinerary into this overall picture.

Whatever may have been the case with biographical fact
which is now irrecoverable, Ovid and Macer are present in
this poem only as literary identities. From the outset (cf. 4),
recognition of the poet is attained through recognition of his
verse, so that his verse becomes the *imago* of the poet's own
self. This notion was developed in the elementary generic differentiation of lines 13–18, which set the idea of 'poetic identity' in the familiar framework of the distinction between epic
and elegy. But while differentiation of this kind clarified the

[88] (1987), 141 n. 1.

individual poet's identity, it also made it possible for practitioners of different poetic genres to share a mutually enriching life together. This point makes an embryonic appearance in line 17, but it is fully developed in the friendship section at 35ff.

Since his verse is the poet's true *imago*, we would expect the poetic texture of *P.* 2.10 to reflect both the shared intimacy of the two poets and the distinctive areas in which they practise their craft. The narrative of the shared journey provides an ideal vehicle for this purpose. The different *itinera* which the two follow in line 18 are fused into the single *iter* which they undertake together at 21ff., just as the generic differentiations of 13–16 are fused in the *communia sacra* (17) which they jointly share as poets. Their union in diversity is reflected not only in the contrasting modes of transport (33–4), but in the details of their shared itinerary. The strong epic associations of 23–4 reflect Macer's distinctive interests, while 25–8 draw heavily on those unique Ovidian hybrids, the *Fasti* and *Metamorphoses*. Dominating this section is the theme of unity amid generic diversity.

In bringing together these different elements, epic and elegiac, which retain their individual identity within the context they both share, Ovid's itinerary proves to be an *imago* of the relationship between the poets themselves. If there is historical fact behind the journey to Asia and Sicily, Ovid is not merely reporting it; he fashions his portrayal of that journey to the point where, within the poem as a whole, it has a significance which diminishes the value of any speculation about its origins.

iv

The complex patterns of meaning which emerge from these readings of *P.* 1.8, *P.* 2.10 and *P.* 4.7 illustrate what is lost if Ovid's exilic 'facts' are allowed to pass unquestioned. In one way, of course, implicit belief in Ovid's factual authority works to the poet's advantage, especially when he portrays his miserable Tomitan existence in such elegies as *Tr.* 5.7 and *Tr.*

5.10; greater sympathy was to be won from the Roman reader who gave easy credence to the proposed 'facts' of his exilic plight. But while Ovid's objective might seem to the credulous reader, whether ancient or modern, to be the simple expression of sincere grief and hardship, the more sophisticated reader will find a different Ovid – an exile who creates an 'unreal' picture of his circumstances in exile by manipulating his 'facts' to creative advantage. This Ovid is no different to the pre-exilic poet who displayed his powers of artistic invention and capability at every turn; and yet within the exilic corpus itself Ovid frequently laments the 'fact' that he is a pale shadow of the creative artist that he once was. The problem which such outpourings pose complicates – and is complicated by – the findings of this chapter; if Ovid is capable of manipulating his exilic 'facts' to characteristically subtle effect in such elegies as *P.* 1.8, *P.* 2.10 and *P.* 4.7, how is that subtlety to be reconciled with his repeated admissions that he has lost his poetic abilities in exile? Another category of exilic 'fact' would seem to be in immediate need of qualification. Could it be, then, that Ovid's pose of literary decline is itself built in to a pervasive scheme of factual 'unreality' in the exile poetry?

2

OVID'S POSE OF POETIC DECLINE

The Tomitan environment as portrayed in the *Tristia* and *Epistulae ex Ponto* is one of unremitting cultural barrenness. Ovid, both as an external observer of this environment and as an enforced victim of it, claims to suffer a debilitating decline in his poetical powers. Living in Tomis, he also claims to be losing his grasp of Latin (*Tr.* 5.7.55ff.) because there is no one with whom he can communicate in his native tongue (cf. *Tr.* 4.1.89–90, 5.2.67, 5.10.37–40); *barbara* [*verba*] (*Tr.* 5.7.59–60) consequently creep into his diction (cf. *Tr.* 3.1.17–18, 3.14.49–50). The *Ars Amatoria* had characterized a *barbara lingua* as the opposite of a style which charmed by its elegant simplicity (3.481–2), and as the kind of weakness in a girl towards which the *magister amoris* could adopt a patronizing disdain. Such condescension was made possible only by the self-assurance instilled by a shared cultural standpoint. When, however, the phrase is translated to the world of the incomprehensible patois of the Pontic tribes (*Tr.* 5.2.67), the effect is to disorientate the poet by making him face the fact of his own linguistic isolation.

This linguistic isolation must, of course, mean cultural isolation as well. Ovid claims to lack books (*Tr.* 3.14.37–8) and a receptive audience before which he can recite his poetry (*Tr.* 3.14.39–40). The environment in which he lives is not conducive to the tranquil occupation of literary composition; constant warfare threatens the poet's security (*Tr.* 3.10.53ff., 4.1.65ff., 5.10.15ff.), and his physical ailments (*Tr.* 3.3.7ff., 3.8.23ff.) are paralleled by the disabling effect which adjustment to life in Tomis has on his poetic abilities. The weight of his *mala* crushes his *ingenium* (*Tr.* 3.14.33–6), depriving it of creative vitality (*Tr.* 1.1.35ff., 1.11.35ff., *P.* 4.2.15–16), and he openly admits the lack of polish and correction in his verse

50

(*Tr.* 5.1.71–2, *P.* 1.5.17–18, 3.9.13ff.). Ovid presents a sorry picture of himself: relegation has a crippling effect on him emotionally, physically, and also, as a poet, creatively.

The elder Seneca terms Ovid *summi ingenii viro* (*Con.* 2.2.12; cf. 2.2.8–9) and Quintilian famously casts him as *nimium amator ingenii sui* (*Inst.* 10.1.88; cf. 10.1.98); but it would seem that neither critic can have based his judgement on the exile poetry. The debilitating effects of Ovid's Tomitan existence appear to deprive him of the two basic requirements for successful composition, *ingenium* and *ars*. Ovid himself contrasts the two terms in passing judgement on Callimachus at *Am.* 1.15.14 (*quamvis ingenio non valet, arte valet*) and, with the opposite effect, in judging Ennius at *Tr.* 2.424 (*ingenio maximus, arte rudis*).[1] The same contrast is drawn by Horace (*Ars* 295ff.) with his point that Democritus held *ingenium* to be a more important commodity in composition than *ars*; elsewhere, of course, Horace supplies the corrective by insisting that both *ars* and *natura* are necessary components of successful writing (cf. 408–11). Callimachus may lack natural talent (*ingenium*) as a poet and Ennius may lack technical skill (*ars*), but Ovid fares worse than both in Tomis by neglecting the Horatian *lima* (cf. *Ars* 291) as well as losing the vitality of his former *ingenium*. Through this negative correlation between the two Peripatetic requirements for successful composition,[2] Ovid's deterioration as a poet in exile would appear to be complete.

Ovid's own insistence on his poetic decline in Tomis long served to confirm the judgement of his harsher critics. More recently, however, reassessment of the literary merit of the exile poetry has exposed the danger of taking Ovid's assertions literally. Luck, for example, has demonstrated that on a technical level the *Tristia* differ little from his earlier verse,[3]

---

[1] On the Ovidian distinction between *ingenium* and *ars* see Pemberton (1931), 525–34 and Cunningham (1957), 258–9.

[2] For the Peripatetic 'compromise' between *ingenium* and *ars* see Brink (1971), 394–5.

[3] Luck (1961), 243–61; so Claassen (1986), 53–278, with thorough analysis of Ovid's style and technique in exile.

while Nagle argues plausibly that 'his self-criticism is strategic, and was meant to arouse in the reader a desire that Ovid's circumstances might improve so that his poetry could, too'.[4] From a literal interpretation of Ovid's declining grasp of Latin and his claim to have composed a poem in Getic (cf. *P.* 4.13.19–20), recent scholarship has moved – as we shall see later – towards a more allegorical interpretation of his development into a Getic poet.

Despite this growing awareness of the strategy which underlies Ovid's pose of poetic decline, insufficient attention has been given to those poems which most emphatically announce that decline. My purpose is therefore to show that such distinctive elegies as *Tr.* 1.1, 4.1, 5.12, *P.* 1.5, 3.9 and 4.2 are implicitly self-refuting because there is a basic discrepancy between the technical skill which Ovid displays in their composition and their repeated and unambiguous insistence on the gradual erosion of that skill. Furthermore, Ovid experiments with the poetic motif of self-depreciation, and I shall argue that his use of the motif can be viewed as an end in itself rather than as a means to the utilitarian end of arousing his reader's pity. Finally, I shall offer a new reading of *P.* 4.13, a poem which has generally been held to mark the final stage, symbolic or otherwise, in the decline of Ovid's abilities as a Latin poet. Far from confirming the demise of Ovid's identity as *Romanus vates* (*Tr.* 5.7.55), the internal evidence of *P.* 4.13 suggests that his *ingenium* retains a capacity for poetic invention which belies any possibility of decadence or decline.

Ovid's self-depreciation

While Ovid's portrayal of his failing poetic *ingenium* is clearly strategic, in that he sets out to win the reader's sympathy for his wretched situation, other subsidiary motives for his pose merit consideration. Could it be, for example, that the theme of decline partly originates in Ovid's ceasing to be a poet of large-scale, episodic narratives like the *Metamorphoses* and

4 Nagle (1980), 171.

Fasti and in his reversion to the small-scale composition of single elegies? Or could the theme denote the change from what was largely impersonal narrative poetry to the introspective poetry of Tomis, with the result that Ovid's debilitating meditation on his unhappy circumstances leads to a decline in the very medium in which he gives expression to his sorrow? The problem in both cases is a lack of tangible supporting evidence for either hypothesis, however plausible. A more promising line of enquiry is to examine Ovid's treatment of a familiar topos which he exploits as an expressive means of asserting the decline of his *ingenium* – the topos of poetic self-depreciation.

The *recusatio* is an obvious instance of poetic self-depreciation.[5] Propertius, for example, stresses the limitation of his capabilities by clearly distinguishing the boundaries of different kinds of verse (2.1.39–42). In *C*.1.6 Horace claims to be unable to celebrate the epic scale of Agrippa's achievements, while in *C*. 2.12 he hands Augustus' achievements over to Maecenas, preferring light love-lyric for himself. Yet these and other *recusationes* are not quite as self-depreciating as they may at first appear to be. As Nagle observes, 'Horace's *recusationes* are a means of refusing to compromise his artistic principles without offending his imperial patron ... There are positive, self-glorifying themes along with the negative, self-depreciating ones, and both are equally conventional.'[6] Thus, what Brink says on Horace, *Ep*. 2.1.257–9 is equally true of Propertius: 'H. declines the subject as being above his powers, and in doing so does, at any rate partly, what he declines.'[7] Like the *recusatio*, the Neoterics' disparagement of their poems as mere trifles is of course an ironic form of self-depreciation. When Catullus calls his poetry *nugas* (1.4), he understates the concept of literary *otium* and plays up to the

---

[5] On apologetic conventions in Augustan poetry see Wimmel (1960), especially his discussion of Ovid's exilic poetics and conventional apologetic elements in *Tristia* 2 (pp. 287–8, 297–300); Curtius (1953), 83–5 supplies various illustrations of literary self-depreciation in antiquity.

[6] Nagle (1980), 141. On the blend of positive and negative elements in Horatian *recusationes* see Smith (1968), 56–65.

[7] (1982), 258.

disreputable associations of *otium* (as opposed to *negotium*) which are illustrated by Cicero at *Off.* 3.1(*otium* and *solitudo* are *duae res quae languorem adferunt ceteris*; the exception is the elder Scipio Africanus, who was accustomed *in otio de negotiis cogitare*).[8] Horace seems to be similarly self-depreciating at *Ep.* 1.19.41–2 when he claims that he is reluctant to recite his verse *et nugis addere pondus*. In this instance, however, the irony implicit in such self-disparagement is exposed by the response to Horace's claim: *rides ... et Iovis auribus ista|servas [scripta]* (43–4). This response suggests that it is not modest appraisal of the value of his 'trifling' verse which keeps Horace from public recitation, but conceit.

In the exile poetry Ovid does more than pay lip-service to the topos of self-depreciation. Far from employing the theme as an occasional ornament which literary precedent obliges him to use, he makes it fundamental to his Tomitan persona by adapting the *recusatio* motif of the poet's enfeebled *vires* and *ingenium* to represent a much more radical, personally damaging and seemingly irreversible decline in poetic creativity. In this respect, Ovid manipulates literary convention in the same way as he manipulates his literary sources through creative reminiscence, and both kinds of manipulative process can be illustrated simultaneously by reference to *Tr.* 5.12.

In this elegy Ovid responds to his addressee's advice that he should console himself by using poetry as an *oblectamen* (cf. 1). He counters by stating that the circumstances in which he writes are hardly conducive to composition (3–4, 19–20), and that his *ingenium* lacks its former vitality in any case (21–2). His lack of books and a receptive audience (53–4) and his failing grasp of Latin (57–8) are further difficulties he faces. All in all, Ovid presents a gloomy picture of himself, his circumstances and his abilities as a poet – in so far as these can be distinguished from one another. But his arguments against the practicability of the suggestion that he should find consolation in writing are 'ultimately subverted by the admission that

---

[8] Cf. Segal (1970), 28 on Catullus 50 and 'the subtle, anecdotal, understated, ostensibly nugatory manner of the *novi poetae* and their Hellenistic predecessors'.

Ovid in fact feels compelled to compose'.[9] Nagle rightly identifies an important aspect of this poem: Ovid's own performance tells strongly against the claims made in the elegy. More surreptitiously, however, Ovid also contradicts the seemingly unambiguous portrayal of his failing *ingenium* in *Tr.* 5.12.

Tr. 5.12 owes much to two of Catullus' poetic epistles, 65 and 68, and there are a number of explicit points of comparison. From poem 68 comes the point of departure, a letter to a friend from the distressed and weary poet, who declines to take up the friend's suggestion made in an earlier letter. Catullus refuses to write a poem of consolation for Mallius because of the distress he has been caused by his own brother's death (19–20); Ovid similarly rejects his addressee's advice that he alleviate his own sufferings by writing (*Tr.* 5.12.1–4). Both poets use the *non sum quod fueram* motif to present their distress as a maturing experience. Catullus describes how the catastrophe of his brother's death distances him from the playfulness of his earlier life and poetry (68.15–20; 25–6); Ovid similarly distances himself from the poetry of his youth (cf. *Tr.* 5.12.43ff.) and his former ambition for *gloria* (41), and the catastrophe of his relegation deprives him of the *vigor* which his *ingenium*, now crushed by *patientia longa malorum*, used to possess (31–2). Catullus can no longer provide *dona beata* (68.14), gifts of poetry which are prefigured in line 10 (*munera ... et Musarum ... et Veneris*); similarly, Ovid is unable to write poetry *quia carmina laetum|sunt opus* (*Tr.* 5.12.3–4, where Catullus' *beatum* is paralleled by Ovid's *laetum*).[10] Both make powerful use of the conventional imagery of shipwreck and stormy seas in the early stages of their respective elegies to depict their overwhelming distress and grief (68.3–4, 13; cf. *Tr.* 5.12.5), and Ovid reproduces the sharp Catullan antithesis between *studium* and *luctus* (*sed totum hoc studium*

---

[9] Nagle (1980), 107.
[10] Fordyce (1961), 364 on 68.14 explains *dona beata* as 'gifts that only the happy can give', citing a possible parallel at Prop. 4.7.60; but in support of the parallel between *beatus* and *laetus* cf. *Aen.* 6.638–9 (*devenere locos laetos ... sedesque beatas*).

luctu fraterna mihi mors|abstulit, 68.19–20; cf. *luctibus an studio videor debere teneri. . .?*, *Tr.* 5.12.9). Ovid's claim that he lacks books in Tomis (*Tr.* 5.12.53) strongly suggests the fulfilment of the Callimachean poet's worst fears. Catullus' letter from Verona pleads the same excuse for his inability to write effectively (68.33–6).[11] Clearly, the relation between the two poems is not merely one of shared mood and pained response.

In Catullus 65 the closeness of the parallel with Ovid is equally evident. The letter to Hortalus is dominated by a central lament (5–14) over what is acknowledged to be an irremediable situation. As is the case when Ovid declares undying fidelity to his absent wife and Roman friends, the sheer hopelessness of Catullus' situation adds a special poignancy to his continuing protestations of fidelity (10–11). In his grief and isolation (1–2), represented by the familiar metaphor of the stormy sea (4; cf. *Tr.* 5.12.5, 50), the poet's *mens anxia* renders him incapable of procuring release from his troubles by writing (3–4; cf. *Tr.* 5.12.3–4). Even so, Catullus, like Ovid, continues to be remarkably productive (15–16), to the extent that his declaration of poetic impotence becomes self-refuting. The poems which are the product of these circumstances bear witness to the soul-searching tension and despair which made them at the same time necessary and yet apparently impossible to write. There is a clear point of contact here with Propertian and Horatian use of the *recusatio*: both Catullus (in 65) and Ovid defeat expectations based on their own self-evaluation.

As some critics have noticed,[12] the interaction of material and themes in these poems is the result of Ovid's conscious reworking of his Catullan models; but allusive reminiscence of Catullus is a means to an end here rather than an end in itself.

---

[11] Cf. Fordyce (1961), 348 *ad loc.*: 'The excuse [for not composing a poem on Mallius' behalf] is revealing evidence of the methods and ideals of the *doctus poeta*; what is expected of him is Alexandrian poetry, translated from, or modelled on, Greek, and for that he needs his library.' The complexities of the *Ibis* surely suggest that Ovid dissimulates when he claims not to have access to books in Tomis – unless he wrote from memory (cf. Kenney (1982), 454). On the obvious importance of books to the Roman *doctus poeta* see Marshall (1976), 252–64.

[12] See Luck (1977), II 320 on *Tr.* 5.12.1ff.; Nagle (1980), 40.

Ovid does not merely use Catullus as an external point of reference to enrich the texture of his own composition with learned allusion, for the reference is not in fact to the odd Catullan phrase, but to what is in itself a major Catullan complexity. Catullus states in poem 65 that he cannot give expression to *dulcis Musarum ... fetus* (3) because of his grief. Yet this same poem most likely introduces (cf. 15ff.) the elaborate Alexandrian adaptation (poem 66) which itself provides evidence of Catullus' sustained devotion to the Callimachean Muses, despite his disclaimer at 65.1–8. And despite his refusal to do what is requested of him in 68.1–40, Catullus most probably goes on to express his gratitude to Allius in a piece which turns into 'a formal elegiac poem, not a translation from Alexandrian poetry like 66 but not less obviously Alexandrian in its inspiration'.[13] It is in order to evoke this complex Catullan sequence, where a *recusatio* is the most improbable prelude to an elaborate and quasi-Alexandrian performance, that Ovid recalls Catullus 65 and 68 in *Tr.* 5.12. His disclaimer in 21ff. is in itself an echo of Catullus' disclaimers at 65.1–8 and 68.1–40. The reader who recognizes this reminiscence sees at once that Ovid's denial that his *ingenium* retains its former vitality cannot be taken at face value; for it is in a context which, paradoxically, laments the decline of his talent that Ovid's creative facility and allusive technique are most fully active.

The technique of literary allusion is therefore one means by which the so-called decline of Ovid's *ingenium* in the exile poetry can be seen to be a more complex phenomenon than it might at first appear. The allusive skill we have observed in *Tr.* 5.12 shows no sign of being radically different from the kind found in, say, *Am.* 2.9 and 3.9.[14] Since Ovid's subtle redeployment of literary reminiscences is a constant and

---

[13] Fordyce (1961), 342. With G. Williams (1968), 229–32, I take it that Catul. 68 should be read as one poem; on the discrepancy of names (Mallius/Allius) see Quinn (1973), 381–2 on 68.41, with a convenient summary of proposed solutions to the problem.

[14] On Ovid's allusive response to Prop. 2.25.5–10 at *Am.* 2.9.19–24 see Morgan (1977), 83; on his creative use of Tibullan reminiscence in *Am.* 3.9 see Taylor (1970), 475–7.

prominent artistic feature in both his pre-exilic and exilic poetry, this aspect of his literary technique constitutes a valid touchstone for the refutation of the pose of decline – and in *Tr.* 5.12 there are further instances of such allusiveness. In a vivid description of the diminished power of his *ingenium*, which is deteriorating with lethargy (*torpet*, 22; cf. *Tr.* 1.3.8) and 'rust' (the metaphorical sense of *rubigo* (21) is yet another borrowing from Catullus 68 (151)), Ovid reworks three illustrative *exempla* which are themselves variations on the standard elegiac similes of ploughing, racehorses and ships (23–8).[15] The field must be ploughed (*renovetur*, 23) if it is to retain its vitality: though in this elegy he depicts his *ingenium* as infertile,[16] the similes themselves bear eloquent witness to the process of poetic adaptation at work here, revealing the fresh vitality of Ovid's poetic invention. Since these three *exempla* are conventionally familiar, they must be revitalized (cf. *renovetur*, 23) so as to avoid the very *rubigo* and *torpor* which afflict Ovid's *ingenium* (21–2). The most conventional of poetic topoi are therefore restructured to emphasize the importance of creative regeneration. That Ovid *does* revitalize these conventional similes is shown by the fact that they are used only in the exile poetry to illustrate the performance (or lack of performance) of poetic *ingenium*. The novel application of these similes shows that Ovid's *ingenium* retains its fertility by revitalizing its resources; and yet, ironically, his *ingenium* is actively engaged in adducing similes to illustrate what is evidently a misleading picture of its sterility.

Another case of Ovidian adaptation can be seen in the reference to Socrates as *Anyti reus* at *Tr.* 5.12.12, a likely imitation of Horace's similar phrase at *S.* 2.4.3. The *Anyti reus* is in

[15] The worn plough regularly illustrates the attritional effects of passing time; cf. Ov. *Am.* 1.15.31–2, *A.A.* 1.474, *Tr.* 4.6.13. For the illustrative racehorse in varying contexts cf. *A.A.* 3.595–6, Hor. *S.* 1.1.114–15, Tib. 1.4.31–2, Virg. *G.* 1.512–14. For the analogy of the leaking boat cf. Ov. *Tr.* 4.6.35–6, 4.8.17–18; the standard illustration is that of the boat being brought into dry dock (cf. Prop. 2.25.7, Ov. *Am.* 2.9.21).

[16] *Fertilis*, applied in line 23 to the field, hints at the poetic fertility which Ovid claims to lack in Tomis; for this figurative sense cf. *P.* 4.2.11 (*fertile pectus habes*).

both cases the archetypal philosopher, and both Horace and
Ovid portray Socrates to ironic effect. While Horace makes
fun of philosophical *praecepta* by comparing them to *praecepta* in cookery, Ovid aims to score points at Socrates'
expense by implying that even the latter's philosophical
armoury would not have stood up to the crushing effects of
Tomitan exile (cf. 13–14) and enabled him to write in such
adverse conditions (cf. 15–16). For all his wisdom (cf. *dictus
sapiens ab Apolline*, 15), Socrates thus 'proves' to be less enduring than Ovid, his poetic counterpart as *Phoebi sacerdos*
(cf. *Am.* 3.8.23).[17] But despite the overt difference between
Socrates and himself which Ovid draws here, the comparison
also suggests an underlying similarity between the two – and
a similarity which lies in more than the fact that both were
officially punished for allegedly corrupting innocent minds in
their respective ways. Socrates famously played down his own
abilities and praised the wisdom of others (cf. *de se detrahens
... plus tribuebat iis quos volebat refellere*, Cic. *Luc.* 15 Plas-
berg), adept as he was at ironic self-misrepresentation: *cum
aliud diceret atque sentiret, libenter uti solitus est ea dissimula-
tione, quam Graeci* εἰρωνείαν *vocant* (*ibid.*).[18] Although Socrates' appearance in *Tr.* 5.12 is designed to reinforce the picture
of the hardship which overwhelms Ovid in Tomis, this Socratic presence also gives a subtle indication of what might, in
general terms, be the model for the kind of dissimulating
irony which Ovid playfully introduces in this and other poems
on the theme of poetic decline.

[17] Ovid ironically forgets that Socrates' misgivings about the value of the written
word (cf. Pl. *Phdr.* 274cff.) suggest that he would have been loath to write in any
case, whether or not under duress. But even though he wrote nothing philosophical, Socrates seems to have composed a hymn to Apollo and versified
Aesop's fables while in prison (cf. *Phd.* 60d); Ovid's point may thus be that even
Socrates, a poet in prison, would not have been able to compose poetry (as Ovid
himself does!) in the harsher conditions of Tomis.
[18] For Socrates conventionally portrayed as the supreme ironist see (e.g.) Pl. *R.* 337a
(αὕτη 'κείνη ἡ εἰωθυῖα εἰρωνεία Σωκράτους), X. *Mem.* 1.2.36 (ἀλλά τοι σύγε, ὦ
Σώκρατες, εἴωθας εἰδὼς πῶς ἔχει τὰ πλεῖστα ἐρωτᾶν), Arist. *EN* 1127b24–6, Cic.
Off. 1.108, Quint. *Inst.* 9.2.46 etc. with Vlastos (1987), 79–96.

Consolidating a line of enquiry

Ovid's dissimulating references to his poetic decline are a pervasive feature of the exile poetry and help to establish a tone of subtle, self-mocking humour which runs through them. This phenomenon is in evidence as early as *Tr.* 1.1.1–14, where Ovid offers a physical description of his shabby exilic book in language (e.g. *incultus*, 3; *infelix*, 4; *hirsutus*, 12) which, in its secondary senses, also signals the allegedly poor quality of its poetic contents.[19] Yet Ovid's subtle manipulation of his language to establish a correspondence here between the physical and poetic complexions of the book is paradoxical in implication: the skill with which he makes the physical description suggest the poor quality of the contents hardly supports the contention that his abilities are in terminal decline.[20]

The same paradox arises more forcefully in *Tr.* 3.14, in which Ovid announces (33) the crushing of his exilic *ingenium* under the weight of his exilic *mala*: the sustained use of the parent–orphan imagery with which this 'deteriorating' poet movingly commends his surviving poetry to his addressee's care in lines 7ff. is among the most impressive things in the whole book. The addressee, introduced as *cultor et antistes doctorum sancte virorum* (1),[21] is cast as the protector of Ovid's bereft offspring, his poetry (cf. *stirps haec progeniesque mea est*, 14), as if all that remains from Ovid's figurative death (cf. *funere*, 20) is a (literary) body which needs priestly hands to preserve it (cf. *retine corpus in urbe meum*, 8).[22] Despite his alleged lack of books (37–8), his lack of a receptive audience (39–40), the unconducive surroundings in which he writes

[19] Cf. Hinds (1985), 14: 'In keeping with the circumstances of its master, the book is to be squalid and unkempt, *incultus* (a word which equally bodes ill for its content).'

[20] So G. D. Williams (1992), 178–89.

[21] van de Woestyne (1929), 31–45 identifies this addressee as C. Julius Hyginus, prefect of the Palatine library; but cf. Nagle (1980), 86 n. 31.

[22] On Ovid's extensive use of the parent–child/orphan comparison in exile see Davisson (1979), 71–7.

(41–2) and his supposed loss of linguistic mastery through Pontic contamination of his Latin (45–50), the force of his poetic imagination tells against our taking his pose of decline seriously. Other elegies show Ovid developing this paradox in a novel way, and conspicuous among these are *Tr*. 4.1 and *P*. 4.2.

i

Tr. 4.1 opens with an appeal to the reader (*lector*, 2) to excuse the *vitia* which allegedly disfigure Ovid's exilic verse and so reflect his exilic circumstances in Tomis (1–2; cf. *non melius, quam sunt mea tempora, carmen*, 105). Ovid had already made a number of similar appeals (cf. *Tr*. 1.1.45–6, 1.11.35–6, 3.1.17–18), but on this occasion he adds the further excuse that his motive for composing poetry in Tomis is no longer the spur of fame, but temporary escape (*requies*, 3) from his woes. The elegy develops into a prolonged statement of gratitude to the Muses who sustain him in Tomis (cf. 19–20, 49–52, 87–8), even though the Muses were partly responsible for causing his relegation in the first place and the exilic relief they bring results in second-rate verse. If such *vitia* are so prevalent in the exilic poetry as a whole, the forewarned reader (cf. 1–2) might reasonably expect to find symptomatic *vitia* in *Tr*. 4.1; and yet he will look in vain because the sophisticated technique with which Ovid demonstrates the alleviating function of the Muse in this poem scarcely indicates that this is a *carmen vitiatum*. Central to Ovid's strategy here is to set two distinct sections of the poem in thematic contrast to each other: lines 5–20 represent the escapist function of his poetry in Tomis, lines 53–106 the harsh Tomitan 'reality'. The contrast between these two sections is reinforced by different generic affiliations which, once identified, illuminate the ambivalent status of Ovid's exilic Muse as a source of both anguish and alleviation in lines 21–52. My starting-point is lines 5–20 and the generic status of Ovid's alleviating Muse.

The shackled labourer who eases his toil through song

(5–6) is Tibullan in origin:

> spes etiam valida solatur compede vinctum:
> crura sonant ferro, sed canit inter opus.
>
> (2.6.25–6)

As a slave to love and similarly sustained by hope in his own erotic toil (cf. 19–20), Tibullus chooses an apt *exemplum* here; just as the slave's song softens the harsh sound of his rattling chains, the ever present symbol of his servitude (26), so Tibullus' own poetic song solaces the disquiet caused by his erotic enchainment. Ovid's repudiation in Tomis of his erotic elegiac past (cf. *ille pharetrati lusor Amoris abest, Tr.* 5.1.22) necessarily modifies the illustrative purpose of Tibullus' slave when the latter is transferred to *Tr.* 4.1.5–6, and the erotic significance of the Tibullan *spes* is inevitably suppressed, even though the underlying implication of the echo is that Ovid still harbours hope of removal from Tomis.[23] Until that hope materializes, however, Ovid's exilic verse serves the same consoling purpose as the labourer's crude song (*indocili numero ... grave mollit opus,* 6), for through his own form of *indociles numeri*, his allegedly unrefined poetry, he softens the hardship (cf. *grave opus*) of his Tomitan existence. But the epic associations of *grave opus*[24] further suggest that Ovid consoles himself amid the martial realities of Tomis (cf. 71ff.) by evoking the softer strains (cf. *mollit,* 6) of a different kind of personal and literary existence. The term *mollis* is standardly used by the Roman poets to distinguish epic weightiness from poetry in the lighter genres,[25] and Ovid applies this distinction in lines 5–14 by retreating into the peaceful world of rural (even distinctively bucolic) *otium* and its accompanying poetics.

---

[23] Cf. *P.* 1.6.31–2, where Ovid again echoes Tib. 2.6.25–6, but with the Tibullan *spes* now explicitly converted into hope of removal from Tomis. Tibullus' allusion to the traditional conflict between Spes/'Ελπίς and (his) Nemesis at 2.6.19–28 (see Cairns (1979), 185) would seem to be redundant in the Ovidian echo – unless Ovid sets *spes* in opposition to the retribution (νέμεσις) brought by his exilic *poena* (cf. *P.* 1.6.27).

[24] For the epic connotation of *gravis* see *Am.* 1.1.1 with McKeown (1989), 12 *ad loc.*, *M.* 10.150, Stat. *Silv.* 1.5.1 etc. with Hinds (1987), 141 n. 58.

[25] See Prop. 2.1.2, Hor. *C.* 2.12.3, Ov. *Tr.* 2.307, 349 etc. with Jackson (1914), 123–4 and Lyne (1978), 108 on *Ciris* 19–20.

CONSOLIDATING A LINE OF ENQUIRY

Compared to the free birds who greet the return of Italian spring with their vernal tunes at *Tr.* 3.12.8 (*indocili ... loquax gutture vernat avis*), the shackled labourer of *Tr.* 4.1.5–6 sings his crude song (cf. *indocili numero*, 6) in poignantly different circumstances. Even so, *indocilis* suggests the αὐτάρκεια of a simple rustic world,[26] far removed from the harsher, more threatening landscape of Ovid's Tomis where the constant threat of war interrupts the ordinary occupations of a peaceful rural existence. Yet these occupations are reconstructed in Ovid's portrayal of the boatman (7–8) and oarsman (9–10) going about their slow tasks (cf. *tardam ... ratem*, 8; *lentos ... remos*, 9) in the unhurried ease of rustic timelessness.[27] Ovid's quest for *requies* in his exilic verse (cf. 3) is converted in this rural picture into shades of bucolic *requies*, while the Tibullan origins of the initial labourer (5–6) lend an elegiac presence to the alleviating strains which form the generic point of departure from the Tomitan battlefield.

The most obvious symbol of this departure is the weary shepherd who soothes his flock in pastoral song (*harundineo carmine mulcet oves*, 12). At *Ecl.* 6.1–8 Apollo diverts Tityrus from epic *reges et proelia* to the *tenuis harundo* of the rustic Muse; in the same way, the shepherd's presence in *Tr.* 4.1 diverts Ovid from his martial preoccupations by representing an alternative form of easing poetics, the alluring and comforting effects of which are encased in *mulcet* (12).[28] The spinner who solaces her toil through song (13–14) belongs to the same Theocritean/Virgilian world as the shepherd,[29] and the

---

[26] Cf. *Aen.* 8.321, where *indocilis* is pejorative in implication, describing the primitive Italian peoples who later evolved under Saturn's rule to Golden Age 'civilization' (see Gransden (1976), 37–9); but Ovid's use of the term in *Tr.* 4.1 carries the same notion of natural simplicity, unconstrained by *ars*, which governs its usage in the idyllic setting of Italian spring in *Tr.* 3.12.

[27] On the apparent timelessness of the 'pastoral moment' see Rosenmeyer (1969), 86–9.

[28] *Mulceo* is regularly applied to Orpheus' powers of diverting song (cf. Hor. *C.* 3.11.24, Virg. *G.* 4.510, Ov. *M.* 10.301, Sen. *Med.* 229); so also to the nymph Canens (Ov. *M.* 14.339) and Arion (*F.* 2.116). At *Ep.* 2.1.212 Horace uses the term of the dramatic poet able to move his audience *ut magus* (213).

[29] See Theoc. 24.75–7 with Gow (1952), 428 (explaining ἀείδοισαι (77) by reference to *Tr.* 4.1.13), Virg. *G.* 1.293–4 with Thomas (1988), I 118 *ad loc.*; extensive examples of the phenomenon are assembled by De Jonge (1951), 44.

programmatic overtones of the slender threads she draws out (13) signal the distinctive mode of poetic song – *deductum carmen* – which Virgil contrasts with epic at *Ecl.* 6.5.[30] The language of deception (*fallitur ... decipiturque labor*, 14) further suggests the pseudo-naive framework in which the bucolic poets disguise their own *labor*/πόνος through the relieving impression of rural simplicity,[31] while the poetic connotation of *labor* finds an Ovidian variation at *Tr.* 3.2.16, *fallebat curas aegraque corda labor*, where *labor* denotes the literary toil with which he beguiled the distress of his journey into exile.[32] Through these associations, the spinner of *Tr.* 4.1 yields a nexus of literary allusions which complicate her simple illustrative function as an exemplar of toil escaped through song; she represents escape to a particular form of relieving poetics.

Tristis Achilles (15) marks Ovid's departure from the bucolic tone of the previous lines, but *tristis* hardly carries the epic connotation which Horace gives the word when he characterizes epic as *tristia bella* at *Ars* 73.[33] No longer the fighting hero but the bereft lover, Achilles alleviates his grief after Briseis' abduction by replacing his *arma* with the lyre, the distinctive symbol of poetry in the lighter genres.[34] In contrast to the epic Muse, his relieving song (cf. *fertur ... curas attenuasse*, 15–16) has more in common with the ge-

---

[30] For *deducere* as a metaphor for finely spun song see (among others) Kenney (1976), 51–2 and Hinds (1987), 18–19, though the metaphor in *deducite ... carmen* (*M.* 1.4) is disputed by Kovacs (1987), 461–2.

[31] Cf. Segal (1981), 6–7 on the paradox of pastoral's unsimple simplification of life, and Hutchinson (1988), 175ff. and 207ff. on Theocritus' artful contrivance of rustic artlessness.

[32] For Ovid's exilic woes 'deceived' by poetic *labor*, cf. *Tr.* 4.10.114, 5.7.39; cf. also *M.* 6.60, *studio fallente laborem*, where Arachne and Minerva weave their respective tapestries with both an enthusiasm which beguiles their toil and an artfulness which belies contrived effort: *ars latet arte sua* (cf. *M.* 10.252).

[33] For *tristis* in this generic sense cf. Virg. *Ecl.* 6.7, *Aen.* 7.325, *Culex* 81 with Cairns (1979), 102–4.

[34] For the lyre set in symbolic opposition to epic cf. Prop. 4.6.32, Hor. *C.* 1.6.10 with Nisbet and Hubbard (1970), 86 *ad loc.*, Ov. *Am.* 1.1.12, *M.* 10.152, *Tr.* 4.10.50, Stat. *Theb.* 10.446 etc.

nerically attenuated proportions of Callimachus' Μοῦσαν λεπταλέην (*Aet.* fr. 1.24 (Pf.)),[35] and Ovid similarly alleviates his own (epic) *curae* by evoking the slender strains of Achilles' lyre. With Orpheus' arrival (17–18), Eurydice supplants Briseis as a figure comparable with the wife from whom Ovid is now separated, even though there would seem to be a reversal of roles: just as Eurydice relied on Orpheus' powers of rescue from the Stygian depths, so Ovid comes to rely on his wife's powers of rescue from an equivalent underworld (cf. *Tr.* 3.3.21–4). Once more, however, Orpheus' alluring song (cf. *cum traheret silvas ... et dura canendo|saxa*, 17–18) acts as a paradigm for Ovid's own self-consoling voice in exile,[36] but with the implication that *dura saxa* are replaced in Tomis by *dura bella*.[37]

When Ovid makes the simple transition from his *exempla* to the equivalent comfort which poetic song brings him in Tomis (*me quoque Musa levat Ponti loca iussa petentem*, 19), the bucolic and elegiac strains which dominate the preceding passage (5–18) find a generic echo in *levat*.[38] But when Ovid subsequently reverts to his hardships in Tomis (53ff.), the escapist poetics of lines 5–18 give way to generic echoes which are more in keeping with the *grave opus* of exilic 'reality'. In the last chapter we saw that in *P.* 1.8 Ovid's dream-like projection of a bucolic existence in Tomis (49ff.) is generically contradicted by an opening section (3–24) steeped in epic allusion. A similar generic contrast prevails in *Tr.* 4.1, but in this instance the programmatic contrast of 'light' and 'heavy' finds

---

[35] With the programmatic hint of *tenuis*, *attenuasse* suggests the generic quality of the song which eases Achilles' cares; for *tenuis* as a token of Callimachean slenderness see Nisbet and Hubbard (1970), 86 on *C.* 1.6.9 and (1978), 270–1 on 2.16.38; cf. Virg. *Ecl.* 1.2, 6.8 (*tenui ... harundine*) with Ross (1975), 19.

[36] For *trahere* applied to Orpheus' alluring song cf Sen. *Her. F.* 572–3; the term is equivalent to Horace's *silvas ducere* (*C.* 3.11.13–14; cf. Ov. *M.* 11.2) and Virgil's *deducere ornos* (*Ecl.* 6.71). On Orpheus' association with Alexandrian poetics see Ross (1975), 23ff.

[37] For the martial epic connotation of *durus* see p. 31 n. 61.

[38] Cf. *levantes* (49). For the programmatic connotation of *levis*, indicating poetry in the lighter genres (cf. *P.* 4.5.1, *leves elegi*, *Am.* 2.1.21, 3.1.41 etc.), see Hinds (1987), 141 n. 58.

a closer structural parallel at *M*. 10.150–4, where Orpheus renounces the weightier strains of epic and the generically stereotypical Gigantomachy (cf. *cecini plectro graviore Gigantas*, 150) in favour of the lighter strains of lyric eroticism (cf. *nunc opus est leviore lyra*, 152).[39] In *Tr*. 4.1 Ovid makes the same generic transition as Orpheus, but in reverse order: after showing a lighter touch in the opening lines, he introduces the menacing tones of epic in lines 53ff.

This generic transition begins in lines 53–60, where elegiac motif evolves into the symbol of Ovid's epic suffering. Since Ovid both rebukes and finds comfort in the Muse which inspired the ill-starred *Ars Amatoria* (cf. 30), the *Ars* provides a suitably ambivalent source of influence in Ovid's enumeration of his exilic woes. The number of sand-grains on the shore (55) serves in the *Ars* to illustrate the countless haunts where the male hunter can go about his business (*A.A.* 1.253–4), the number of fish in the sea (56) the countless girls to be found in Rome (*A.A.* 1.58), while the number of emerging flowers in spring (57) represents the myriad colours of enticing female garb at *A.A.* 3.185–7. Ovid's catalogue of the four seasons (57–8) carries a further resonance of *R.A.* 187–8, where autumnal fruits, summer harvests, spring flowers and winter fires provide a seasonal timetable for the lover who turns to farming to escape his erotic ills. Even though Ovid's illustrations in lines 55–8 find parallels in a range of sources,[40] the conspicuous transformation of erotic *exempla* in this exilic context reflects the transformed circumstances of both poet and accompanying Muse (cf. *comes nostrae ... fugae*, 20): traces of Ovid's erotic Muse survive in suitably chastened form.

In *Tr*. 1.5 Ovid uses similarly exaggerated illustrations to portray the epic scale of his sufferings in exile (cf. 47–8), and by surpassing Ulysses in a prolonged syncrisis of compared hardships he explicitly announces the generic category of his

[39] For the programmatic contrast between *gravis* and *levis* or their cognates cf. Hor. *C*. 2.1.40, Ov. *Am*. 1.1.1, 19, 3.1.69–70, 3.15.17–20, Sen. *Ag*. 334, 338 with Tarrant (1976), 237–8 *ad loc.*, Stat. *Silv*. 1.4.36, 1.5.1 etc.

[40] De Jonge (1951), 58–60 cites extensive parallels.

woes.[41] His appeal to epic role-models is less overt in *Tr.* 4.1, but his choice of language in line 59 (*[mala] toto patior iactatus in orbe*) leaves no doubt about his generic pretensions. *Iactatus* revives the description of Aeneas as *et terris iactatus et alto* at *Aen.* 1.3, though Ovid's global extension of his sufferings (*toto ... in orbe*) implies that he surpasses both Ulysses and Aeneas in his own epic wanderings towards the Pontic coast (cf. 60). With *nec tamen, ut veni, levior fortuna malorum est* (61), Ovid signals the epic quality of his *mala* through the equivalence of *nec levior* and *gravis*, and the generic point is reinforced when he states that the dangers (*pericula*, 65) which he faces in Tomis are *veri ... graviora fide* (66); apart from the programmatic hint in *graviora*,[42] his hyperbole in lines 65–6 echoes the epic pretension to unbelievable suffering which precedes his syncrisis with Ulysses in *Tr.* 1.5 (cf. 49–50). In the intervening lines (62–4) Ovid's recognition that he is living out the black destiny spun on the day of his birth (cf. *cognosco natalis stamina nostri*, 63) parallels Alcinous' recognition at *Od.* 7.196–8 that Odysseus must live out the dark fate which birth allotted him: Ovid is in Odysseus' position of having to fulfil an epic destiny.[43]

The contrast which Ovid draws in lines 71–4 between his juvenile games with arms (*nec nisi lusura movimus arma manu*, 72) and his old age (cf. *senior*, 73) under arms in Tomis marks his transition from *lusus* to *seria* as both poet and campaigner.[44] As a youthful love-elegist, Ovid's aversion to a military career (cf. *Am.* 1.15.3–4) was of course complemented by his aversion to martial epic (cf. *Am.* 2.18.1–4), and both aversions are simultaneously represented at *Tr.* 4.1.71 (*aspera militiae iuvenis certamina fugi*). When Ovid dons arms in Tomis (73–4) in language which ironically recalls his youthful games (*induimus trepida ... arma manu*, 76; cf. *lusura movimus arma manu*, 72), his drastic transformation from elegiac *lusor* to real

---

[41] The poem is discussed in Chapter 3.

[42] See p. 62 n. 24.

[43] See Heubeck, West and Hainsworth (1988), 333 on Homeric μοῖρα as the heroic (and now Ovidian) birthright.

[44] On *ludere* and its cognates as terms of generic contrast with epic *seria* see Wagenvoort (1956), 30–42.

soldier is reflected in the epic allusions which permeate his martial narrative (73–84) in fitting generic accompaniment to his *seria arma*.

With *canitiem galeae subicioque meam* (74) Ovid directly echoes *Aen.* 9.612, where Numanus Remulus proudly claims that even in old age the Rutulians reach for their war-helmets (*canitiem galea premimus*). The echo is of course ironic: far from exuding Rutulian hardiness, Ovid has more in common with Priam, a *senior* like himself (cf. *Aen.* 2.509) who takes up arms against the invading Greeks with the same enfeebled trembling (cf. *trementibus aevo ... umeris, Aen.* 2.509–10) which debilitates Ovid (cf. 76). The poisoned arrows of the enemy both here (77) and elsewhere in the *Tristia* (e.g. 3.10.63–4, 5.7.15–16) find various parallels in the *Aeneid*,[45] but lines 77–84 are modelled more specifically on Virgil's account of Turnus' attempt to infiltrate the Trojan camp in *Aeneid* 9. Like the enemy horsemen encircling Tomis (*hostis ... saevus anhelanti moenia lustrat equo*, 77–8), Turnus rides round the Trojan camp looking for a way in (cf. *huc turbidus atque huc|lustrat equo muros* (*Aen.* 9.57–8). Turnus is subsequently compared to a wolf prowling around the sheepfold and vainly seeking to steal inside (59–66).[46] Ovid modifies the Virgilian simile by allowing the enemy outside Tomis greater success than Turnus; whereas the latter is cast as a foiled predator, the Tomitan enemy fall wolf-like on the stragglers left outside the walls as if on sheep outside the fold (cf. 79–82). Although Ovid's idyllic retreat in the first section of the poem portrayed Orpheus as drawing the woods in seductive song (cf. *cum traheret silvas*, 17), the verb *traho* denotes savage violence in the contrasting world of Tomis (cf. *pecudem ... per silvas fertque trahitque lupus*, 79–80); and while the shackled labourer (*vinctus ... compede fossor*, 5) eases his toil through escapist song, his counterpart in lines 83–4 is chained by the neck (*coniectaque vincula collo|accipit*), his voice symbolically suffocated.

---

[45] See 10.140, 12.857 with De Jonge (1951), 65 on *Tr.* 4.1.77.

[46] The Virgilian simile is itself an allusive blend of Apollonian (cf. 1.1243–9) and Homeric (cf. *Od.* 6.130–6; *Il.* 11.548–55 and 17.657–64) influences; see Conington and Nettleship (1898), III 158 on *Aen.* 9.59.

Since the Muse who eases these epic hardships (cf. *in tantis hospita Musa malis*, 88) through the alleviating poetics of lines 5–20 was Ovid's criminal accomplice in the *Ars Amatoria* (cf. *mecum iuncti criminis ... rea*, 26), she shares an ambivalent relationship with the poet in exile as both the cause of his epic sufferings (53–86) and their reliever (5–20). This ambivalence is pictured in the intervening section (21–52), where the juxtaposition of love and resentment (cf. *carmen demens carmine laesus amo*, 30) explains the generic opposition between the two surrounding sections. The damage done by Ovid's poetry (cf. *carmine laesus*) anticipates the epic hardships of lines 53ff., while his continued devotion to poetry (cf. *carmen demens ... amo*) is repaid by the charm-like diversion of lines 5–20.[47] The lotus provides a suitably double-edged point of comparison for the Muse in lines 31–2: her lotus-like influence, so harmful in the *Ars Amatoria* (cf. *lotos ... illo, quo nocuit, grata sapore fuit*, 31–2), now becomes medicinal in Tomis by diverting Ovid from his woes. But Ovid's subsequent comparison with the infatuated Bacchante (41–4) captures the ultimate futility of his escapist efforts through his Muse, for just as the Bacchic reveller will wake up to feel the wound which her ecstasy numbs (cf. *suum ... non sentit saucia vulnus*, 41), so Ovid recovers from his own form of Bacchic diversion (cf. 43–4) to feel the smarting of his exilic wounds (cf. *corque vetusta meum, tamquam nova, vulnera novit*, 97); the draughts of forgetfulness (cf. 47) are blended with the certainty of painful recollection.

Ovid's love–hate relationship with his Muse as portrayed in lines 29ff. carries its own form of painful reminiscence. The *dementia* which holds the elegiac lover in the grip of his own torment (cf. *Am.* 2.9.27–8) now characterizes the exile's anguished devotion to his Muse (cf. *carmen demens carmine laesus amo*, 30). Just as Cupid turns his shafts on his faithful soldier in *Am.* 2.9 (*quid me ... laedis...?*, 3–4), so Ovid is wounded by his Muse's own form of erotic betrayal; and yet in exile he continues to cherish the cause of his own injuries

---

[47] *Carmen* of course carries the suggestion of the diverting 'spell' or 'incantation' (see *OLD* s.v. 1b), with properties akin to the lotus (31–2) and Lethean draughts (47–8).

(*quodque mihi telum vulnera fecit, amo*, 36), just as he continues to soldier on in the service of his persecuting master at *Am.* 2.9.29ff. The erotic implication of line 36 is signalled by the explicit amatory analogy drawn in lines 33–4, where the truism that the lover pursues the cause of his own ruin (*materiam culpae persequiturque suae*, 34) is borne out in Ovid's reversion to the erotic subject-matter (*materia*) which led to the *culpa* of exile. His *furor* (37) in exile is his continued infatuation with the Muse which destroyed him, its *utilitas* (38) the forgetting of his woes (cf. [*furor*] *mentem ... praesentis casus immemorem ... facit*, 39–40); and yet the erotic echoes of lines 29ff. revive the memory of the very woes which Ovid is trying to forget.

The balanced structure of *Tr.* 4.1, in which Ovid's ambivalent relationship with his Muse (21–52) reconciles the two generically contrasted sections of lines 5–20 and 53–86, is supposed to represent the work of a poet in decline. His lack of an audience and linguistic isolation (89–90) revive the familiar causes of his broken *ingenium* (cf. *Tr.* 3.14.33ff.), while the anger which leads him to destroy much of his defective verse (101–2) is directed against the waning talent of his creative hand (cf. *manus demens ... irata sibi*) as well as the *studia* which have destroyed him (cf. *manus ... studiis irata*, 101). But the allusive manner in which Ovid portrays the alleviating function of his Muse through generic contrast in this elegy hardly supports his opening claim that his verse is riddled with faults. The poem's internal evidence betrays the irony of Ovid's closing plea for his alleged *vitia* to be excused; and this closing irony merely confirms what the initiated reader (cf. *lector*, 2) will have suspected all along.

ii

Cornelius Severus, the epic poet who is Ovid's addressee in *P.* 4.2,[48] clearly has the literary credentials of an initiated reader.

---

[48] For the distinction between this Severus and the Severus addressed in *P.* 1.8 see p. 26 n. 49. Dahlmann (1975) offers a thorough analysis of the identity question and of C. Severus' extant fragments.

A pivotal theme of this elegy is again the decline of the poet's *ingenium*, though on this occasion the pretext for its introduction is an explanation of why Ovid has not yet named Severus in his poetry (3–4). The motif of poetic fertility and infertility is usually central to Ovid's portrayal of this theme, and here it enables him to establish a contrast with Severus' prosperity as a poet. This contrast adds a literary dimension to the familiar antithesis of good and bad fortune, and the contrast finds expression in subtle changes of linguistic usage. The term *otia* (cf. *quaque infelicia perdam|otia materia . . . ?*, 39–40) now denotes the time-vacuum which Ovid has to fill in Tomis, as opposed to the programmatic kind of 'leisure' which the poet requires for composition,[49] while the epithet *infelicia* reinforces the contrast with the [*felicia*] *otia* which are so conducive to composition; [50]*infelix* can describe the unproductive sterility of plants or soil,[51] suggesting that the *otium* which usually generates sophisticated composition is now sterile and infertile. Severus, on the other hand, continues to cultivate his *fertile pectus* (11), and no poet achieves a harvest which is *uberius* (12). In a direct comparison with Ovid's frozen stream of inspiration, Severus emerges as the more felicitous poet: *bibitur felicius Aonius fons* (47).

In this relatively simple way, then, Ovid exploits the technical nuances of poetic diction to contrast himself unfavourably with Severus; and yet various factors again suggest that Ovid's portrayal of his sterile *ingenium* is a dissembling pose. Take, for example, lines 15–16, the very couplet in which Ovid states that his *ingenium* is not as responsive as before. The motif of futility in the pentameter (*siccum sterili vomere litus aro*) can be compared to various other instances where the same motif expresses the idea of a pointless waste of energy, though elsewhere in Ovid the motif does not have an obvious literary relevance. At *Tr.* 5.4.48 'ploughing the sand' illustrates the pointlessness of cultivating a futile relationship;

---

[49] Cf. *Tr.* 1.1.41 for this usage; see *OLD* s.v. 2a for further examples.
[50] For *felix* used of poetic productivity cf. 47, *Tr.* 2.533, *F.* 1.585; see *OLD* s.v. 7b for *felix* applied to 'well-turned' literary productions.
[51] See *OLD* s.v. 1 for examples.

at *Her*. 5.115–16 Oenone portrays herself as warned that her pursuit of Paris will be profitless; and at *Her*. 17.139–40 Helen asks Paris *quid bibulum curvo proscindere litus aratro|... coner...?* More relevantly, Propertius also provides an analogy for the same motif in 2.11, where he tells Cynthia that other poets merely sow seed in the sterile earth (2), and that if she rejects him she will be left unknown and unsung. This Propertian example is particularly significant because it offers a parallel for the special application of the motif to denote the waste of effort on the part of a poet who lacks *ingenium*.[52]

How is Ovid's allusion in line 16 to these earlier instances of the motif to be interpreted? On the one hand, it could be argued that Ovid's allusive technique here suggests an unbroken thread of continuity in his creative work, though such continuity is seemingly contradicted by the waning of his poetic talent which is explicitly (and, on this reading, ironically) announced in the preceding line (*nec tamen ingenium nobis respondet, ut ante*, 15). On the other hand, the objection remains that Ovid's use of such a trite motif in line 16 (and, indeed, his use of the proverbial 'adding leaves to trees' motif in line 13)[53] actively shows that his *ingenium* has lost its fresh vitality. Such an objection is easily countered, however: Ovid's deliberate choice of 'trite' illustrations to portray the supposed lethargy of his *ingenium* proves to be a brilliantly imaginative touch designed to support the dissimulating assertion of his poetic decline.

The transferred epithet *sterili* conceals a complex nexus of allusions. The phrase 'ploughing the sand' is usually accompanied by an instrument. The plough of *P*. 4.2.16 (*sterili vomere*) also occurs at *Her*. 17.139, where it is qualified by the simple *curvo*; at *Her*. 5.116 the instrument is the oxen pulling the plough, though to no effect (*quid facis, Oenone? ...|nil profecturis litora bubus aras*). What Ovid does at *P*. 4.2.16 is to combine the adjectival description of the futility of the oxen's

---

[52] Helzle (1989), 69–70 supplies additional examples of the 'ploughing the sand motif'.

[53] On the proverbiality of this motif see Helzle (1989), 69 *ad loc*.

labour at *Her.* 5.116 with the instrumental plough of *Her.* 17.139 (*curvo . . . aratro*), and the adjective he chooses for this purpose is the very *sterilis* which Propertius uses for the motif at 2.11.2 (*laudet* [*te*], *qui sterili semina ponit humo*). In Propertius, of course, there is no instrument, and *sterili* qualifies *humo* conventionally enough. In transferring Propertius' *sterili* to the same metrical *sedes* in his own use of the motif at *P.* 4.2.16, Ovid applies the epithet to the instrument – not, however, to the oxen familiar from *Her.* 5.116, but to the much less appropriate plough of *Her.* 17.139. In its new application at *P.* 4.2.16 *sterilis* is most naturally read as an adjective transferred from the (infertile) sandy shore, which is precisely the application it had in Propertius. In effect, Ovid combines allusions to all these earlier instances of the motif simultaneously, and the very words which describe the infertility of his *ingenium* ironically imply the very opposite because of their allusive subtlety.

Lines 17–20 yield what is perhaps an even more subtle instance of creative reminiscence. Ovid compares the interruption in his flow of poetic inspiration to the effect of silt which clogs the veins (*venas*, 17) in springs and holds up the flow of water. *Vena* recurs in line 20, but in a figurative sense derived from Horace, denoting the 'flow' of poetic inspiration.[54] This is no simple case of semantic juggling, for the reference to the silt clogging the watercourse and figuratively blocking the flow of inspiration invites comparison with lines 108–12 of Callimachus' *Hymn to Apollo*.[55] There Apollo says of the great Assyrian river that τὰ πολλά|λύματα γῆς καὶ πολλὸν ἐφ' ὕδατι συρφετὸν ἕλκει (108–9), as opposed to the trickling stream ἥτις καθαρή τε καὶ ἀχράαντος ἀνέρπει|πίδακος ἐξ ἱερῆς (111–12). If πόντος (106) is interpreted as indicating Homer's poetry, then in literary terms the Assyrian river 'presumably represents the imitation of traditional epic, a genre which in

---

[54] See *OLD* s.v. 7 with Nisbet and Hubbard (1978), 298 on *C.* 2.18.9.

[55] Helzle (1988), 75–6 and (1989), 12 adduces the comparison to state that 'Ovid may . . . present himself as un-Callimachean on the surface, but at the same time also as more Callimachean than Callimachus'. I broadly agree, but my emphasis will differ.

its lengthy course has lost all its vitality ... The fine spray from the pure spring stands for Callimachus' own poetry: on a small scale, but highly refined, written for the few who are able to appreciate the poet's learning and subtlety.'[56] Few Callimachean critics would today differ greatly from Williams' interpretation; fewer still would deny the significance of these lines for subsequent Hellenistic and Roman poetics.[57]

If we accept that in the *Hymn to Apollo* the waters of the pure spring form an allegory for the trickling stream of Callimachean verse, Ovid's claim in *P.* 4.2 that his flow of poetic inspiration is reduced to a mere trickle (17–20) can be seen to work against his pose of decline. His initial insistence on the 'clogging up' of his *pectora* (19) turns into a carefully contrived statement of allegiance to Callimachean poetics, for the disruption which the figurative *limus* (his exilic hardship) brings to the seat of his creative powers modifies the association between Callimachus' λύματα γῆς and turgid, large-scale composition of poor quality: *limus* now marks the interrupted flow of inspiration in a Roman poet writing in the Callimachean manner. But the effect of the figurative 'silt' of vexation is to reduce, and not to block entirely, the flow of Ovid's verse: *carmen vena pauperiore fluit* (20). The initial sense conveyed by *pauperiore* here, as by *paupere* at *P.* 2.5.21 ([*ingenium*] *vena ... paupere manat*),[58] is one of quantity: the poet's flow of song is reduced by the clogging silt. But in both cases the word also has qualitative overtones which, as we shall see, are far from being pejorative.

The significance of the elegist's poverty for generic differentiation is clearly demonstrated at *Tr.* 2.335–8. In describing what he presents as his ill-fated attempt at writing an epic on Augustus, Ovid sets out the difficulties involved in such an enterprise as follows:

> divitis ingenii est immania Caesaris acta
> condere, materia ne superetur opus.
>
> (335–6)

---

[56] F. Williams (1978), 89.
[57] Cf. Wimmel (1960), 227 and Cairns (1979), 125ff.
[58] On the metaphor here see Wimmel (1960), 231.

Unable to sustain his heavy load and lacking a suitably en-riched *ingenium*, he returns instead to the lighter genre of love-elegy (339). Small-scale writing is here equated with an impov-erished talent, so that at *Tr.* 2.73–6 Ovid distinguishes himself from those who sing Augustus' praises with richer resources than he himself has at his disposal (*ingenio . . . uberiore*, 74); a poetic pauper, Ovid is unable to offer an epic celebration of Augustus, and the deified emperor must be won over *minimo . . . honore* (76). The most extended application of this motif appears in Propertius 2.10, where the poet claims that he will turn to celebrating Augustus' military achievements in grand, epic style (3–4), or at least that he will do so if his powers are up to the task (5–6). He goes on to construct a form of proem to his proposed work, but suddenly comes to a halt: it tran-spires that this is a project for the future (19–20), and he ends with an apology for the small-scale inferiority of his present offering, the result of his impoverished talent. Like a wreath which is placed at the foot of a god's statue because its head cannot be reached (21–2), Propertius' is a lowly gift in the sense that he cannot reach the heights of acceptable epic per-formance: *nos nunc . . . pauperibus sacris vilia tura damus* (23–4). The elegist is a creative pauper, working within a narrow compass as opposed to the wide dimensions and fertile rich-ness of the epicist's terrain.

Ovid's use of this motif both in *Tristia* 2 and in *P.* 4.2 coincides in essential detail with the picture mapped out by Propertius. Combining the latter's poetic *paupertas* with the Horatian poetic *vena* (cf. *C.* 2.18.10), Ovid can be seen clearly to be making some kind of statement of literary identity at *P.* 4.2.20. The initial reading, on which the phrase *vena pau-periore* refers to the flow of Ovid's inspiration being blocked by the figurative 'silt' of distress, and so provides fresh evi-dence of the decline of his *ingenium*, will not survive a close examination of the literary pedigree of these terms in Pro-pertius, Horace and Ovid himself. Far from denoting poetic decline, a *vena pauperior* denotes the very opposite in the lan-guage of programmatic poetics; and Ovid's use of the phrase in a 'decline' context shows how a veil of dissimulation is drawn over Ovidian literary usage to make it suggest to the cursory reader the opposite of what a sympathetic and informed reader will find there. At *P*. 4.2.20 the seemingly meagre flow of song serves only to consolidate the generic distinction between the elegists and writers in a more exuberant vein, and thereby to define Ovid's literary allegiances by differentiation from those of poets on the scale of Homer – who is ironically mentioned in the very next line (21).

By adapting the Callimachean reminiscence to make his own literary point, then, Ovid adjusts the motif of filth defiling his stream of composition so that the *limus* reduces his flow of song to slender proportions, and the trickling stream which results corresponds to Callimachus' ὀλίγη λιβάς. Ovid's allegiance as a poet is therefore further defined: it lies with Callimachus' small-scale refinement, or the Μοῦσαν λεπταλέην (*Aet*. fr. 1.24 (Pf.)), even though his veil of ironic dissimulation suggests that he is beyond any form of programmatic allegiance in Tomis. The irony of his self-disparaging pose is reinforced by the damning term *vitiata* in line 19 (*pectora sic mea sunt limo vitiata malorum*). The technical sophistication of lines 17–20, exploiting such features as the figurative senses of *limus* and *vena*, the literary overtones of *dives*|*pauper* and the simultaneous evocation of Callimachus, Propertius and Horace, ironically suggests the absence of *vitia* in the Horatian sense of literary blemishes.[59]

But *vitiata* possibly contains a further implication. The elder Seneca says of Ovid, in a context describing the unbridled *licentia* which the poet allowed himself, *aiebat interim decentiorem faciem esse, in qua aliquis naevos fuisset* (*Con*. 2.2.12). Could it be that Seneca refers here to an important feature of Ovidian poetic technique which is evident as early as the *Amores*? In *Am*. 3.1 the appearance of Elegia is disfigured by the *vitium* of her disfigured feet (7–8), but *pedibus vitium causa decoris erat* (10): the *vitium* of lameness paradoxically enhances Elegy's physical appearance. And so when Cupid steals a foot from every other line of Ovid's hexametrical

[59] For this connotation of *vitium* cf. *S*. 1.4.9, *Ep*. 1.19.17 and *Ars* 31 with Brink (1971), 115 *ad loc*.

poetry at *Am*. 1.1.3–4, his theft can be interpreted retrospectively as introducing a literary *vitium* into idealized hexametrical perfection. This *vitium*, pictured at *Am*. 1.1.3–4 as a shortcoming, turns out to be *the* essential characteristic of the verse itself: 'Elegy would not be elegy without the elegiac metre. The *vitium* is *causa decoris*.'[60] Recognition that *vitium* is essential to the identity of Ovid's elegy very probably lies behind the Ovidian *dictum* cited by Seneca, and it also raises a point which is relevant to the interpretation of *vitiata* at *P*. 4.2.19. The damage brought about by the 'silt' of excess is a *vitium* which serves the ironic purpose of marring the very poetic structure – Ovidian elegy – of which it is an essential characteristic. Moreover, the substitution of the *vitium* of poetic decline for the *vitium* of metrical impropriety establishes Ovid's identity as an *exilic* elegist: just as his amatory verse was characterized by the *vitium* of 'disfigured' metre, so his exilic verse is characterized by the *vitium* of an infertile *ingenium*.

The many ambivalences locked up in the dissimulating language of line 19 can be compared with the simpler case of the *vena pauperior* in 20, where a basic idea of Callimachean poetics is introduced by way of Horace and Propertius, but dissembled to give the impression of an *ingenium* in terminal decline rather than one fertilized in the Callimachean manner. The dissimulation in 19 proceeds along the same lines, but the allusions are more densely packed together and the irony surrounding *vitiata* has, as we have seen, possibly more complex ramifications. These ramifications enable *pectora* ... *vitiata* (19) to be viewed as a programmatic statement of poetic identity which distinguishes Ovid from Severus, the epicist whose hexameters are not 'crippled' by the *vitium* which Cupid imposes on Ovid's verse in *Am*. 1.1.

But does Ovid go further than this and distinguish his own literary allegiance from that of Severus? The poem suggests that too rigid a distinction should not be drawn between the two, just as it is misleading to characterize either Callimachus'

[60] Cunningham (1957), 254.

OVID'S POSE OF POETIC DECLINE

prologue to the *Aetia* or the end of the *Hymn to Apollo* as
straightforward diatribes against epic; in both cases it would
seem more likely that Callimachus is drawing a distinction
between 'good' and 'bad' poetry and not regarding genre as
an absolute criterion of quality.⁶¹ We should not assume,
then, that because Severus is termed *vates magnorum maxime
regum* (1) he cannot share with Ovid a common allegiance
to Alexandrian poetic theory and to the Callimachean canon
which values τέχνη above scale and sheer length (cf. *Aet.* fr.
1.17–18 (Pf.)). What, for example, of the *Aeneid*, which is
acknowledged to be a highly allusive poem in the Alexandrian
manner?⁶² This reservation about drawing too rigid a generic
distinction between Ovid and Severus needs to be stressed
because there is just a suggestion in some of Severus' surviving
fragments of what might be termed an allusive Alexandrian
technique. In the long fragment on the death of Cicero (fr.
13), for example, *abstulit una dies* (10) quotes Ovid's adaptation at *P.* 1.2.4 of Virgil's *abstulit atra dies* (*Aen.* 6.429), which
in turn recalls Lucr. 3.898–9, and *facundia linguae* (11) has
been taken to be a reminiscence of the phrase at *P.* 1.2.67 and
2.3.75.⁶³ Also, the final line of the fragment (25) bears obvious comparison with *Aen.* 12.951–2.⁶⁴ True, such instances of
Severus' allusiveness are too few to offer real insight into his

---

⁶¹ Cf. Knox (1986), 10, arguing that the issue of generic differentiation is not raised
in the prologue to the *Aetia* and that neither ἓν ἄεισμα διηνεκές (3) nor Ovid's
rendering (*perpetuum ... carmen, M.* 1.4) need refer to epic; but the epic associations of βασιλῆ (3) and ἥρωας (5) would seem to indicate that διηνεκές is not in
fact generically neutral (see Hinds (1989), 270). The crucial point, however, is
that even if (*contra* Knox) generic differentiation *is* at issue in the prologue (cf.
Hutchinson (1988), 79 n. 103), τέχνη remains the ultimate criterion by which *any*
poem's quality is to be gauged, regardless of length or scale (cf. 17–18). Thus, in
the *Hymn to Apollo*, the Assyrian river as an allegory for meandering imitation of
Homer (see F. Williams (1978), 89) need hardly represent a Callimachean tirade
against epic *per se*, but an attack on second-rate epic which lacks Homeric τέχνη.
⁶² See Clausen (1987), 14.
⁶³ Most of these allusions are noted by Courtney (1993), 326 *ad loc.* Although
Courtney argues (p. 320) from the view that Ovid's Pontic poems are the earlier,
it is not impossible that Severus is being quoted by Ovid in the above instances
(the evidence for chronology offered by Sen. *Ep.* 79.5 is not relevant here). In *P.*
4.2 Ovid certainly writes as though Severus were already an established poet (cf.
P. 4.16.9).
⁶⁴ See Courtney (1993), 327.

78

general poetic technique, but they nevertheless suggest that Ovid may acknowledge that epic is a different kind of poetry from his own, and yet still recognize in Severus a poet who shares a cultural background and outlook similar to his. In this respect, the kind of relationship drawn between the epicist and elegist in *P*. 4.2 finds its closest analogy in the harmonious relationship which, in the last chapter, Ovid was seen to share with the epic poet Macer in *P*. 2.10.

The fuller picture of Ovid's relationship with Severus is not, then, unconnected with his continuing interest in Callimachean poetics. Ovid's allegiance to Callimachean principles is an established feature of his verse as early as the *Amores*,[65] and it is a remarkable testimony to his poetic consistency that interest in the Callimachean programme continued to be central to his literary outlook even throughout the poems of exile. There is, however, at least in the case of *P*. 4.2, a noticeable change of approach. The subtle allusions to key Callimachean terminology continue to be central to Ovid's technique, but we have seen how the effect is now more ambivalent and imprecise when it comes to applying these allusions to an understanding of Ovid's own literary position. It is a widely acknowledged feature of the exile poetry that earlier Ovidian themes tend to be put into reverse, and at first we might suspect the same to be happening at *P*. 4.2.19–20: Ovid's Callimachean *ingenium* would seem to be firmly on the wane. But there is a large measure of dissimulation in these statements, and the closer reading we have given to these lines shows how they enhance the very talent they set out to depreciate.

Ovid's unpolished Muse

The technique of dissimulation with which Ovid depreciates the quality of his exilic poetry requires him to claim that he is reluctant to polish and revise his Tomitan verse. The polished execution of such elegies as *Tr*. 4.1 and *P*. 4.2 hardly supports such a claim, however; and in those elegies where Ovid openly

---

[65] See especially Lateiner (1978), 188–96 on *Am.* 2.19.

insists on the unpolished condition of his verse, especially *P*. 1.5 and 3.9, his use of Horatian models to suggest inadequacies in his own poetry serves ultimately to undermine the likelihood that his depiction of such inadequacies is either accurate or plausible. This Horatian presence is first apparent in *Tr*. 1.7, and its ironic significance in this elegy will prove to be typical of Ovid's treatment of Horatian material elsewhere in the exile poetry.

i

In his illuminating discussion of *Tr*. 1.7, Hinds plausibly argues that lines 35–40 are to be read as if they were a new preface to the *Metamorphoses* 'which will make pointed reference, like the beginning of *Tristia* 1 itself, to its author's exile; and which, again like the beginning of *Tristia* 1, will claim a reflection of the author's woes in the poem's own rough and unfinished state'.[66] This last point about the incompleteness of the *Metamorphoses* requires elaboration, since Ovid's method in treating the alleged imperfections of the *Metamorphoses* will help us to evaluate the parallel inadequacies claimed for the exile poetry.

For the purpose of my argument the crucial lines, which Hinds does not discuss, are 29–30. Here, two images are combined: the poem was not 'hammered out' on the anvil (*ablatum mediis opus est incudibus illud*, 29), nor was it given the attention of the 'file' (*defuit ... scriptis ultima lima meis*, 30). As Nagle notes,[67] the couplet is modelled on Horace, *Ars* 441. In distinguishing the true friend and critic from the false one, Horace writes of the former

> delere iubebat
> et male tornatos incudi reddere versus,

where *tornatos* ('turned on the lathe') represents the kind of fine 'polishing' which the terms *limatus* and τορευτός de-

[66] (1985), 26.
[67] (1980), 128 n. 29.

note.[68] Bentley objected to the Horatian text, as he might well
have done to the related Ovidian couplet, on the grounds that
lathing is incompatible with hammering on the anvil, and that
the two operations are harshly combined in the same line;[69]
but Ovid's couplet, reproducing the Horatian reference to
both *incus* and *lima/tornus*, strongly suggests that the combination of anvil and lathe must stand, uncomfortable as it is.
Confirmation of Horatian influence at *Tr.* 1.7.29–30 comes
not only from the unusual nature of the combination, but also
from its uniqueness: Ovid never uses the anvil image again,
although the *lima* motif recurs on a number of occasions (e.g.
P. 1.5.19, 2.4.17).[70]

In the Horatian context the rigorous Quintilius would demand that badly 'lathed' lines be put back on the anvil to
be refashioned. At *Tr.* 1.7.29–30 Ovid depicts the *Metamorphoses* as a work which is still in need of such corrective treatment, snatched as it was from the anvil and the attention of
the file; the 'canons of Alexandrian criticism'[71] which the true
Horatian critic will use have not been applied to the *Metamorphoses* (or so Ovid claims) any more than they will be applied
to the exilic elegies. But how seriously should Ovid's insistence
on the imperfections of the *Metamorphoses* be taken? Such
imperfections are certainly not referred to in the poem itself as
they are in the exile poetry, and, as Kenney has indirectly
shown in his analysis of the style of the *Metamorphoses*,[72]

---

[68] For *lima/limatus* as literary terms see Brink (1971), 321 on *Ars* 291; for *tornatus*
see Brink (1971), 414 on *Ars* 441.

[69] Bentley's objections, along with counter arguments, are summarized by Brink
(1971), 414–15 on *Ars* 441.

[70] Luck's note on *Tr.* 1.7.29–30 ((1977), II 66–7) is seriously defective. To his parallels for the motif of 'hammering on the anvil' applied to poetry, add Crinagoras'
epigram on the *Hecale*: Καλλιμάχου τὸ τορευτὸν ἔπος τόδε δὴ γὰρ ἐπ' αὐτῷ|ὡνὴρ
τοὺς Μουσέων πάντας ἔσεισε κάλως (*A.P.* 9.545.1–2). Τορευτός ('worked in relief',
LSJ s.v. I; metaph. 'elaborate', s.v. II) denotes the finely crafted 'finish' of Callimachus' verse; see Gow and Page (1968), II 220 on *A.P.* 9.545.1. The 'high finish'
of the term is also represented by Horace's *caelatum opus* at *Ep.* 2.2.92 (see Brink
(1982), 320). Luck also omits the Prop. 2.34.43–4: *incipe iam angusto versus in-
cludere torno,|inque tuos ignes, dure poeta, veni*. The poem subjected to the lathe
(*tornus*) is the τορευτὸν ἔπος, embellished by *limae labor*.

[71] Brink (1971), 412.

[72] (1973), 116–53.

they are hardly self-evident in the poem either. In fact, there are many indications in the poem itself, most obviously the sense of finality which comes with the postlude at 15.871ff., to suggest that Ovid saw the work as a finished whole;[73] and in so far as the so-called 'alternative' sections – mostly to be found in Book 8 – are genuinely Ovidian, they are more likely to derive from a subsequent revision of a completed and published text than from an initial draft being left incomplete.[74] Moreover, the probable falsity of Ovid's claim that he tried to burn the *Metamorphoses* serves only to undermine our confidence in the truth of his continuing assertions of the work's defects. That there is an allusion at *Tr.* 1.7.15ff. to Virgil's insistence on the burning of the *Aeneid* after his death because of its imperfections and incompleteness is now universally acknowledged.[75] Ovid uses this allusion to revive one myth and then to apply it to himself in order to enhance the credibility of another myth – that the *Metamorphoses* anticipates the sense of poetic incompleteness which characterizes the *Tristia* and *Epistulae ex Ponto*.

Ovid thus directs us towards a certain interpretation of the role of the *Metamorphoses* in *Tr.* 1.7 which helps to establish the persona of the poet in exile as artistically self-critical, perhaps ironically so. The *Metamorphoses* constitutes a literary analogue for the transformation which Ovid undergoes in his personal circumstances; and yet the poem itself also changes its complexion to match its author's transformation. Ovid is

---

[73] Kovacs (1987), 462–4 argues on the strength of *Iovis ira* at *M.* 15.871 that the *Metamorphoses* was 'first published to the world after his exile'. True, *M.* 15.871 would seem to be prophetic if the *Metamorphoses* had been published in its extant form prior to Ovid's relegation; but Kovacs takes no account of *Tr.* 1.1.117–20, where Ovid's reference to the *Metamorphoses* in his introductory exilic elegy clearly assumes his reader's prior (and pre-exilic?) acquaintance with the work.

[74] For alleged evidence of a double recension (and of Ovid's failure to bring the *Metamorphoses* to polished completion) see Enk (1958), 324–46 and Blaensdorf (1980), 138–51. But cf. Murgia (1984), 228: 'The existence of "double versions" is not a peculiarity of the transmission of Ovid ... Each example deserves to be weighed separately, but in the *Metamorphoses*, since in five examples clustered in a single book [8] French mss have wordier versions, and in some at least the wordier versions can be proven to be interpolated, all the versions so attested must labor under a particular weight of suspicion.'

[75] See Evans (1983), 43–4 and 185 n. 27, Hinds (1985), 22, Kovacs (1987), 463 n. 10.

transformed, after his exile, into a poet who claims to be in decline and technically ill-equipped for his task. If, then, the *Metamorphoses* is to survive and continue to be the poet's *maior imago* (11), accurately portraying his true appearance (cf. 26), the poem must also change its *frons* to that of Ovid's exilic state. In *Tr.*1.7 Ovid accordingly rewrites the inscribed *frons* (cf. 33) of the *Metamorphoses* (35–40) to transform it retrospectively into a poem which is 'more pessimistic – more suited, in fact, to an age of *Tristia*'.[76] He must therefore stress the (probably fictitious) notion of technical imperfection in the *Metamorphoses* (22, 27–30) in order to direct attention to an element in the poem which will justify the new legend on its *frons*; reduced to an unpolished and unkempt state, it will thus continue to be an *imago* of its author. *Tr.* 1.7 helps to consolidate at an early stage in Ovid's first exilic book the connection between the poet's exilic *frons* and the technical quality of his compositions; but it also points to the connection itself being an instance of contrived dissimulation. The reference to the lack of polish in the *Metamorphoses* is itself an artful Horatian reminiscence, and the introduction of the motif of technical deficiency in this early poem shows it to have been a feature of the whole initial conception of the exilic theme, as opposed to being a spontaneous and inevitable reaction to the difficulties Ovid faces in surviving as a Latin poet among the unresponsive Getae.

ii

Horatian reminiscence is a decisive influence in *P.* 1.5 and 3.9, where Ovid alludes to specific lines and passages and draws on much of Horace's technical vocabulary in order to portray his own failure to correct and revise his exilic elegies. The parallels between Ovid and Horace are well known,[77] but Ovid's ironic exploitation of the Horatian canons of correct *ars* requires clarification. There is, of course, an irony implicit in

[76] Hinds (1985), 26.
[77] See conveniently Nagle (1980), 128–30.

Ovid's many reminiscences of Horatian material: he exploits such points of reference only to announce his neglect of the literary *praecepta* on revision and correction which Horace gives; and yet this allusiveness requires the application of the very techniques which Ovid denies he employs. Predictably, the way in which Ovid responds to the Horatian material he echoes complicates the portrayal of his poetic decline.

Ovid's depiction of his poetic madness in *P.* 1.5 is a case in point. Why does he continue to write poetry when his poetry has brought him no profit, but only harm (27–30)? Popular opinion would seem to be correct:

> an populus vere sanos negat esse poetas,
>   sumque fides huius maxima vocis ego,
> qui, sterili totiens cum sim deceptus ab arvo,
>   damnosa persto condere semen humo?
>
> (31–4)

Ovid has of course already characterized himself as mad because he continues to write poetry both on his way to, and in, Tomis (cf. *Tr.* 1.11.11; 2.15; 4.1.37–8), and this *dementia* motif is part of the general *infelicitas* of his exile: the implied suggestion of *stultus*|*insanus* which *infelix* can sometimes carry was never more appropriately stressed than in Tomis (cf. *quid mihi vobiscum est, infelix cura, libelli...?*, *Tr.* 2.1).[78] But poetic madness is traditionally associated with inspiration,[79] not with creative decline or the insanity which drives Ovid to write even though he seems to gain no benefit from his poetry. This Ovidian form of madness both complements and helps to explain his rejection of the recommended techniques of revision and correction: he is 'mad' to go on writing, in part because the quality of what he produces is so poor (cf. 33–4).

The various contrasting points here can be conveniently elucidated by reference to Horace's ironic treatment of poetic inspiration at *Ars* 295ff. Democritus was one of those for whom *ars* and *ingenium* were polarized opposites (cf. 295–6),

---

[78] Cf. Ov. *Am.* 2.9.39–42, where *infelix* (39) anticipates *stulte* (41), Virg. *Aen.* 5.465 (*infelix, quae tanta animum dementia cepit?*); see further *TLL* 7(1).1364.24ff.

[79] See, e.g., Hor. *C.* 3.4.5–6, *S.* 2.7.117. For background see Dodds (1951), 80–2 and Brink (1971), 328–33 with Videau-Delibes (1991), 371ff.

since he held that poetic talent was a matter of inspiration and not technique. Since he also equated inspiration with madness, he effectively (Horace concludes) required genuinely talented poets to be insane (296). Taking their cue from this, people with literary ambition but little talent affect signs of madness in order to appear the literary geniuses they are not (297–8). For Ovid and Horace, of course, the Democritean opposition of *ingenium* and *ars* can have made no more sense than it would to any other poet who had learnt from Callimachus, but Democritus serves the purpose for Horace of having established a prejudice in the popular mind: all real poets are mad eccentrics. Of course, artistic impostors can easily turn this prejudice around and persuade the gullible that all madmen and eccentrics are real poets; and it is something of this kind which Ovid presents himself as doing to the Tomitans (and to his Roman readers) at *P*. 1.5.31–4. Writing as he is for no visible audience and with no apparent result (cf. 27ff.), and without even satisfying his own artistic standards in the process (cf. 15ff.), Ovid applies to himself this popular prejudice that poets must be mad to carry on as they do (31). But in invoking the prejudice, he gives it an ironic twist: popular recognition of his madness would in fact confirm the genuineness of his poetic talent – at least on the so-called 'Democritean' criterion of *Ars* 295ff. – and not its decline or the futility of its exercise. The very madness of persevering with verse in uncongenial circumstances and with a declining talent gives Ovid a welcome endorsement of the poetic status which he fears lost.

What we have in lines 31–2 is not simply an allusion to Horace, but allusive manipulation and adaptation of Horatian irony. Both Ovid and Horace would share an equally ironic view of the Democritean disjunction and emphasis, but what Horace disdains Ovid turns to his own advantage: his verse may (he admits) be defective and futile, but even so – or rather, because of this – he remains a poet in the public mind. This is an aspect of Ovidian technique in *P*. 1.5 which militates against his claim that he is reluctant to use the 'file' to polish his verse. His adoption of Horace's *sanos . . . poetas* (31;

cf. *Ars* 296), with its approximation to, and yet departure from, the Democritean/Horatian conception of poetic madness, typifies the way in which he applies the file and brings *sub iudicium singula verba* (20). It is ironic that Ovid may receive popular acclaim as a poet for his 'madness' and not for his verse, but there is a further irony in the possibility that his continuing awareness of technical propriety (cf. 13–20) may confirm that public opinion was correct on this occasion, though for the wrong reason.

Again, in *P.* 3.9 Ovid depicts himself as reluctant to endure *longi ... laboris onus* (20) and to make corrections to his verse. He outlines the technical deficiencies of his poetry by subtle evocation of Horatian *praecepta*, and, as in *P.* 1.5, such reminiscences serve only to demonstrate his continued commitment to the studied application of poetic *labor*, rather than his resignation to its absence.[80] Take, for example, his claim that he is aware of the shortcomings of his poetry, despite the fact that every poet tends to think more highly of his work than he should (7–8). This seemingly candid admission takes up a point made at *Ep.* 2.2.106–8, where Horace declares that poets of poor quality have a high opinion of themselves and, unless told of their *real* quality, *laudant quidquid scripsere beati* (108).[81] Ovid creates this point of association with Horace, and yet he also responds positively to his model; unlike the poets whom Horace criticizes, he states that he does not persist in writing in blissful ignorance of his *delicta*, nor does he value his own compositions too highly (11–12). Ovid seems momentarily to have taken the Horatian point to heart, and, as a consequence, to be candidly honest about his own poetic self-evaluation. But his frankness is once again deceptively ironic: by acknowledging his faults and saying how bad his verse is, he is in effect showing how, in Horatian terms, he is elevated *above* bad poets.

Ovid also turns Horatian irony to his own advantage. At *Ars* 295–308 Horace portrays the careful polishing of verse as

---

[80] Block (1982), 22 takes the same line.
[81] Nagle (1980), 129 sees the connection.

quite inconsistent with the Democritean notion that poetry is produced in an inspired frenzy and that native genius (*ingenium*) is therefore to be more highly valued than laborious technique (*ars*). Horace's reaction to this un-Callimachean primitivism is decidedly ironic: if inspired poetry involves madness (cf. *bilem*, 302), then he would rather be without it and remain sane, and, in consequence, become a critic rather than a writer of poetry. Brink rightly detects the ironical tone of Horace's self-depreciation as a poet in lines 303ff.: 'This ironic diminution of his own status H. has practised throughout his career from *S.* 1.4.13ff. onwards ... Few instances are as amusingly and disarmingly ambiguous as the present one.'[82] Ovid reacts to Horace's irony with an irony of his own. As in *P.* 1.5, he depicts himself as mad because he continues to write verse among the unresponsive Getae (*vix ... mihi videor, faciam qui carmina, sanus*, 31); once again, this is not the madness of inspired Democritean frenzy, but that of trying to write in unconducive surroundings and circumstances. Ovid is having it both ways: although his madness is part of his pose of poetic decline, his being *insanus* gives him, in Democritean terms, the creative edge over Horace, who claims to be unable to write for want of inspirational madness. While Ovid seems to be fully acknowledging the defects of his poetry according to Horatian canons, his 'insanity' nevertheless enables him to continue writing and so to succeed where Horace depicts himself as 'failing'.

The pointed edge of Ovid's irony is sharpened by the way in which he takes issue with Horatian *praecepta* in lines 23–6. Horace describes the type of critic who is scrupulous and fastidious as 'an Aristarchus' (*Ars* 450). But Ovid, having already admitted that he is not up to the task of applying *ars* to the correction of his work (15–18), compares fluency of composition as opposed to the laborious industry of correction to the superiority of Homer *over* Aristarchus (23–4). The astonishing and ironic consequence of this preference is that Ovid now seems to be siding with Democritus, who considered *in-*

genium misera ... fortunatius arte (*Ars* 295). As if following Democritus' *dictum*, Ovid depicts himself as valuing inspiration and native talent (*ingenium*) over technique (*ars*), and so to be reversing at *P.* 3.9.23–6 a central canon of Horatian literary criticism. Inverting the familiar pattern of the hackneyed images of inspiration, Ovid will not allow the cool, detached labour of studied *cura* to restrict or impair (cf. *laedit*, 25) the hot passion of the swelling creative impulse (cf. *cum ... suo crescens pectore fervet opus*, 22). And yet no one is going to be deceived into taking this kind of Democritean association at face value, for Ovidian irony is playing a gently mocking game here at the expense of Horatian didacticism. His technical negligence (19–20) is, like his artistic 'madness' (31), the adoption of a 'Democritean' mask to conceal the poetic art behind it. The dissimulation here is obviously more concerned with projecting the persona of a poet whose artistic values (like most other aspects of his life) have become the reverse of what we might have expected in a poet of Ovid's stature. Technical skill has gone the way of poetic *gloria* and *laus*, along with the other accoutrements of the Augustan *vates*. Horatian literary canons are used as a foil for Ovid's new and contrasting literary persona, but the heavy irony tells against the notion that Ovid is constructing a new *Ars Poetica*.

Ovid's irony at the expense of Horatian criticism extends to the way in which he distances himself from some of Horace's canons and, in doing so, aligns himself with others. Take, for example, the fault (*vitium*) of monotonous repetition of theme in the exile poetry (37ff.). There is a good reason why Ovid should be reluctant to undertake the editing and pruning of his work in the Horatian manner. If repetition is a *vitium* in his poetry, it is not one he will want to correct, since the recurrent tone of complaint and melancholy is an artistic device used in the exilic elegies to portray the monotony of the situation in which the poet finds himself. The *vitium* of monotonous repetition therefore enables him to establish the frozen consistency of his poetic character and environment within his material. The latter point is reproduced in lines 35–6, though appropriately it is an established and recurring theme throughout the exilic elegies (cf. *carmine temporibus conveniente suis*, *Tr.* 3.1.10; so *Tr.* 5.1.5–6), forging the identity between Ovid's *carmen* and his own condition. In consequence, Ovid rejects one Horatian canon – the application of *limae labor* – only to approximate to another, that of making tone and style consistent with thematic material (cf. *Ars* 105–7, 119–24).

Horatian influence may be further detected in Ovid's treatment of the concept of poetic *utilitas*. In *P.* 3.9 his alleged motivation for writing is not *gloria* but *utilitas officiumque* (55–6). *Officium* denotes the social and moral duty which is inherent in the profession of being a poet, and so the phrase *utilitas officiumque* corresponds at least in this respect to Horace's parallel phrase *munus et officium* at *Ars* 306.[83] *Utilitas* has a two-fold significance. As Nagle has shown,[84] it denotes the writing of poetry as an end in itself, enabling Ovid to divert himself from meditation on his distress; but the term also denotes the functional use of his poetry as a means to an end, as Ovid can hope to influence his friends to work for his transfer or recall from Tomis. This dual connotation is present at *P.* 1.5.53–4:

> magis utile nil est
> artibus his, quae nil utilitatis habent.

Poetry is *utilis* in the sense that it enables Ovid to forget his misfortunes (cf. 55), but *inutilis* in the sense that it has not as yet succeeded in securing his removal from Tomis.

Given the wider Horatian influence in *P.* 1.5 and 3.9, the theme of *utilitas* in both poems would seem to offer yet another illustration of Ovid's ambiguous relationship to Horatian literary vocabulary and precept. In Horatian poetics *utilis* is applied to the instructive subject-matter of poetry, and

---

[83] See Brink (1971), 336 for *officium* in this sense of social/moral obligation, whereas *munus* carries 'a predominantly juridical and religious significance'. For Ovid, *officium* of course represents his binding duty to his friends – and their reciprocal duty to help secure his removal from Tomis (see Evans (1983), 149–50).

[84] (1980), 71.

dulcis is applied to the embellishment of style (cf. *qui miscuit utile dulci,\lectorem delectando pariterque monendo, Ars* 343–4). *Dulcis* and *utilis* are terms used in the *Ars* to develop the distinction made at 333–4, to the effect that poets aim either to benefit (*prodesse*) or to please (*delectare*) their audience, *aut simul et iucunda et idonea dicere vitae*. Since to provide *utilia* is to provide *idonea ... vitae*, *utilitas* is what constituted the ὠφέλησις of poetry in Hellenistic literary theory, as opposed to ἡδονή.[85] But Ovid, unlike poets who seek to benefit or entertain others, restricts the *utilitas* of his poetry to benefiting himself. This is a modification of poetic *utilitas* as it is presented by Horace, and the novel adaptation of the term to the poet's own advantage arises out of the novel circumstances in which the exilic poet has to compose: there is no way in which he can continue to be *utilis urbi* (cf. *Ep.* 2.1.124), and so he becomes *utilis sibi*.

Such modification is typical of the broader use which Ovid makes of Horatian material in *P.* 1.5 and 3.9. The passages discussed above reveal the limitations implicit in assuming that Horatian influence is demonstrable only where basic similarities are evident in the material. Horatian literary *praecepta* provoke from Ovid an ironic response which, though appearing for the most part to ignore them, in other respects pays them subtle homage. His allusions to the terms of Horatian criticism play an essential part in shaping our response to his seemingly frank admission of the declining standards of his workmanship – and an informed response will, I argue, call into question the credibility of that picture. It is difficult to see how Ovid's subtle evocation of Horace, and the game of reversal which he plays with the canons of Horatian *ars*, can suggest anything other than the preservation of the *ingenium* and *ars* he fears lost. After all, a poet genuinely driven by circumstances to depart from the principles of composition he had faithfully followed in all his earlier works would be likely to ignore the Horatian literary *praecepta*, and not

[85] For background see Brink (1971), 352–3 and (1982), 163–4.

be drawing our attention back to them through constant allusion.[86]

Ovid as a Getic poet

Ovid's persistent claims that in Tomis his grasp of Latin has seriously weakened and his *ingenium* has become sterile reach their climax in *P.* 4.13, where he states that he has written a Getic poem in Latin metre on the apotheosis of Augustus and recited it before a Getic audience. There is no surviving evidence of any such poem, and, indeed, it seems extremely unlikely that Ovid did actually undertake the project. What, then, are we to make of his assertions?

Lozovan rightly questions the assumption that Getic was a language which could be accommodated in Latin metre,[87] and it is surely special pleading to argue, as Wilkinson does, that Ovid could have imitated 'not the quantitative metre of the Greeks and Romans, but one of the accentual metres native to Italy'.[88] To believe that Ovid wrote an imperial eulogy in Getic, we have to assume that Getic had a suitable vocabulary and idiom for such *laudes*. His grasp of the language would have to be quite extraordinary if he was to portray such evocative Roman concepts as *virtus* (27), *imperium* (28) and *pudicitia* (29) successfully. We would also have to accept that Ovid, although evidently a late learner, had mastered such traditional techniques of royal/imperial eulogy as may have been found in Getic. Straightforward transference of the Latin idiom for imperial *laudes* into Getic would not be sufficient to win the acclaim of the local audience. The Getae acknowledge the quality of Ovid's performance (21–2), but this would

---

[86] Cf. Helzle (1988a), 127–38, comparing *P.* 3.9 with Hor. *Ars* 438–56 and arguing that through Horatian allusion Ovid casts himself as both an accomplished poet and a mad poetaster; Ovid uses the guise of mad poetaster to persuade Augustus to recall him. The significant point in Helzle's argument is that Augustus' own reading of *P.* 3.9 is brought into question: did Ovid assume that Augustus was unable to recognize dissimulation and poetic irony?

[87] (1958), 402.

[88] (1955), 363.

surely only be possible if he had mastered the Getic idiom for royal *laudes*.[89] Such mastery would itself require more than linguistic expertise; for Ovid to make a success of his project, he would need an extraordinary 'feel' for Getic diction, and this despite his reluctance to learn the local language in the first place.[90] These reservations about the feasibility of the project do not imply any cultural condescension towards the Getic population, but merely recognize the extent to which Latin imperial eulogy was formally and stylistically a Hellenistic/Roman phenomenon.[91] And yet, as Nagle observes,[92] the question of whether or not Ovid wrote a poem in Getic is ultimately of secondary importance; the crucial point is that he claims to have done so.

Orthodox opinion on *P.* 4.13 is conveniently summarized by Evans: 'As a culmination to earlier apologies where he decried conditions of composition, the weakening of his poetic *ingenium*, and the barbarization of his style, he now presents himself as *paene poeta Getes*, no longer to be considered a Latin poet to be judged by Rome's civilized standards.'[93] Having complained about the lack of an audience receptive to his Latin poetry (cf. *Tr.* 3.14.39–40, 4.10.113–14), Ovid at last wins the approval of a Getic audience by his recitation of a poem in the Getic language (*P.* 4.13.21–2). This express need for an audience (cf. *excitat auditor studium*, *P.* 4.2.35) sets Ovid on a path which leads to what Lozovan presents as his gradual 'gétisation',[94] while Herescu goes further, taking *P.* 4.13.17–18 to mean that Ovid writes bad Latin poetry precisely because he is becoming a Getic poet. His transforma-

---

[89] Della Corte (1976a), 215–16 assumes as much in claiming that Ovid's successful Getic poem was a translation of a Latin version mentioned at *P.* 4.6.17–18 and 4.9.131–2.

[90] Cf. *Tr.* 5.7.55–64, where *cogor* (56) hardly suggests a polyglot's thirst for learning a new tongue.

[91] This is in effect recognized by Adamesteanu (1958), 391–5, who believes in the Getic poem but, in an attempt to create a cultural context for it, places Ovid in the public *gumnasion* before an audience of Greeks and half-Greeks. These hardly correspond to the *inhumanos ... Getas* of *P.* 4.13.22.

[92] (1980), 138 n. 42.

[93] (1983), 165.

[94] (1958), 402.

tion into a Getic poet constitutes a conscious break with the past: if he is to be rejected as a Latin poet, he will become a Getic poet, overcoming his fears of 'une dégradation de l'artiste et un avilissement de son art'.[95]

The standard interpretation of *P*. 4.13, then, is that it brings to a dramatic climax the process of Ovid's gradual decline as a Latin poet during his Tomitan exile. But this approach fails to take into account the pervasive force of Ovidian dissimulation which is actively present in this poem, as in so many others in the exilic collection. Whereas critics such as Evans, Lozovan and Herescu detect only negative features in his portrayal of himself as *paene poeta Getes*, I propose to show that, on the contrary, there are strongly positive aspects to the picture of Ovid's conversion into a Getic poet. Ovid states that the faults which riddle his Latin verse are attributable to the fact that he has become *paene poeta Getes*; and yet there is evidence to suggest that his description of his Getic poem in this elegy is designed, paradoxically, to show that his Latin poetry is free from the literary defects (*vitia*) which he claims for it.

Ovid's portrayal of Carus, his addressee and the author of a poem on Hercules,[96] gives initial guidance to his overall strategy here. Carus' distinctive abilities immediately reveal the authorship of his verse: *prodent auctorem vires* (11). A parallel is immediately drawn between Carus' *vires* as a poet and the heroic *vires* of his subject, Hercules:

> vires, quas Hercule dignas
> novimus atque illi, quem canis ipse, pares.
> (11–12)

This parallel at once establishes a correspondence between the poet and his subject-matter, with Hercules' *vires* being celebrated in an artistically contrived medium which displays the

---

[95] Herescu (1959), 74. Cf. (1958), 404–5, where he claims that Ovid's originality as a poet lies partly in his being probably the only Roman author who wrote in a foreign language other than Greek; equally eccentric is his claim ((1958a), 93–6) that Ovid was the first Romanian poet.

[96] For Carus cf. *P*. 4.16.7–8 and see *RE* 3.1631.46ff. with Bardon (1956), 66; Ovid is our only source of information on him.

equivalent *vires* of its author.[97] This relation between Hercules and the poet Carus serves, I suggest, as a model for Ovid, who adopts this same correspondence between author and subject-matter as a basis for his account of his Getic poem.

The imperial household whose praises Ovid sings in Getic (25–32) represents a unique form of poetic subject-matter. Augustus had been consistently invoked by Ovid as both the mainstay and figurehead of Roman power (cf. *P.* 2.8.19–20), Livia continues to be portrayed as a woman uniquely equipped to be Augustus' consort (cf. *Tr.* 2.161–4), and Tiberius, even before his accession, was depicted along with Drusus and Germanicus as a worthy successor of the Augustan heritage (cf. *Tr.* 2.165ff.). What kind of poetic celebration will do justice to the unparalleled status of the imperial family, at this crucial moment of transition from one reign to the next? In *Tristia* 2 Ovid claims to have attempted an epic composition in celebration of *immania Caesaris acta* (335), but his lowly literary powers were not up to the task (cf. 337–8). If he is to undertake imperial eulogy, then, he must resort to an alternative medium which lies within his powers of successful execution, and the consequence in *P.* 4.13 is that he depicts himself as having devised a unique literary combination defined as *structa ... nostris barbara verba modis* (20) – Getic language set in Roman metre.

Ovid therefore follows Carus' own procedure in his poem on Hercules. Carus celebrates Hercules' *vires* in a poetic achievement distinguished by the Herculean performance of his artistic *vires*. Ovid similarly sets up a correspondence between his own distinctive literary abilities and the distinctive status of his imperial subject-matter by devising a unique literary combination in which to sing the praises of the unique Augustan household. The theme of a poem's structure reflecting or complementing the nature of its contents is itself basic to Ovid's presentation of *P.*4.13 to Carus: his distinctive

---

[97] For *vires* in this poetic sense see *OLD* s.v. *vis* 27, adding Hor. *Ep.* 2.1.258–9 and Ov. *Tr.* 2.531–2, where *vires* is applied to Ovid's natural aptitude for elegy rather than epic (*natura ... ingenio vires exiguas ... dedit*).

OVID AS A GETIC POET

mode of elegiac epistle, with its formalistic connotation of
elegiac lament, complements his mournful tone (cf. *color*, 3) as
the mark of Ovid's authorial identity (cf. *unde saluteris ...
index|... structura mei carminis esse potest*, 3–4). Given his
poetic decline, this elegiac structure is distinctively Ovidian
not because of its remarkable quality (cf. *non ... mirifica est*,
5), but because it is *non publica* (5) in a range of senses – a
private exilic communication which is composed in extraordinary circumstances.[98] Reapplied to the structure of Ovid's
Getic poem (cf. *structa*, 20), the phrase *non publica certe est* (5)
again functions as the distinguishing mark of Ovidian authorship; but on this occasion Ovid's decidedly public performance ironically limits the sense of *non publica* to the extraordinary fusion (cf. *[structura] mirifica*, 5) of Getic language and
Roman metre.

The novelty of Ovid's alleged achievement is explicitly announced in *novitas* (24), which signals not only the originality
of his chosen format, but also its oddness as an unusual literary phenomenon.[99] Divine inspiration, defined in line 24 as
the inspiration provided by Augustus' *numen*, helps Ovid to
execute his novel literary enterprise and gives a new twist
and an unexpected dimension to *Am.* 3.9.17–18 (*sacri vates et
divum cura vocamur,|sunt etiam qui nos numen habere putant*).
But it is the conception of Augustus as a divinity, rather than
Augustus' Muse-like support, which provides the true inspiration for Ovid's Getic poem. Augustus' *novitas*, in the sense
that as a recently deified emperor he is a phenomenon without
parallel, is appropriately celebrated in a poem which has
novitas of its own as a literary phenomenon without parallel.

[98] On the competing nuances of *publica* [*carmina*] in exile ('public' but 'common-
place') see Evans (1983), 95.
[99] For the former sense of *novitas* see *OLD* s.v. 4b; for the latter, s.v. 2b. Accepting
that Gilbert (1896), 62 is right to punctuate after *laudes*, I detect an ambiguity in
line 23. *Laudes* could be a noun: 'You want to know of my subject-matter? Eulogy
– I spoke about Caesar Augustus' (for the plural cf. Hor. *Saec.* 75–6, *Dianae|
dicere laudes*). *Laudes* could also be a potential subjunctive: 'You want to know of
my subject-matter? You would praise it – I spoke about Caesar Augustus' (for
laudes in this sense cf. *P.* 2.5.1 on Ovid's alleged poem in honour of Tiberius'
Pannonian triumph: *illic, quam laudes, erit officiosa voluntas*). A neat play: Ovid
invites praise for his praises.

The correspondence between the inner structures of the poems of Carus and Ovid is complemented by a further correspondence between the *materia* of Ovid's Getic poem and Carus' Herculean theme. The typological depiction of Hercules as an earlier Augustus is familiar from the *Aeneid* and elsewhere,[100] and the association is implicit in *P.* 4.13 as well. Augustus' apotheosis is described in lines 25–6 as the separation of the mortal *corpus* from the immortal *numen*, which then proceeded to its place among the gods. In Hercules' case too, his immolation and cremation on Mt Oeta bring about the discarding of his mortal form and the ascension of his spiritual being to heaven, as Ovid himself had already described at *M.* 9.239–72 (cf. *mortales ... exuit artus*, 268; *parte sui meliore viget*, 269).[101] It is certainly plausible to take this Herculean apotheosis as the primary model for that of Augustus in lines 25–6, and by associating the two in this way, Ovid can be seen to be suggesting more than simply an extension of the comparison of Augustan and Herculean *acta*. The ascension of Augustus was observed immediately after his cremation, or so Suetonius claims: *nec defuit vir praetorius, qui se effigiem cremati euntem in caelum vidisse iuraret* (*Aug.* 100.4). The connection with Hercules will have suggested itself naturally to the poetic mind, as Augustus emerges from the flames of the pyre as an immortal being. Ovid, then, exploits what may well have been on the way to becoming received as popular tradition, and he applies the Herculean apotheosis to Augustus to strengthen the already evident correspondence with Carus' subject-matter.

Both the inner structures and the subjects of Carus' poem on Hercules and Ovid's Getic poem can be seen to offer these correspondences, but while these parallels may be evident enough, Ovid's overall purpose in shaping them has yet to be

---

[100] On the Virgilian comparison see Galinsky (1972), 132ff. and Lyne (1987), 27–35. Cf. Hor. *C.* 3.3.9ff., 3.14.1ff., *Ep.* 2.1.10ff. (with Brink (1982), 39–42). Hirst (1926), 347–57 detects an Augustan allusion when Livy applies the term *augustior* to Hercules and Romulus.

[101] For the immolation on Mt Oeta cf. S. *Tr.* 1185ff., Lucian *Herm.* 7; for the apotheosis cf. E. *Heracl.* 910ff. The growth of the myth is discussed briefly by Easterling (1982), 17–19.

established. Though he claims that his Latin poetry is defective (cf. *vitiosa ... carmina*, 17–18), Ovid avoids one particular *vitium* in this elegy, namely the incongruity which results from a poet treating his chosen subject within an inappropriate poetic medium or a medium which is beyond his natural powers of execution. In Horatian terms, the ideal poet has both to choose a theme appropriate to his powers (*sumite materiam vestris, qui scribitis, aequam|viribus*, *Ars* 38–9) and to observe the norms of diction appropriate to the different poetic genres (*Ars* 73–88). Carus fully complies with Horace in the harmonious interaction he achieves between Hercules' *vires* and his own equivalent powers of poetic expression (cf. 11–12), and Ovid proves to be similarly responsive in his Getic poem. Lacking the *vires* to celebrate the deified Augustus in the suitable or expected medium of epic, he purports to have taken the radical step of creating a new and unique genre which matches the uniqueness of his subject-matter without straining his own artistic *vires*. Even though Ovid apologizes (cf. *pudet*, 19) for having set *barbara verba* in Roman metre in his Getic poem, the result is a performance which scrupulously observes Roman literary protocol through the necessary application of Horatian canons.

By reporting his Getic poem in the elegiac format of *P.* 4.13, however, Ovid achieves a further effect which renders the question of whether or not he actually wrote in Getic entirely irrelevant. Ovid ingeniously surmounts the traditional problem of how a lowly elegist is to rise to Augustan *laudes* without depreciating them through generic diminution. Propertius provides one solution to the elegist's dilemma in 2.1 by claiming that he would sing of Augustus' and Maecenas' achievements (25–6) – if only he had the power (cf. 39–42). By thus envisaging an Augustan epic within his *recusatio*, Propertius successfully broaches an epic task without compromising his lowly generic status as an elegist. Ovid modifies this Propertian tactic in *P.* 4.13 by replacing Propertius' elegiac allusion to the epic which might have been with a description of his extraordinary Getic poem. Like Propertius, Ovid succeeds in devising his own form of Augustan eulogy within

an elegiac framework, though his Getic performance represents a breathtakingly original alternative to the standard epic
which Propertius envisages. Even if Ovid really did write the
Getic poem, the more important point is that by reporting it
in elegy he finds a new answer to an old problem: one way of
writing Augustan *laudes* in elegy is to give an elegiac description of a separate poem which, in its generic form, is ideally
equipped for such *laudes*.

Viewed in this light, Ovid's claim that he has written a
poem in Getic need not be interpreted as the lowest point of
his poetic decline in exile. His self-portrayal as *paene poeta
Getes* is a dissimulating guise which belies his observance
of Roman literary protocol in the construction of his Getic
poem, and the claim that his Latin verse is distinguished only
by its faults (cf. 14) is not only unsupported by evident *vitia*
in this or any other exilic elegy, but also belies the Horatian
canons which he implements to avoid the cardinal *vitium* of
celebrating Augustus in an inappropriate medium. Indeed,
Ovid's dissimulation in *P*. 4.13 may even extend to his treatment of the imperial family in lines 25ff., despite the implied
compliment of Augustus' comparison with Hercules. Ovid
portrays himself as a loyal supporter of the Augustan/
Tiberian dynastic family. Such an allegiance, we suppose, can
only help him to win the support of Carus, who has a certain
amount of influence in imperial quarters (cf. 47–50). But does
Ovid's claim that he has celebrated Augustus' achievements
and apotheosis in *barbara verba* have any bearing on the nature of the *acta* which are thus celebrated? When Ovid puts
into the mouth of a local tribesman the statement that he
should have been restored by Augustus (37–8), does the poet
imply that the wild Getae have a sympathetic sensibility which
Augustus himself lacked? Does the fact that Ovid can win
over the local peoples and receive their acclaim for his poetry
by the shaking of their quivers (35) imply that he can succeed
where Roman arms fail? If we do detect such implications, is
it any surprise that Ovid writes *carmina nil prosunt* (41) and
finds himself in the sixth winter of his relegation? The crude
answer on each count is that Ovid is engaged in mischievous

dissimulation. A more subtle response, however, is to accept that Ovid's dissimulating technique in exile does not operate within rigidly drawn limits, but beguiles the reader in its range of application, and each case must be judged on its own (possibly finely balanced) merits. In the case of Ovid's pose of poetic decline, however, his dissimulation is certainly not in doubt: *P.* 4.13, like the other poems examined in this chapter, proves that Ovid remains firmly in control of the abilities which are misleadingly portrayed as all but destroyed by exile.

3

FRIENDSHIP AND THE THEME OF
ARTISTIC MOTIVATION

If Ovid's pose of poetic decline in the *Tristia* and *Epistulae ex Ponto* is an extended exercise in dissimulation, how is this pose to be reconciled with his insistence on the ingenuous and candid openness of committed friendship? Clearly, the poet himself drew a sharp distinction between dissimulation as a literary device and dissimulation as a contemptible trait in a faithless character. This latter condition is that of the un-named addressee in *P.* 4.3, a figure who chooses to pretend not to know Ovid after his downfall (cf. *dissimulas etiam, nec me vis nosse videri*, 9). On the other hand, Ovid's friendship with his addressee in *Tr.* 3.6 is so well known that the latter could not deny it even if he wished to do so: *foedus amicitiae nec vis ... nostrae|nec, si forte velis, dissimulare potes* (1–2); similarly, the unnamed addressee of *Tr.* 4.4 could not deny the long-standing association between his father and Ovid, an association which the son has inherited (cf. *hoc certe noli dissimulare*, 28). Fabius Maximus, the addressee of *P.* 1.2, cannot turn a blind eye to Ovid's wife after his relegation without betraying the loyalty and trust on which committed friendship is based: *non potes hanc salva dissimulare fide* (146). And yet how can Ovid reasonably appeal to the candid faith and loyalty (*fides*) of his addressees when he himself is so skilful an exponent of ironic dissimulation in both his pose of poetic decline and his account of environmental conditions in Tomis? *Fides* in friendship is cast as inviolate, but *fides* in the sense of Ovid's commitment to the accurate reporting of his exilic circumstances would seem to be another matter.

The ironic effect of Ovid's dissimulation in exile is compounded by his many protestations to the contrary. Even though his pose of poetic decline hardly survives careful scrutiny of his verse, and despite the fact that his depiction of environmental conditions in such elegies as *Tr.* 3.10 clearly owes more to literary informants than to first-hand experience,[1] his exilic *vox* unashamedly rejects the licence allowed to all poets at *Am.* 3.12.41–2:

> exit in immensum fecunda licentia vatum
> obligat historica nec sua verba fide.

Just as Ovid is transformed from the youthful love poet into the grave exilic elegist, so his once playful Muse is transformed into the sober reporter of exilic *seria*:

> Musa mea est index nimium quoque vera malorum,
> atque incorrupti pondera testis habet.
>
> (*P.* 3.9.49–50)

In *Am.* 3.12 Ovid's attempt to stave off competition for Corinna lies behind his claim that poets are not to be taken at their word as *testes* (19) and that their outpourings should carry no weight (*pondus*; cf. 20); but in exile his Muse becomes a faithful witness of weighty authority. Elsewhere, his exilic book reports back to Rome with the express statement that it offers a true reflection of its master's condition:

> haec domini fortuna mei est, ut debeat illam
> infelix nullis dissimulare iocis.
>
> (*Tr.* 3.1.5–6)

Through statements of this sort (cf. *Tr.* 3.1.9–10, 5.1.5–6) Ovid stakes a claim for the trustworthy authority of his exilic Muse and seems to guide his ingenuous reader's response to his supposedly candid narrative.

But is Ovid's claim that his exilic Muse faithfully reflects his exilic fortunes (*P.* 3.9.49–50) another instance of the very dissimulation which he eschews? The couplet rejects the *fecunda licentia vatum* of *Am.* 3.12.41, but while every writer must be allowed the privileges of self-assessment and re-direction in the overall strategy of composition, it remains difficult to envisage a transition from the sophisticated grasp of the complex possibilities of language and verse to a naive, monochrome and representational view of a poem's function. Yet

---

[1] See p. 10ff. *supra.*

this is the guileless posture which Ovid goes on asserting in the exile poetry, even while he supplies the reader (as we saw with his pose of poetic decline) with more than enough evidence to form a contrary opinion of his poetic technique.

Cornelius Severus, the addressee of *P*. 4.2 and a poet in his own right, receives an elegy in which Ovid beguilingly portrays his complete literary demise. Ovid's shame at not writing a poem to Severus before (cf. 3–4) suggests that they have shared a close relationship, and poetic communication serves to bridge the physical divide. To suggest that Ovid either means to deceive Severus into believing that his poetic powers really are on the wane or that Severus' own literary sensibility would not have equipped him to detect, even in part, the finer nuances of Ovidian irony in the poem does a disservice to both. Ovid's use of dissimulation in this and other poems to his various Roman friends is a pose which is neither malicious nor meant deliberately to deceive; after all, *dissimulatio* was perceived as an attractive, sophisticated and witty affectation in discourse, relying for its urbane, ironic effect on the dissimulator's ability to offer a transparent misrepresentation of reality which will only mislead the naive.[2] Despite Ovid's own insistence that he writes poetry in Tomis for the utilitarian purposes of diverting himself from his misery and enlisting his friends' sympathy and support, a poem such as *P*. 4.2 resists simple characterization as a piece written only for such pragmatic ends. In the cultural wasteland of Tomis, Ovid's dissimulating epistle to Severus represents a sophisticated form of literary contact with Rome which keeps a friendship alive and a shared poetic sensibility mutually satisfied; Severus might reasonably be expected to see through – and to relish – Ovid's transparent breach of poetic *fides*.

My theme in this chapter is Ovid's cultivation of friendship in the exile poetry not as a means to an end, but as an end in itself. While the formal code of *amicitia* undeniably enables

---

[2] So Cic. *Brut.* 292, *de Orat.* 2.269: *urbana etiam dissimulatio est, cum alia dicuntur ac sentias ... cum toto genere orationis severe ludas, cum aliter sentias ac loquare.*

Ovid to make utilitarian demands of his friends at Rome, whether to approach Augustus on his behalf or to protect his general interests, my priority is to show that such *utilitas* is of limited significance in his poetic communication with loyal friends, and that simple acceptance of *utilitas* as his sole – or even prime – motive for writing poetry in Tomis is as misguided as taking his pose of poetic decline at face value. The expectations which Ovid might have of Cornelius Severus' literary sensibility apply to his other addressees as well: beyond Ovid's alleged motives of *utilitas officiumque* (*P*. 3.9.56),[3] the gentle testing and ironic beguiling of his reader's perceptions remain the artistic challenge.

But who are Ovid's addressees in the *Tristia*? How seriously are we to take his claim that he preserves the anonymity of his friends in order to protect them from official persecution? In the first part of this chapter the prevalent assumption that Ovid conceals specific addressees under the veil of anonymity in the *Tristia* will be contested, and *Tr*. 1.5, my main exemplifying text, will develop the ironic contrast which has already been alluded to between Ovid's unwavering commitment to *fides* in friendship and his ambivalent commitment to poetic *fides*. Readings of *Tr*. 3.4, 4.7 and 5.13 will subsequently illustrate Ovid's artistic priority in elegies which deliver overtly straightforward messages to their unnamed addressees. Few poems are more pointed in their appeals for help than *P*. 2.9, an address to a Thracian king, Cotys, in which Ovid asks for protection in exile; but we shall see that Ovid appeals primarily to Cotys' literary sensibility in a complex form of quasi-Augustan *supplicatio*. If Cotys can provide physical protection, the Muses are Ovid's permanent source of general alleviation and support – and also of anguish. Their paradoxical role as friend and enemy will be considered in due course; at the outset, however, *Tr*. 1.5 provides initial orientation for Ovid's artistic ordering of the theme of friendship in the exile poetry.

---

[3] For discussion of these terms see Evans (1983), 149–50.

Truth and untruth in *Tr.* 1.5

Ovid's addressee at the start of *Tr.* 1.5 is depicted as an intimate friend, but he remains unnamed.[4] Ovid's ostensible reason for preserving the anonymity of his addressees in the
Tristia – to avoid endangering them through named association with him (cf. *Tr.* 3.4.63–6, 4.5.13–16) – is commendable
for its tact, but it nevertheless remains open to question on
various grounds. It is surely hard to imagine that the friends
who stood by Ovid after his downfall would be unknown in
official circles – if, that is, their identity was actually sought,
for offering words of advice and comfort to a friend in distress
was not a criminal offence, as Ovid himself recognizes at *P.*
3.6.13–14. It transpires that Augustus had not in fact forbid-
den Ovid to communicate with his friends by letter (cf. *P.*
3.6.11–12); but is it really feasible that throughout the whole
duration of the *Tristia* Ovid's irrational fear (cf. *pavor attonito
rationis ademerat usum*, *P.* 3.6.47) led him to persist with the
veil of anonymity without any inkling, guidance or instruction
to the effect that the tactic was unnecessary? No; we should at
least consider the possibility that the disguised name is not
intended simply to protect Ovid's friends, but a device used to
achieve a different or perhaps additional effect.

One suggestion along these lines is that by writing to unnamed addressees in the *Tristia* Ovid gives his elegies 'a gener-
ality of appeal which they would lack if addressed to particular individuals'.[5] But could not Ovid have learnt from, say,
Catullus or Horace's *Epistles* I that a general audience is especially attracted by the impression that it is gaining privileged
access to the literary or moral formation of a distinguished,
named addressee, and that to conceal the addressee's identity
is simply to reduce potential interest among this wider read-

---

[4] Different names have been suggested. Koch (1865), 27 n. 1 tentatively proposes
Sextus Pompeius, the addressee of *P.* 4.1, 4.4, 4.5 and 4.15. Graeber (1881), xxi
favours Celsus on the strength of the similarities between *Tr.* 1.5.5ff. and *P.*
1.9.13ff.; so (e.g.) André (1968), 18, Della Corte (1973), 222 and Verdière (1983),
140. But the similarities between *Tr.* 1.5 and *P.* 1.9 need only imply that Ovid's
anonymous friend in the former is the typological equal of Celsus in the latter.
[5] Evans (1983), 58.

ership and to lose a device for applying the technique with subtle variations in a succession of poems? Another suggestion is that Ovid conceals the identity of his friends in order to set the conflict between himself and Augustus in sharper relief;[6] but the weakness of this view is evident from reading the *Epistulae ex Ponto*, in which the naming of addressees enables Ovid to create a network of alliances which, among other things, successfully emphasizes the isolation of the *princeps* in his stubborn adherence to the original sentence passed on the poet. I suggest we consider a third possibility.

Could the veil of anonymity in the *Tristia* be a device which Ovid uses to establish his addressees' identity as moral types rather than specific, named individuals? In these *publica carmina* (*Tr*. 5.1.23), allegedly 'ordinary' poems written for a general audience,[7] the question of identity by name is surely of secondary importance to anyone outside Ovid's private circle; more instructive for the detached reader is the quality of person whom Ovid addresses in each elegy. Whoever (if anyone specific) Ovid's initial addressee in *Tr*. 1.5 may be, his moral identity matters more to the poet in exile than his named identity. He is a model friend whose character is defined by his actions – the haste with which he comes to console Ovid after disaster strikes (3–4), the encouragement he offers (5–6), and his unstinting commitment to the fallen poet (8). These, as well as such epithets as *memorande* (1) and *carissime* (3), are the *signa* which Ovid refers to with the words *scis bene, cui dicam, positis pro nomine signis* (7) – the *signa* or indications within the poem which delineate his addressee's character as an ideal and valued friend. Similarly, Ovid identifies his addressee in *Tr*. 4.4 by defining his moral character; his *morum nobilitas* (2) and the *candor* which he inherits from his father (3) are the *signa* (cf. *positis pro nomine signis*, 7) which constitute his moral identity and require the reader to recognize personal worth without the preconceptions imposed by prior awareness of the *nomen* (cf. *tua te bona cognita produnt*, 9).

---

[6] Marg (1959), 350.
[7] For the play on *publica* see p. 95 with n. 98.

Attempts to identify the father and son[8] obscure a crucial point in *Tr*. 4.4: moral excellence is shown to be an inheritance more valuable than material advantage.

The anonymous addressees of such elegies as *Tr*. 1.8 (a false friend), *Tr*. 3.5 (a mere acquaintance who shows the devotion of a true friend) and *Tr*. 4.7 (a friend who has failed to write to Ovid) conveniently illustrate the range of typological reference to different kinds of friend which is employed in the *Tristia* as a whole.[9] Within this picture Ovid identifies his addressees by showing *what* they are rather than *who* they are, and the opening address to his friend in *Tr*. 1.5, the first exilic elegy in which he reflects at length on the nature of friendship, is where that typology begins. The advantage of this typological interpretation of the start of *Tr*. 1.5 is that it eases the transition from a single addressee to the plural *pauci* in line 35. After depicting his addressee at the beginning of the poem as an ideal friend, Ovid channels the didactic force of this illustration and his lecture on the demands of committed friendship into the imperatives *succurrite* and *date* of lines 35–6. He has provided a model for the *pauci* to emulate, and with the introduction of these few Ovid replaces a type of individual with a collective, generic type.

Tr. 1.5 is divided into two separate elegies in a number of mss, but not because of any perceived difficulty over the transition from a single addressee to the multiple *pauci*. Rather, the break comes after line 44 because of the seeming incom-

---

[8] Diggle (1980), 409 states without argument that *Tr*. 4.4 is addressed to the same friend as *Tr*. 1.5; but cf. Graeber (1881), 17, Della Corte (1973), 293 and Verdière (1983), 141–2, accepting M. Valerius Messalla Messallinus as the addressee in *Tr*. 4.4, Celsus in 1.5. So Syme (1978), 122 on Messallinus: '[*Tr*. 4.4] eschews the name but at once discloses the person'. But if Messallinus' name is so apparent, why the veil of anonymity? Could it *really* have fooled those with a need to know, if such there were?

[9] Graeber (1884), 9 and Némethy (1913), 31 speculate that the Macer addressed in *P*. 2.10 is the recipient of *Tr*. 1.8 because of verbal similarities between the two poems (*Tr*. 1.8.29–30/*P*. 2.10.9–10; *Tr*. 1.8.31–2/*P*. 2.10.41–2); but there are complicating parallels with other elegies (e.g. *Tr*. 1.8.31–2/*P*. 2.4.9–10). Némethy (1913), 70, Della Corte (1973), 267 and Luck (1977), II 192 accept Carus, the addressee of *P*. 4.13, as the recipient of *Tr*. 3.5 because of a parallel play on *carus* (*scis carum veri nominis esse loco*, *Tr*. 3.5.18; cf. *P*. 4.13.2); but there is no compulsion to see the name Carus at *Tr*. 3.5.18. The identity of Ovid's addressee in *Tr*. 4.7 is even more uncertain.

patibility between the poem's two thematically differentiated sections. After his discourse on the art of true friendship in the first part of the elegy (1–44), Ovid portrays the extent of his sufferings as an exile in the second part (45–84) by means of an elaborate syncrisis between himself and Ulysses. Modern editors have resisted the proposed division, and rightly so: despite the somewhat abrupt transition between the two sections, *casibus* (43) is taken up by *casus* (45), and Ovid takes his cue from the terse reference to his sufferings in line 43 to give an account of those sufferings from line 45 onwards.[10] But after his opening discourse on *fides* as the bedrock of committed friendship, the exaggerated description of his exilic sufferings which follows poses a test of *fides* in a different sense. Is he to be trusted when he claims to have suffered even more than Ulysses? If not, the unequivocal commitment to *fides* in friendship would seem to be ironically juxtaposed with his equivocal commitment towards *fides* as the credibility of a poet reporting the incredible. The poem's conceptual coherence lies in reconciling these juxtaposed elements, and Ovid's use of mythological reference in the two distinct sections of the elegy conveniently clarifies – and, I suggest, resolves – the problem of their reconciliation.

The use of myth in lines 19–24 is as typological as the description of the initial addressee's distinctive actions and character (cf. 3–8). Theseus and Pirithous (19–20), Orestes and Pylades (21–2) and Euryalus and Nisus (23–4) are all literary stereotypes used here and elsewhere in the exile poetry (e.g. *Tr.* 1.9.27–34, 5.4.25–6, *P.* 2.3.41–6, 2.6.25–6) to illustrate the unwavering commitment of true friendship.[11] From one perspective myth is of course untrue and defies belief, and this perspective works to Ovid's advantage in *Am.* 3.12 when he

[10] Schulz (1883), 2 n. 2 accepts the division; but see *contra* Ehwald (1884), 158 and (1887), 137. *Tr.* 1.5 is printed as a single elegy in the editions of Owen (1889, 1915) and Luck (1967) I; Ehwald and Levy (1922) have dual numeration after 44 and mark the second part of the poem (Vb).

[11] Cf. Bion fr. 12 (Gow), where Theseus and Pirithous (2–3), Orestes and Pylades (4–5) and Achilles and Patroclus are exemplary friends; though absent at *Tr.* 1.5.19–24, Achilles and Patroclus are introduced to similar effect at *Tr.* 1.9.29–30, 5.4.25 and *P.* 2.3.41.

depicts Scylla (21–2), Perseus (24), Proteus (35) and others as figures who have no greater claim to 'real' existence than the Corinna paraded so desirably in his erotic verse. From another perspective, however, the fictional origins of Theseus and his peers are wholly irrelevant to the truths which such figures represent to the moralizing mind of the poet in exile. The first truth illustrated by Theseus and his like is *fides*, or truth in friendship, termed *verus amor* in line 21; the further truth is gnomic, that genuine friendship or *fides* undergoes its ultimate test in adversity (25–6). From this second perspective, myth offers a yardstick against which Ovid can reasonably measure what he portrays as his own experience. *Haec ... nunc mihi sunt propriis cognita vera malis* (31–2): bitter experience has finally brought home to him the lesson which mythology, in the form of figures like Theseus and Pylades, had previously taught (cf. *exemplis quondam collecta priorum ... vera*, 31–2).

In the second part of the poem, however, mythology is a token of falsehood. Whereas the *exempla* which he cites in lines 19–24 illustrate truth in friendship, Ovid now draws on Ulysses as an exemplar of fictional suffering against which the poet can establish the 'reality' of his own hardships:

> adde, quod illius pars maxima ficta laborum:
> ponitur in nostris fabula nulla malis.
>
> (79–80)

Throughout the syncrisis (57–84) Ovid carefully regulates the portrayal of his sufferings to match and supersede those of Ulysses (cf. *Neritio ... mala plura tuli*, 58). His tone is more boastful than grief-laden: 'we find ourselves congratulating him on each new point he wins in this odd contest of rivalry'.[12] He belittles the extent of Ulysses' wanderings (59–60) in order to magnify the extent of his own journey to Tomis (61–2); he disparages the isolated insularity of Ulysses' home (67–8) only to stress the greatness of Rome and the pain of

---

[12] Wilkinson (1955), 319. Cf. Rahn (1958), 115–19 and Evans (1983), 40 ('Ovid's comparison sets him directly in a Ulysses role').

exclusion from the global metropolis (69–70); he appears to pride himself on being able to claim a greater oppressor than Neptune – Jupiter/Augustus – for the divine dimension of his sufferings (77–8). Further, he conveniently imposes his own interpretation on the Homeric portrayal of Odysseus by pretending that Ulysses made for home as a joyful victor (cf. *laetus*, 65) well supported by a loyal band of fellow travellers (63); the many dark moments of Odysseus' journey are suppressed, and the fact that he was the sole member of his party to make it back to Ithaca at the end of his epic journey is carefully overlooked in Ovid's revision of the Homeric story.[13] Ovid is engaged in an exercise of wilful one-upmanship which reaches its contrived climax in lines 81–4: whereas Ulysses reaches his homeland, Ovid's Tomitan sojourn has no end in sight.

There is an interesting poetic strategy at work here. Just how effective is the ploy of emphasizing the intensity of one set of misfortunes by putting them into fictional rivalry with those of Ulysses? The obvious answer is that hyperbole of this kind quickly undermines the apparent point of comparison. Mythical *exempla* can be used to give guidance, but when our experiences are set in immediate competition with them we can easily find ourselves fictionalizing our own lives rather than adding a dimension of reality to the myth. Imitation is by far the safer policy. Hence Ovid reasonably urges Albinovanus Pedo, his addressee in *P*. 4.10 and the alleged author of a *Theseis*,[14] to follow Theseus' example (*quem ... refers, imitere virum*, 73) through active imitation (cf. *est ... ex illo nobis imitabile quiddam,|inque fide Theseus quilibet esse potest*, 77–8); similarly, Horace casts Ulysses as a model of forbearance in adversity (*Ep*. 1.2.17–22), an *utile ... exemplar* for

---

[13] See Davisson (1982), 32–3 for further misrepresentations of Homer in Ovid's parallel syncrisis with Ulysses at *P*. 4.10.9–30. Ovid is equally contemptuous of Jason's hardships in another syncrisis – and hyperbolical self-projection – at *P*. 1.4.23–46.

[14] Another of his epics has yielded the famous fragment on the dangers of navigation in the North Sea; see Courtney (1993), 315–19 with Bramble (1982), 489–90. Courtney also records as a possible fragment of Pedo the line which Bentley contrived out of Senecan prose (see *fr. inc*. 24, pp. 462–3).

others to emulate.[15] Theseus and his like serve this simple
didactic purpose in lines 19–24, but Ovid's self-election as a
greater Ulysses in the syncrisis of lines 57–84 is equivalent to
claiming that it really is possible to be a truer friend than
Theseus. Now that Ovid has redefined the limits of epic suffering by supplanting Ulysses as an acknowledged paragon of
superhuman endurance, Horace's *utile ... exemplar* at *Ep.*
1.2.17–22 would seem to be outdated – unless, of course, Ovid
merely succeeds in raising his sufferings to the level of hyperbolical absurdity.

Ovid's pretension to epic suffering is expressed in tones suitably replete with epic mannerism and motif in lines 45–56,
but with a studied artificiality and density of allusion which
ultimately detract from their credibility (cf. 49–50). His initial
claim that anyone wanting to know all his afflictions will be
disappointed because they are too numerous to mention (45–
8) instantly suggests comparison with the Homeric Odysseus.
When Arete asks Odysseus to identify himself and to describe
his wanderings (*Od.* 7.237–9), he first declares the difficulty of
the enterprise:

> ἀργαλέον, βασίλεια, διηνεκέως ἀγορεῦσαι
> κήδε', ἐπεί μοι πολλὰ δόσαν θεοὶ οὐρανίωνες.
> (241–2)

Then, with τοῦτο δέ τοι ἐρέω ὅ μ' ἀνείρεαι ἠδὲ μεταλλᾷς (243),
Odysseus goes on to tell of his encounter with Calypso and the
storm which subsequently brought him to Phaeacia. The common narrative ploy of starting with a disarming appeal to the
supreme difficulty of the task is introduced at *Tr.* 1.5.45–6 by
way of a prelude to the curious re-ordering of the Odyssean
labores which is to come in lines 57–82. Like Odysseus, Ovid
has to satisfy the demands of an audience (*ille petit*, 46), and
here identifies himself with the reticent stance adopted by

---

[15] Horace further describes Ulysses as *patiens* (*Ep.* 1.7.40) and *laboriosus* (*Epod.*
17.16). For Ulysses as a Stoic hero see Cic. *Tusc.* 2.50–1, Sen. *Dial.* 2.2.1 with
Stanford (1963), 121–7; for Ulysses as an ethical role-model in Cynic as well as
Stoic thought see Castiglioni (1948), 31–43; for Stoic elements in Ulysses' character in the *Metamorphoses* see Stephens (1958), 279–82.

Aeneas when Dido asks him to describe the fall of Troy, so that Ovid embarks on the tale of his own *casus* partly under Virgilian auspices also (cf. 45–6 with *Aen.* 2.10–13). The two great sources of epic influence are each to be significant in the approaching syncrisis, where Odysseus' list of sufferings is interwoven in successive couplets with echoes of the debilitated Virgilian hero (cf. 64, 66, 75); and to launch the syncrisis at 53–4 Ovid re-uses one of the most familiar of epic invocatory motifs.[16]

Introducing the catalogue of ships in *Iliad* 2, Homer invokes the Muses to help him rise to his momentous task. Without their help,

> πληθὺν δ' οὐκ ἂν ἐγὼ μυθήσομαι οὐδ' ὀνομήνω,
> οὐδ' εἴ μοι δέκα μὲν γλῶσσαι, δέκα δὲ στόματ' εἶεν,
> φωνὴ δ' ἄρρηκτος, χάλκεον δέ μοι ἦτορ ἐνείη.
>
> (488–90)

Although the motif of the many-mouthed poet was an established fixture in Roman literature by Ovid's time,[17] his specific point of reference at *Tr.* 1.5.53–4 is the Homeric form of the invocation. Line 53 is a virtual translation of *Il.* 2.490, and Ovid may even have coined the word *infragilis* to echo the Homeric ἄρρηκτος directly.[18] Through this evocation of Homer Ovid achieves a paradoxical effect which hinges on his lowly status as an elegist. He claims to suffer on an epic scale, but his suffering defies adequate expression in elegy, and the

[16] In other places too this section of the poem combines Homeric and Roman influences. Ovid's comparison of his countless troubles to dust-particles (48) is a possible evocation of Achilles' words to the embassy at *Il.* 9.385: he will not return to the Greek fold, οὐδ' εἴ μοι τόσα δοίη ['Αγαμέμνων] ὅσα ψάμαθός τε κόνις τε. But Catul. 61.199–203 offers a closer parallel for stars and sand/dust combined as symbols of countlessness: *ille pulveris Africi|siderumque micantium|subducat numerum prius,|qui vestri numerare volt|multa milia ludi.* For further examples of the motif see Luck (1977), II 154 on 47f., adding *Il.* 8.555 (ἐν οὐρανῷ ἄστρα; cf. *in aethere sidere, Tr.* 1.5.47). Ovid's comparisons smack of literary cliché which does little to enhance the 'reality' of his woes.

[17] Cf. Enn. *Ann.* 469–70 Sk., Hostius fr. 3 Courtney (p. 53), Virg. *G.* 2.42–4, *Aen.* 6.625–7, Ov. *A.A.* 1.435–6, *F.* 2.119–20, *M.* 8.533–5. Skutsch (1985), 627–9 supplies further examples and bibliography on the motif.

[18] That *infragilis* is specially devised to render the Homeric term is suggested by its uniqueness. Ovid never uses the word again; it occurs in the *Consolatio ad Liviam* (*infragilem ... animum*, 354), but few would now argue (against Schoonhoven (1992), 22–39 and others) that the *Consolatio* is Ovidian.

Homeric disclaimer in *Iliad* 2 must accordingly undergo a shift of generic emphasis when it is echoed in lines 53–6: even if Ovid had a tireless voice, he would still be unable to recount all his troubles, not because of the usual restrictions experienced by the epic poet, but because the epic weight of his sufferings places an excessive strain on his elegiac powers (*materia vires exsuperante meas*, 56).[19] And yet lines 53–4 unmistakably echo the language of epic, and the ultimate effect of lines 53–6 in the light of their dependence on Homer is to prepare the way for a concise and highly personalized elegiac substitute for the Homeric catalogue in *Iliad* 2.

Humility is ironically fused with hyperbole when Ovid invites the *docti poetae* of line 57 to undertake the epic task which is apparently beyond him (cf. *pro duce Neritio ... mala nostra ...|scribite*, 57–8); the syncrisis with Ulysses (57–84) is his own solution to the problem of how to portray the epic scale of his hardships without straining his lowly powers of elegiac song. The same device is used to resolve a similar problem elsewhere. When the Nones of February are reached in *Fasti* 2 and there is a need to celebrate Augustus' accession to the title of *pater patriae* in 2 B.C, we have first an echo of the Homeric invocation motif (*F.* 2.119–20), though a less explicit one than at *Tr.* 1.5.53–6. Then, stressing the limitations of an elegist (123; cf. *Tr.* 1.5.56), Ovid acknowledges that epic is the proper medium for his Augustan theme and that he is taking generic liberties in using elegy (125–6). So how can he substitute for an epic celebration of Augustus an elegiac equivalent which will not detract from the emperor's greatness? He constructs a line-by-line comparison between Augustus and Romulus, and Augustus is the outright winner on every count (131–44).[20]

[19] The elegiac significance of line 56 is underscored by comparison with *Tr.* 2.335–6. To write an epic on Augustus requires rich talent, *materia ne superetur opus* (336); lacking that talent, Ovid abandons his epic effort and reverts to love elegy (339). His alleged attempt at an epic in celebration of Tiberius' Pannonian triumph is abandoned for the same reason (*P.* 2.5.27–32; cf. *materiae gracili sufficit ingenium*, 26).

[20] But for discordant hints in Ovid's effusive praise of Augustus at *F.* 2.119–44 see Harries (1989), 166–7.

In the light of *Fasti* 2, the syncrisis with Ulysses in *Tr*. 1.5 proves not to be a unique literary device which Ovid invents to portray his unique sufferings, but a borrowed formula for the elegiac structuring of epic subject-matter. In the course of the syncrisis Ovid's awareness of his generic limitations is itself one form of appeal to his reader's sympathy: elegiac poets such as he are hardly equipped to face epic sufferings. The generic point is made when he draws a contrast between Ulysses' hardiness (*illi corpus erat durum patiensque laborum*, 71) and his own weakness (cf. *invalidae vires ingenuaeque mihi*, 72), between Ulysses' experience in war (*ille erat assidue saevis agitatus in armis*, 73) and his own preference for the 'softer' life (cf. *adsuetus studiis mollibus ipse fui*, 74). The language in these lines is rich in programmatic implication and contrast: while such terms as *durus* and *arma* locate Ulysses in the world of epic, the words *adsuetus studiis mollibus* locate Ovid in the antithetical world of elegy.[21] The latter's inexperience in war inevitably follows from the Roman elegists' traditional aversion to arms,[22] and his physical weakness (72) complements his lack of vocal power (56); the epicist requires vocal resources which far exceed those of the feeble elegist.

Ovid tries to disarm his sceptical readers in lines 49–50 by conceding that the scale of his sufferings will defy belief, even though they are true (*quamvis acciderint*, 50). But the sheer scale of the hardships which he claims for himself, his supercilious condescension towards Ulysses, his self-appointment as a real-life exemplar of heroic endurance without equal in myth, his allusive construction of an elegiac narrative which is epic in pretension – all these factors undermine whatever credibility Ovid momentarily commands with his disarming tactic in lines 49–50. The only valid point of comparison between Ovid and Ulysses here is their shared capacity for beguiling rhetoric, but Homeric evidence suggests that Ulysses is the

---

[21] For the programmatic connotation of *durus* see p. 31 n. 61; for *mollis*, p. 62 n. 25.
[22] For the literary effects of this aversion (soldiering in love, rejection of epic etc.) see conveniently Lyne (1980), 67–71 (on Tibullus and Propertius) and 284–6 (on Ovid).

more persuasive practitioner. Odysseus charms his Phaeacian audience when he tells of his wanderings (cf. *Od.* 11.333–4, 13.1–2), and Alcinous speaks for all when he praises his song for both its evident truthfulness and its elegance (11.363–9). Whether or not Odysseus really has told the truth is open to speculation,[23] but at least the Phaeacians believe so. By any-one other than a reader of Phaeacian ingenuousness or im-pressionability, however, Ovid will be taken at his word when he forecasts that his sorrows will defy belief (*fidem*, 50), de-spite his insistence that they are all true (cf. *acciderint*, 50).

In the light of Ovid's unequivocal commitment to *fides* in friendship in the first part of *Tr.* 1.5, his subsequent attempt to induce belief in the unbelievable marks an ironic change of direction. Equivocal in his commitment to *fides* in the sense of his own credibility as a poet, he now draws on mythology as a fictional construct against which he can assert the alleged 'reality' of his own exilic circumstances; myth is no longer a source of gnomic truth (cf. 31–2), but of patent falsehood (cf. 79–80). Despite the impression of thematic incoherence which led to the poem's division in certain mss, it is ambivalence in the use of myth and in the commitment to *fides* which both connects and destabilizes the complementary sections of the poem.[24]

How, then, is this reading of *Tr.* 1.5 to be reconciled with Ovid's claim that *utilitas* is his motive for persevering with poetry in Tomis? No longer driven by the spur of fame (*Tr.* 1.1.49, 4.1.3, 5.1.75 etc.), he allegedly writes to escape his cares (*Tr.* 4.1.3–4, 39–40, 4.10.117–18, 5.7.67 etc.) and as an act of duty and utilitarian appeal to his friends at Rome (cf. *utilitas officiumque*, *P.* 3.9.56). Ovid's opening discourse on friendship in *Tr.* 1.5 would seem to meet the terms of this

[23] For discussion of the narratological problems which complicate Odysseus' tone before the Phaeacians see Goldhill (1991), 47ff. and 47 n. 85 for further bibliography.

[24] The same distinction between different senses of *fides* prevails in *P.* 4.10, a parallel poem. Ovid encourages Albinovanus Pedo to display the loyalty (*fides*) of a Theseus (73); and yet Ovid's triumph in his syncrisis with Ulysses (9–30) exagger-ates his burden of suffering beyond the bounds of credibility (*fides*; cf. 36). Ovid's poetic *labor* answers the question of line 82 (*quis labor est puram non temerasse fidem?*) through its own ironic breach of faith.

utilitarian strategy, but the ensuing description of his sufferings (45ff.) is more problematical. Even if any of his friends
were gullible enough to work for Ovid's removal from Tomis
on the basis of such a hyperbolical account of what is con-
ceded to be unbelievable (49–50), his subtle testing of *fides* in
different senses renders the poem more (or perhaps less) than
a utilitarian *cri de cœur*. This is not to suggest that *utilitas* is
a negligible motivating force in the *Tristia* and *Epistulae ex
Ponto*; but the theme of *utilitas* also works to support Ovid's
pose of poetic decline by drawing yet another veil over the
quality and artistic objectives of the exile poetry. Despite its
ostensibly practical purpose, then, *Tr.* 1.5 assumes a select
audience of loyal friends who are as refined in literary sensibility as they are personally dependable – and the same expecta-
tion is made of loyal friends throughout the exile poetry.

The art of friendship

At *P.* 2.4.11–12 Ovid fondly recalls lingering conversations
with his addressee, Atticus:

> saepe citae longis visae sermonibus horae,
> saepe fuit brevior quam mea verba dies.

Since Ovid regularly submitted his poetry to Atticus' judgement (cf. *nova iudicio subdita Musa tuo est*, 14), the clear inference is that their conversations embraced literary matters. *P.*
2.4 represents Ovid's attempt to keep their shared communication alive (cf. *accipe conloquium*, 1),[25] and the elegy is itself
an affirmation of the literary and personal ties which bind
them. Literary reminiscence is combined with personal reminiscence in lines 11–12, for the couplet echoes Callimachus'
own fond recollection of the conversations which he had
shared with Heraclitus of Halicarnassus until well after sunset.[26] We noticed earlier that the same echo recurs in *P.* 2.10

---

[25] For the ancient letter portrayed as a substitute for conversation see Thraede
(1970), 39–47, 52–61.

[26] Cf. ἐμνήσθην δ'ὁσσάκις ἀμφότεροι|ἥέλιον λέσχη κατεδύσαμεν, *A.P.* 7.80.2–3 =
Epigr. 2.2–3 (Pf.). With Gow and Page (1965), II 191 I read ἥέλιον λέσχη for ἥλιον
ἐν λέσχη, taking λέσχη to mean 'conversation' (cf. Call. fr. 178.16 (Pf.)) rather
than 'a place where people converse' (cf. Hes. *Op.* 493).

when Ovid remembers past conversations with the poet Macer (37–8);[27] it is also heard at *Tr*. 5.13.27–8.[28] In all three cases the echo lends allusive support to the message which Ovid sends his addressees: the bonds of personal and literary friendship remain unbroken by exile, and shared acknowledgement of the Callimachean connection is the point of reassuring contact – even if a piquant irony is that Ovid reverses the Callimachean picture by emulating Heraclitus in his own figurative death and by addressing his surviving friends from beyond the Tomitan grave.

Ovid's portrayal of his earlier intimacy with Atticus culminates in an appeal for continued loyalty and support (31–4). Strategic as the poem clearly is in this respect, Ovid simultaneously preserves the essence of their former relationship: he used to submit his poetry to Atticus' criticism, and *P*. 2.4 is another such offering. Far from merely providing allusive decoration, the Callimachean presence here is typical of the subtle artistry which complicates Ovid's overtly strategic purpose in other exilic elegies on the theme of friendship. In the light of *P*. 2.4, such poems as *Tr*. 3.4, 4.7 and 5.13, three elegies on friendship with overtly simple messages, may reasonably be suspected of masking a veiled complexity.

i

In *Tr*. 4.7 Ovid mildly rebukes his anonymous addressee for failing to send word since his arrival in Tomis two years before.[29] During those long years (cf. *tempore tam longo*, 3), measured out by the slow movement of the seasons (1) and the stars (2),[30] Ovid has waited in vain for his friend to apply his *dextra officiosa* to its required *officium* (3–4). By not writing,

[27] See p. 44.
[28] For the epigram's influence on the exile poetry see further G. D. Williams (1991), 169–77.
[29] The date of composition would seem to be A.D. 11 if, as De Jonge (1951), 162 supposes, Ovid was relegated towards the end of A.D. 8 and the two winters which have passed (cf. 1) were those of A.D. 9 and 10.
[30] Cf. Claassen (1986), 293–8 on the 'timeless now' of Ovid's Tomitan sojourn.

this friend risks breaking the bonds of *amicitia*; the bonds which Ovid would prefer to break are of course the *vincula* (cf. 7) sealing a reassuring letter. Ovid's insistent questioning of why (*cur?*, 3, 5, 7) his friend has failed to write inevitably leads to uncertainty and hopeful speculation: the friend's letters must have gone astray (9–10), or so Ovid prays (*di faciant ut . . .* , 9). *Quod precor, esse liquet* (11): Ovid is confident that his own explanation of his friend's silence is the right one. But what if his addressee has withdrawn his affections? Such a possibility is unthinkable, or so Ovid tries to convince himself in a desperate act of self-assurance; he would believe in the existence of all the fictional monsters he lists in lines 11–18 before accepting that his friend is disloyal.

The eleven monsters listed – Medusa, Scylla, the Chimaera, the Centaurs, Geryon, Cerberus, the Sphinx, the Harpies, the Giants, Gyas and the Minotaur – belong to the irrational horror-world of the disordered mind, which is where Lucretius had placed them (4.739–43).[31] The monstrous effect of Ovid's catalogue is enhanced by his piling of polysyllabic epithets one upon another in an extraordinary verbal sequence in lines 15–18: five adjectives of five syllables and one of six syllables are grotesquely amassed in only two couplets.[32] Further, the second half of line 18 is a deafening echo of *A.A.* 2.24 (*semibovemque virum semivirumque bovem*), a line famously quoted by the elder Seneca (*Con.* 2.2.12) as one of the three verses which the poet's friends urged him to emend but which he insisted on retaining. By echoing so notorious a line at *Tr.* 4.7.18 and by creating the same jarring verbal effect in line 16 (*tergeminumque virum tergeminumque canem*), Ovid applies what Seneca was later to describe as a self-indulgent *vitium* to creative advantage in his horrific catalogue; his irregular styl-

---

[31] Ovid may also rely on Virgil for the hellish effect here, for six of the monsters listed also lurk in the Virgilian underworld (*Aen.* 6.285–9).

[32] *Serpentipedes* (17) is an Ovidian coinage and hapax (so De Jonge (1951), 168) which gives verbal expression to the Giants' singular monstrosity. If *anguineis*, the reading of some mss, is accepted in line 12 instead of *anguinis*, the word is another Ovidian invention (see De Jonge, (1951), 165 *ad loc.*), perhaps devised to similar effect.

istic affectation complements the grotesqueness of the monsters he describes.[33]

The dramatic effect of Ovid's chosen *adunata* here is to picture the emotional chaos which would result if his confidence in his friend's devotion and *pietas* (5) were ever shown to be misguided. The alternative to the structured world of reciprocated *amicitia* which is bound together by the *vincula* of shared consolation and trust is the nightmarish fantasy which unleashes monstrous *vincula* like the grotesque union of snake and lion (13–14) and man and horse (15). Myth held no such horrors when Ovid was a youthful love elegist, secure of his place in Rome's cultural and social milieu. To return once more to *Am.* 3.12, Ovid reminds his rival suitors that since poets are free to invent what they will (*exit in immensum fecunda licentia vatum*, 41), Corinna need be no more real than the mythical figures he lists in lines 15–40. In *Tr.* 4.7, however, Ovid attempts to safeguard a relationship which is more urgent and meaningful in his Tomitan isolation than his early flirtations with Corinna, and because of this greater urgency the poetic licence to imagine what he likes is no longer the supportive ally that it was in *Am.* 3.12. Now his imagination runs riot (cf. *exit in immensum*) to more personally damaging effect, and the resulting crisis overshadows the closing lines of the poem (21–6). Everything – the distance which separates poet and addressee (*innumeri montes*, 21), the countless possible reasons for the friend's silence (*mille ... causis*, 23; cf. 25) – is conceived on the vast scale of Ovid's monstrous exaggerations in lines 11–18. In the light of that gigantic nightmare, the vocatives *carissime* (19) and *amice* (26) evoke a world of structured and ordered friendship to poignantly contrasting effect.

Ovid's frequent use of *adunata* in the exile poetry has not always been correctly understood. Among the more banal of earlier views was that the motif is 'doubtless due in part to the poet's unhappy lot, which denied him more fruitful themes,

---

[33] Cf. Rosati (1979), 130–1: 'In questi versi [*Tr.* 4.7.11–18] ... l'artificio linguistico invade vistosamente il testo, la forma dell' espressione vuole aderire, farsi duttile al suo contenuto.'

and in part to the attempt to compensate by its use for declining poetic powers'.[34] Modern critics counter by demonstrating how Ovid uses *adunata* to different effect in different elegies with subtle *variatio*,[35] and a sample comparison of *Tr.* 4.7 with two conspicuous instances of the motif in *Tr.* 1.8 and *P.* 2.4 bears out the point.

Tr. 1.8, an address to a false friend, starts from the premise that 'false friendship' is a contradiction in terms. When the evidence of experience becomes irresistible and the poet has been confronted by the impossible (9–16), the whole structured order of the physical world goes into reverse along with his naive assumptions about life (5–8). Here, the impending *adunata* open the poem (1–4), so that the reader arrives on the scene at the dramatic moment when impossible consequences are just about to happen and after the impossible betrayal has already taken place (cf. *sum deceptus*, 9). The poem's temporal sequence is as retrogressive as the disorder pictured in the *adunata*, for it begins with a vision of the future (*haec ego vaticinor*, 9) and moves through the present state of rejection and alienation (cf. *iacet*, 16) to recalling the miserable circumstances of Ovid's departure from Rome (17ff.), before turning back through present bitterness (37ff.) to a further glance at the future (47–50). This poetic mirror of the reversal of nature actually succeeds in representing the reversal of the poet's hopes and expectations in a way that the *adunata*, which are by definition unrealizable, never can. This elegy is the first in which *adunata* are used to make natural disorder a macrocosmic paradigm for the disordered psyche of a faithless friend,[36] but the rhetorical ploy of representing the undesirable by the impossible is not in itself entirely con-

---

34 Canter (1930), 40. Wilkinson (1955), 360 cites figures of speech (presumably including *adunata*; cf. Coon (1928), 3–20) to illustrate the monotony which allegedly pervades the exile poetry.
35 So Davisson (1980), 124–8, Claassen (1986), 178. For general remarks on Ovid's use of *adunata* in exile see Dutoit (1936), 118–23, 155–6.
36 Cf. Davisson (1980), 125: 'Here we find a strong statement, early in the exile poetry, that nature's laws and the character of friends are equally changeable. This initial clue should warn us that the impossible, including unthinkable disloyalty, may be possible in this corpus.'

vincing. The conventional *adunata* here serve their function only in the wider poetic context.

P. 2.4 offers a more successful variation on the theme. In this instance Ovid refuses to believe that Atticus could have forgotten him; he would sooner believe that the ordered workings of the seasons, climate and nature (25–8) could change their normal pattern. As in *Tr*. 1.8, the implication is that Atticus' disloyalty is unnatural and therefore unthinkable, but the fuller context of *P*. 2.4 nevertheless distinguishes Ovid's *adunata* in lines 25–8 from his earlier usage of the motif. For one thing, the seasonal disruption envisaged in lines 25–6 – winter days lengthened, summer days shortened – bears a striking relation to the picture of timelessness drawn earlier in the poem. As we saw earlier, Ovid recalls in lines 11–12 how the hours passed all too quickly and the day seemed all too short when he and Atticus were engaged in their lingering conversations (the contrasting senses of time being emphasized by the juxtaposition of *citae longis* in 11 and *verba dies* in 12). Time was of no consequence when they enjoyed each other's company in leisurely ease, and with the same disregard for worldly distraction (*negotium*) which characterizes Catullus' relationship with Calvus in poem 50. The ordering principle of *constans fides* (cf. 33) provides the foundation for the intimate and self-regulating conversations between Ovid and Atticus; but what if *fides* should ever be shaken? The casual disregard for time in cultivating an intimate relationship (11–12) is now replaced by the anarchic dissolution of the temporal sequence (25–6).[37] Similarly, the familiar significance of geographical locations, reinforced by the associations of friendship (19–20), is to be disrupted as sites lose their most well-known characteristics (cf. 27–8).

When Ovid uses *adunata* in *P*. 2.4, then, he does not simply redeploy a formula whose function in the whole of the exile poetry is programmatically explained to blanket effect as early as *Tr*. 1.8. The choice of particular *adunata* now actively contributes to the interpretation of the elegy offered to Atticus,

[37] So G. D. Williams (1991), 172–3.

and the locating of the motif in the later part of the poem enables Ovid to avoid here what we saw to be the odd and self-defeating effect introduced at the very opening of *Tr.* 1.8: the first two-thirds of *P.* 2.4 are devoted to constructing such a vivid and detailed *imago* of the friendship between Ovid and Atticus (cf. 7–8) that we really feel the breaking of so firm a bond to be as impossible as the eventualities listed in lines 25–8. While the *adunata* in *Tr.* 1.8 sat rather uncomfortably with the material which followed, the effect in *P.* 2.4 is to intensify the inner strength of the relationship which the poem celebrates and which is firmly established before the *adunata* are reached.

The creative use of the motif in *P.* 2.4 raises similar expectations of *Tr.* 4.7. The crucial word in the latter elegy is *mutatum*:

> haec ego cuncta prius, quam te, carissime, credam
>   mutatum curam deposuisse mei.
>
>   (19–20)

Eight of the eleven monsters listed in lines 11–18 also appear in the *Metamorphoses*,[38] and their collection here in a kind of chamber of horrors in part warns the addressee of the dehumanizing metamorphosis which overtakes anyone who puts aside the responsibilities of friendship (cf. 20).[39] Also, five of the monsters are partly human in appearance,[40] so that the margin between the human and the monstrous is already obscured within the given examples, and the possibility of a transition from the former to the latter looks all the more menacingly real. As the addressee is drawn by his own negligence nearer to the world of deformed monstrosity, the enormous distance separating him from Ovid assumes new significance:

---

[38] The point is noted by Davisson (1980), 126 and Claassen (1986), 178–9. The monsters are Medusa (*M.* 4.615ff.), Scylla (13.730ff.), the Chimaera (6.339, 9.647–8), the Centaurs (12.210ff.), Geryon (9.184–5), Cerberus (9.185), the Giants (1.151ff.) and the Minotaur (8.155ff.).

[39] *Mutatum* (20) may also suggest another exilic adaptation of an erotic elegiac motif. The shifting allegiances of the Roman elegiac lover are similarly described (*cur sim mutatus quaeris? quia munera poscis*, Ov. *Am.* 1.10.11; cf. Prop. 1.4.1–2).

[40] I include the Harpies; cf. *Aen.* 3.216, where they are depicted as monstrous birds with the faces of maidens. Ovid describes them similarly at *M.* 7.4.

innumeri montes inter me teque viaeque
fluminaque et campi nec freta pauca iacent.
(21–2)

Every feature nature can provide seems to be set between
them, representing the gulf which divides possible betrayal by
the addressee from the poet's continuing fidelity.

ii

Tr. 5.13 shares certain basic similarities with *Tr.* 4.7. Superficially, the poem offers another mild rebuke to a friend for
failing in his duty to communicate, though on this occasion
the grievance is that his addressee has written too rarely (11)
rather than not at all (cf. *Tr.* 4.7.3–8). Ovid prays that the
complaint is misguided (17), and the words which answer his
parallel prayer in *Tr.* 4.7 are repeated to the same reassuring
effect: *quod precor, esse liquet* (19; cf. *Tr.* 4.7.11). Once more
adunata seem to express his confidence in his friend's continued loyalty (21–2; cf. *Tr.* 4.7.11–18), and the predictable
appeal for more correspondence follows (29–30; cf. *Tr.*
4.7.25–6). Despite these similarities with *Tr.* 4.7, however, *Tr.*
5.13 carries a very different message, and Ovid's claim that he
is ill in mind and body (3–4) is the point of departure.

Adjustment to the harsh climatic and environmental extremes of Pontus means that Ovid loses the delicate balance
of his constitution and succumbs to constant illness (cf. *Tr.*
3.3.3ff., 3.8.23ff., 4.6.43, *P.* 1.10.3ff. etc.). At *Tr.* 5.13.3–6 this
is reflected in the unmediated extremes of suffering which
plague him; his feverish burning (5) is as immoderate as the
icy coldness which causes these ironically scorching effects (cf.
6). But whether or not Ovid is as ill as he claims to be, the
epistolary format of *Tr.* 5.13 lends itself to creative exploitation of the language of sickness and health. The conventional
opening greeting (*mittit tibi Naso salutem,* 1) is followed by a
simple play on *salus* which enables Ovid to introduce his illness (*mittere si quisquam, quo caret ipse, potest*);[41] in hoping

---

[41] Although the formula *aliquis alicui salutem dicit* is common (cf. Cicero's letters *ad Atticum, passim*), Lanham (1975), 31 claims that in Classical Latin only Ovid uses the formula *salutem mittere*; *mittere* may be meant to emphasize the distance which separates him from his addressees (so Davisson (1981), 18).

his friend is well (7), Ovid seeks medicinal comfort for himself in a standard epistolary formula (*si vales, valeo*); and in the hope that his friend fares better than he (*meis distent ut tua fata*, 34), Ovid uses the conventional farewell (*vale*, 34) to wish on his addressee the good health he himself lacks.[42] In the same way, the *adunata* in lines 21–2 are selected to reinforce the poem's concern for health with another literary device: the herbs *apsinthium* and *thymum* were common ingredients in medical potions, as is attested by many examples in Celsus, Pliny, Caelius Aurelianus and other medical writers.[43] But there is a nexus of relevant images in line 22; apart from its medical significance, *dulce thymum* is familiar from poetic expressions of affection,[44] and is also an image redolent of eloquent literary discourse.[45]

Various other factors suggest that the relationship envisaged here between poet and addressee is as literary as it is personal. The knowledge of Callimachus which is required of the reader when conversations lingering after sunset are fondly recalled in lines 27–8 follows an allusion to Horace in line 14. At *S*. 1.6.66–7 Horace claims that his moral character is above reproach – except, that is, for a few minor blemishes which he compares to moles on a handsome body (*... velut si\egregio inspersos reprehendas corpore naevos*). By borrowing the Horatian terminology for a single blemish on an otherwise spotless character (*quod si correxeris unum,\nullus in egregio corpore naevus erit, Tr.* 5.13.13–14), Ovid softens the impact of his rebuke to his friend for not writing regularly enough: his friend's character, with this one minor and easily corrected failing, is even more exemplary than Horace's. More significant for present purposes, however, are the traces of elegiac love-sickness in Ovid's portrayal of his illness:

[42] For further epistolary features in *Tr.* 5.13 see Davisson (1985), 238–46.

[43] For the medical uses of *apsinthium* see *TLL* 2.322.5–23 (the Pontic variety was especially prized; cf. Plin. *Nat.* 27.45); for *thymum* see Plin. *Nat.* 21.154–7, Larg. 15 and 182, Cels. 2.21 (p. 93 Marx), 4.2 (*tum commodum est hysopum vel nepetam vel thymum vel apsinthium ... decoquere eaque gargarizare*, p. 158 Marx).

[44] Cf. Virg. *Ecl.* 7.37, *Nerine Galatea, thymo mihi dulcior Hyblae*, and Otto (1890) s.v. *Hybla* 2.

[45] Cf. Hor. *C.* 4.2.29, Quint. *Inst.* 12.10.25. As Horace shows, the image arises from the rhetorical association of *mel* (cf. Cic. *Orat.* 32, *sermo est ille quidem melle dulcior*, and Otto (1890), s.v. *mel* 1).

'Lines 3–5 would fit equally well in an amatory elegy. The ambiguity of line 5 [*lateris cruciatibus uror*], which could just as well describe the symptoms of physical lust as of pleurisy, is only resolved by line 6. These two couplets are intentionally constructed to remind the reader of the amatory convention.'[46] But to what effect?

In the context of the exile poetry as a whole, the erotic presence in *Tr.* 5.13 serves a familiar purpose. The chastened love elegist renounces his erotic past (cf. *ille pharetrati lusor Amoris abest*, *Tr.* 5.1.22), and in Tomis the staple themes of amatory elegy undergo a parallel form of literary metamorphosis. The *exclusus amator* gives way to the *poeta relegatus*, erotodidaxis is replaced by instruction on how to win over Augustus (cf. *P.* 1.2.67ff., 2.2.39ff.) and Livia (cf. *P.* 3.1.113ff.), Getic warriors wield arrows more formidable than Cupid's; and the symptoms of love-sickness give way to the harsher ailments of exile.[47] At first this redeployment of material may seem to confirm the poverty of Ovid's exilic *ingenium*; but I shall argue that in *Tr.* 5.13, as elsewhere, we find great artistry applied to creating a novel, and highly personal, crisis out of familiar thematic motif. This is evident in part from the impact which these one-time love symptoms at 3–6 have on the broader scheme of the poem; but their localized meaning is, as we shall see, conditioned by the opening play on *salus*.

Ovid uses this *lusus* in at least three pre-exilic contexts, twice in the *Heroides*, once in the *Metamorphoses*.[48] At the start of *Heroides* 4 the sick Phaedra at once reveals the radical contradiction in her character. In greeting Hippolytus,

---

[46] Nagle (1980), 62. Bakker (1946), 170 suggests that Ovid's physical symptoms are those of pleurisy. For discussion of the familiar ailments of elegiac love-sickness see Sabot (1976), 502–9.

[47] These and other erotic adaptations in exile are amply discussed by Nagle (1980), 42–70.

[48] *Her.* 13 and 18 also begin with the *salutem mittere* formula, but not with the explicit play on *salus* (Jacobson (1974), 146 comments that '13.1 *may* be a play on the two senses of *salus*' (my emphasis)). The authenticity of what a few mss offer as the opening couplet of *Her.* 11, where the play on *salus* does recur, is hotly debated; see Kirfel (1969), 71–4 and Jacobson (1974), 166 n. 25 with Kenney (1970), 196. Since the couplet remains controversial, it is excluded from the present discussion.

she simultaneously seems to be sending him the good health which she will only possess if, as she admits, he first sends it to her:

> Qua, nisi tu dederis, caritura est ipsa, salutem
> mittit Amazonio Cressa puella viro.

Phaedra goes on to describe the bitter division within her in the figurative language of erotic illness, afflicted as she is by the wound of secret love (20) and burning with its feverish effects (19–20; cf. 33, 52). For Paris, however, in the opening couplet of *Heroides* 16, the motif has a different significance:

> Hanc tibi Priamides mitto, Ledaea, salutem,
> quae tribui sola te mihi dante potest.

The hexameter here offers a self-contained greeting which arouses no suspicion and, as will be the case with Paris himself, the negative side is initially held back. What the pentameter soon reveals is the hollowness of the gesture so confidently made in the first line, as if at the outset to warn the reader of what the rest of the poem abundantly confirms, that everything Paris says is to be taken with a large pinch of salt. In *Metamorphoses* 9, however, when Byblis writes to Caunus declaring incestuous passion for her brother, she begins her letter with an echo of Phaedra's, so revealing the confusion and lack of focus within what is quickly shown to be her own guilt-ridden self:

> quam, nisi tu dederis, non est habitura salutem,
> hanc tibi mittit amans; pudet, a! pudet edere nomen!
> (530–1)

Wounded by Cupid's arrow (540), Byblis is likewise consumed by the feverish flame of desire (541) to debilitating effect on both mind (540) and body (535–7), and the form in which her condition is narrated has the consequence of complicating the generic status of the *Metamorphoses* through elegiac infiltration.[49]

---

[49] See Tränkle (1963), 460–5 for the erotic elegiac affiliations of the Byblis story, Paratore (1970), 304–6 for the influence of the *Heroides* on Byblis' letter.

The use of the *salus* motif at *Tr.* 5.13.1–2 bears a closer resemblance to the subtle reservation of Paris than to the contorted openings favoured by Phaedra and Byblis, and here also this feature is, as we shall see, consistent with the picture of a character who conceals a potentially duplicitous nature behind a facade of simple self-confidence. The love-sick women of *Heroides* 4 and *Metamorphoses* 9 have a presence of a different sort in this elegy. Ailing in mind and body and feverishly burning (5–6), Ovid transfers the symptoms of love-sickness which afflict Phaedra and Byblis to his exilic sickbed, so that another cluster of erotic motifs undergoes novel acclimatization to the poet's exile.

Quite apart from the erotic associations of *querela* (17),[50] the complaint that his friend has not written frequently enough (11–12) is itself paralleled in the *Heroides* when Hypsipyle rebukes Jason for not writing (cf. 6.3–18). The formative influence of the *Heroides* in *Tr.* 5.13, however far-reaching in point of detail,[51] modifies the theme of the artist destroyed by his own *Ars/ars*:[52] Ovid falls victim to the very ills which he had inflicted on Phaedra in *Heroides* 4, the figurative language of love-sickness now assumes literal significance for the poet in exile, and the despairing tones which Ovid had ascribed to Phaedra are now reclaimed as his own. But when Ovid draws on the *Heroides* once more in *P.* 1.10, another poem on illness and the only other exilic elegy to open with the play on *salus* which we find in *Heroides* 16 and *Tr.* 5.13, the nature of his poetic illness is very different. The ailment in *P.* 1.10 is a general lethargy (*languor*, 4) rather than the feverish burning and mental and physical *contagia* which prevail in *Tr.* 5.13 (cf. *nec dolor ullus adest, nec febribus uror anhelis*, *P.* 1.10.5). The parallel with the *Heroides*, so inventively drawn in *Tr.* 5.13, is now a spent literary force, and

---

[50] On Propertius' use of the term see Saylor (1967), 142–9; on Ovidian use in the *Heroides* see Baca (1971), 195–201.

[51] See Rahn (1958), 105–20 on the general relationship between the *Heroides* and Ovid's exilic epistles.

[52] Cf. *Tr.* 2.2, 3.3.74, 3.14.5–6, *Ibis* 6, *P.* 2.7.48.

Ovid acknowledges as much by no longer sharing the symptoms he once ascribed to Phaedra.[53]

The opening couplet of *Heroides* 16, the first line of which carries self-assured overtones which are seriously qualified in the second, already encapsulates the way in which Paris will consistently fail to meet the expectations he encourages others to have of him. When this version of the *salus* motif is adopted in the opening couplet of *Tr.* 5.13, the reader is alerted to the possibility that this elegiac epistle will also be in part concerned with complicating the initially simple image of authorial identity. In lines 25–6 Ovid gives his addressee a gentle warning:

> tu tamen, ut possis falsae quoque pellere culpae
> crimina, quod non es, ne videare, cave.

Although his loyalty is not in doubt (cf. 9–10, 21–4), the addressee's failure to write conveys the misleading impression that he is less than fully committed to their friendship. But in the light of the parallel with the duplicitous language of Paris, Ovid's warning that his addressee should guard against seeming to be what he is not, or seeming to be a disloyal and forgetful friend, has ironic implications for the poet himself.

In *Tr.* 5.1 he distances himself from his youthful love-elegy (7–8) and from the tradition of elegists – Gallus, Tibullus and Propertius – with whom he was once proud to be associated (17–20; cf. *Tr.* 4.10.51–4). And yet the allusive presence of so many erotic motifs in *Tr.* 5.13, with no attempt made to conceal their literary origins in their new exilic context, suggests that Ovid's break with his erotic past is not quite as complete as he would have us believe in *Tr.* 5.1 and elsewhere (cf. *Tr.* 1.1.67, 3.1.3–4, 3.3.73–6 etc.). In *Tr.* 5.13 it is the poet who gives the impression of being what he is not, or what he claims

---

[53] But though the connection with *Her.* 4 is modified, Ovid's weariness (3–4), insomnia (21–3), loss of appetite (7–8) and pallor (25–8) continue to carry traces of erotic elegiac illness; see Nagle (1980), 61–2 with Videau-Delibes (1991), 328–30. The specific ailments drawn from the *Heroides* in *Tr.* 5.13 thus give way to a more general condition of erotic/exilic malaise.

no longer to be – an elegist as committed to traditional motifs as ever he was. *Quod non es, ne videare, cave*: Ovid lays the injunction on his addressee without quite complying with it himself, and the double standards which operate in *Tr.* 5.13 make this friendship poem a witty exercise in ironic hypocrisy, in fact not so different in this respect from the overall impression conveyed by *Heroides* 16.

iii

Ovid offers a warning of a different sort to his addressee in *Tr.* 3.4: *vive tibi et longe nomina magna fuge* (4). Bitter experience has allegedly taught the poet the dangers of courting friends in high places, and *Tr.* 3.4 represents a general discourse on the theme, at least in lines 1–46. Thereafter Ovid offers a description of the geographical and physical conditions which prevail in Tomis (47–52), an escapist picture of his wife and friends at Rome (53–62), and an explanation of why he is reluctant to name his friends in his verse (63ff.). The ostensible change of direction in lines 47ff. has led editors from Heinsius to the present day to follow those mss which divide the poem after line 46,[54] even though Ovid's account of Pontic conditions (47ff.) is introduced by the bridging reference to *Scythicus ... Pontus* (46). Moreover, the change from a single to a multiple addressee (*amici*, 63) poses no great difficulty; as we saw earlier, Ovid makes a parallel change, without consternation to modern editors, in *Tr.* 1.5. But if *Tr.* 3.4 is read as a single elegy,[55] how are its two differentiated sections to be reconciled?

An integrated approach requires a balanced understanding of the poem's shifting emphases. An important point of reference whose significance will only gradually become apparent is the Epicurean imperative λάθε βιώσας (fr. 551 Usener), which is echoed in lines 25–6:

---

[54] So Owen (1889) and (1915), Ehwald and Levy (1922), Luck (1967), I, André (1968) and Della Corte (1973); but cf. Merkel (1837), 166.
[55] So Herrmann (1924), 46–7, Bouynot (1957), 216–17, Evans (1983), 57–8.

THE ART OF FRIENDSHIP

crede mihi, bene qui latuit bene vixit, et intra
fortunam debet quisque manere suam.

Ovid's intermediary source here is Horace. In *Ep.* 1.17 and
1.18 Horace offers tactful advice to his two addressees, Scaeva
and Lollius, on how to conduct themselves with appropriate
decorum in *amicitia* with their social superiors. In both poems
the alternative to a life in high society is an existence of quiet
self-sufficiency in accordance with Epicurean precept (*nec
vixit male qui natus moriensque fefellit*, *Ep.* 1.17.10; cf.
secretum iter et fallentis semita vitae, Ep. 1.18.103).[56] Now
that Horace has retired to a life of philosophical contempla-
tion in the country (cf. *Ep.* 1.1.1–19), his advice to Scaeva and
Lollius is coloured by his own *modus vivendi*, and his self-
imposed 'exile' from Rome provides the situational parallel
which underlies Ovid's adaptation of Horatian moralizing in
Tr. 3.4. But whereas Horace offers detached reflections on
φιλία καθ᾽ ὑπεροχήν from his voluntary place of retreat, Ovid
is of course left to reflect on his own folly in his enforced place
of exile. He belatedly learns the truth of Horace's advice to
Fuscus at *Ep.* 1.10.32–3:

fuge magna: licet sub paupere tecto
reges et regum vita praecurrere amicos.

Ovid directly echoes *fuge magna* when he urges his addressee
at *Tr.* 3.4.4 *vive tibi et longe nomina magna fuge*; and with the
words *vive tibi* in lines 4 and 5, as well as *mecum vixi* in line
15,[57] Ovid again draws on Horace (cf. *sit mihi quod nunc est,
etiam minus, et mihi vivam|quod superest aevi, Ep.* 1.18.107–8)
for the Epicurean guidance which might have saved him.

---

[56] Cf. Macleod (1979), 19, setting Horace's Epicurean allusions in *Ep.* 1.17 and 18 in
a broader philosophical context: 'In effect, in these *Epistles* Horace has written in
his own manner a *De Amicitia*, in the tradition that flows from *Nicomachean
Ethics* viii–ix; the type of friendship concerned is what Aristotle terms φιλία καθ᾽
ὑπεροχήν [cf. *N.E.* 1158b11–12].'
[57] Luck (1977), II 186 on 15f. rightly accepts *mecum*, proposed by Heinsius in place
of *tecum* as reported by the mss. The Epicurean implication of *vive tibi* is repeated
in *mecum* to complement Ovid's portrayal of his tranquil existence before he
courted disaster (cf. 15–16).

Ovid's poem has its beginning in Horace's ironic presentation of a familiar maxim, but it is a mistake to see *Tr.* 3.4 as simply illustrating Horace on a more elaborate scale. Horatian irony may appear to qualify the didactic tone of the *Epistles*, but didacticism remains a controlling force to the extent that the poems succeed if they persuade the reader to assimilate their moral content. In this respect, Ovid emerges from *Tr.* 3.4 as having become one of Horace's most responsive readers, but his transformed circumstances have altered his evaluation of his mentor's didactic methods. What was once learnt from Horace is now confirmed by Ovid's own experience: the whole emphasis of *Tr.* 3.4 is on the impact and proven reliability of direct experience as adding a new dimension to the refinements of Horatian poetic tuition.

The practical question immediately at issue is how we attain the truer awareness (*cognitio*) of the real worth of friendship and of individual friends. Ovid has already attained this kind of awareness in the case of his present addressee (cf. *cognite*, 2). Two familiar approaches to *cognitio* can conveniently be linked with the acquisition of wisdom through study (*studium|doctrina*) and through practical experience (*usus*). The general superiority of *usus* over *studium* is, of course, attested before Ovid. Speaking of training Roman orators, for example, Cicero says *excitabat eos* [sc. *oratores*] *magnitudo, varietas multitudoque ... causarum, ut ad eam doctrinam, quam suo quisque studio consecutus esset, adiungeretur usus frequens, qui omnium magistrorum praecepta superaret* (*de Orat.* 1.15). A central concern of *Tr.* 3.4 is to embody this notion in poetic form as another means of emphasizing the reality and intensity of the exilic condition.

From the opening couplet we find *cognitio* located in the middle of the harsh realities of Ovid's present existence (*tempore duro|cognite, res postquam procubuere meae,* 1–2). He is therefore *usibus edoctus* (cf. 3), and the Horatian moral *praecepta* which, as we have seen, follow in lines 4–5, 15 and 25–6 consequently acquire additional authority from being confirmed by the poet's own experiences. The mutual support of *studium* and *usus* is designed to give a new significance to different kinds of didactic *exempla* in lines 3–36 by tying them in closely with self-referential admissions: similes (9–12) and myths (19–24, 27–30) are interwoven with recurring appeals to direct, personal experience (13–16, 35–6, 41–2), with the effect of establishing Ovid's *cognitio* of his friend, though mediated through the *studium* of Horatian ethical poetry, on the firmer, truer foundation of *usus*.

The initial aim is to reinforce the λάθε βιώσας dictum, as is evident from the cumulative message of the *exempla* in lines 31–2:

> tu quoque formida nimium sublimia semper,
> propositique, precor, contrahe vela tui.

Both metaphors – rising to precarious heights and trimming the sails of overweening ambition – find literal expression in the preceding *exempla*. Horace had drawn on the nautical illustration to exemplify wise *mediocritas* in *C.* 2.10 (cf. *sapienter ...|contrahes vento nimium secundo|turgida vela*, 22–4),[58] and Ovid follows him in lines 9–10: the wise sailor lowers the yard-arm (cf. *demissa antemna*) in the face of excessive winds, and the broader the sail, the more urgent the precaution (10). The metaphor of poetic voyaging in the *Ars Amatoria* is suggestive in this connection.[59] Ovid failed to trim his sails in the *Ars* and the result was his own form of shipwreck (cf. *Tr.* 1.5.36, 1.6.8, 2.18, *P.* 2.6.11 etc.); while his (poetic) craft (*cumba*, 16) sailed before a lesser breeze, he was safe.[60]

---

[58] For the literary history of the nautical metaphor see Nisbet and Hubbard (1978), 166 on 23.

[59] For the sailing metaphor see 1.6 (Ovid is the Tiphys of love), 771–2, 2.9–10, 429–32, 3.25–6, 99–100, 499–500, 747–8; cf. *R.A.* 69–70, 811–12. The lover must learn to trim and unfurl his sails according to the prevailing winds (cf. *A.A.* 2.337–8, 514, 725–6, 3.584).

[60] *Cumba* denotes Ovid's light elegiac craft at *A.A.* 3.26 and *Tr.* 2.330. This poetic connotation is implicit in his use of *cumba* at *Tr.* 1.1.85: just as the Greek survivors of the shipwreck at Caphereus fear to return to Euboean waters (83–4), so Ovid's craft dreads to return, in the form of *Tristia* 1, to the place where it was wrecked – the imperial palace (85–6). Cf. *P.* 2.6.11–12: now that Ovid is shipwrecked, what benefit is there in learning the course which his (poetic) *cumba* ought to have steered?

The man who keeps his feet on the ground both literally and figuratively soon recovers from a rare fall *in plano* (17), the earth barely touched (*tacta ... humo*, 18). The moral implications of the phrase *in plano*[61] are immediately borne out in Elpenor's contrary example: drunk to excess, he crashes to the ground from the roof of Circe's palace (*tecto ... ab alto*, 19), and the shade who meets his master in the Underworld is crippled by his own lack of self-mastery (*occurrit regi debilis umbra suo*, 20; cf. *Od.* 11.60ff.). In lines 21–4 Icarus gives literal meaning to the dangers of striving to reach *nimium sublimia* (31; cf. *petit infirmis nimium sublimia pennis, Tr.* 1.1.89); whereas Daedalus moderates his course with the same caution which the prudent sailor shows in lowering the yard-arm (*demissa antemna*, 9; cf. *demissius ille volabat*, 23), Icarus of course rises (*hic alte ... volabat*, 23) and falls to physical extremes which are as immoderate (cf. *immensas ... aquas*, 22) as his own ambitions.[62] Then there is Phaethon (29–30): in *Tr.* 1.1 Ovid had already exploited the Jovian/Augustan connection to compare himself with Phaethon (*me quoque, quae sensi, fateor Iovis arma timere*, 81; cf. 79–80), and in *Tr.* 3.4 the comparison suggests itself once more, but with a shift of emphasis. When Ovid introduces Phaethon as one who brought transforming grief upon his father and siblings (29–30), and when he introduces Eumedes as the father of a son (Dolon) who was manifestly misguided in trying to steal Achilles' horses (27–8), the new point of comparison lies between the poet's intimate circle (cf. 59ff.) and the grieving relations of his mythological counterparts.[63]

---

[61] *In plano/-um* as a figurative token of humility would seem to be a post-Classical usage (cf. Sen. *Cl.* 1.5.3, *Dial.* 9.10.6, both cited by Tarrant (1976), 189 on *Ag.* 85); but it is surely implicit in Ovid's literalism in line 17. And does Ovid take up that implication in hoping that his addressee will progress 'without obstruction' (*pede inoffenso*, 33), without any stumble as he walks *in plano*?

[62] Cf. Daedalus' words to Icarus at *M.* 8.203–6: *medio ... ut limite curras ... moneo, ne, si demissior ibis,|unda gravet pennas, si celsior, ignis adurat.|inter utrumque vola!*. Ovid's own fall (cf. *res ... procubuere meae*, 2) immediately suggests comparison with Icarus.

[63] Cf. *Tr.* 4.3.65–6: just as Phaethon was not rejected by his loved ones after his Jovian destruction, so Ovid's wife should not be ashamed of her husband (cf. 61–2).

In lines 37–40 the *studium* of learned allusion is offset by an appeal to personal recollection, as the repeated emphasis on visual awareness (37, 39) supplies the bond which twice binds together writer and addressee in the closest of relationships (*ego te*, 37; *nostra tuas*, 39). The point becomes an important one, for later in the poem we find that dependence on the reliability of visual perception is the only basis on which the exiled poet can now reconstitute a faith in the only relationships which greatly matter to him, those with his home, wife and friends. What forms the most cogent evidence that '4A' and '4B' are an integrated whole is that '4B' offers the convincing explanation for the direction taken in '4A'. In the total isolation of exile, denied the intellectual stimulus and social intercourse of Rome, Ovid finds in visual memory the only access he has to familiar points of association outside the self.

Everything in the second half of the poem is directed to emphasizing the detached loneliness of the poet's visual imagination. *Amicitia* is now possible only with a disembodied *nomen* (45–6, giving *Nasonis ... tui* in 45 – the only mention of the poet's name – a curiously hollow ring). Separated by a distance of stellar magnitude (47) and by virtually insurmountable geographical features (49–50), Ovid is symbolically placed on the borderline between the human and the non-human (51–2). All that remains to him of the humanity he has known is what is accessible through the visual imagination: *sunt animo cuncta videnda meo* (56). The significance of visual recollection in lines 37–40 is now fully realized, as the repeated *vidi* of 37 and 39 is taken up by the repeated *ante oculos* of 57 and 59. Unsettling though such an *imago* may seem (cf. 59–60), the emphasis is put squarely on the make-believe reality it now holds for the poet (cf. *sicut praesentis*, 59), arousing emotional responses like an actual person (60–2).

With his own name left behind in Rome (cf. 45–6), Ovid finds himself in a place where names are anyway few and unintelligible (50). The maxim *longe nomina magna fuge* (4) echoes with a self-mocking literalness as the nameless poet writes from a nameless place to a nameless addressee. The reluctance to name friends in the verse (63ff.) is thus also broadly connected to the first part of the elegy: 'In the opening lines Ovid cautions his friends about associating with the mighty; at the end he assures all his friends that he will not endanger them by associating their names with himself.'[64] But how real was that danger? We saw earlier that Ovid's ostensible motive of protecting his friends through anonymous address was open to question on various grounds, not least because it is hardly likely that his former associates were either totally unknown in official circles or beyond discovery by routine enquiry at Rome.[65] Paranoia apart, Ovid's reluctance to name his friends would seem to be a futile exercise – unless, of course, that anonymity disguises the fact that he is addressing moral types rather than specific individuals. In this and various other ways his silence is open to creative interpretation in the *Tristia*, and 3.4 illustrates as much. With emphasis now put on faith in the visions of the *animus* (cf. 74), recourse must be had to 'friendship' which is merely an introspective conversation with the self (69–70) and which parallels the enclosed world of visual recollection (cf. 55–6).

Ovid is also confident that his friends would not want to be named in his exilic verse (65–6). The situation was different in times past:

> ante volebatis, gratique erat instar honoris,
> versibus in nostris nomina vestra legi.
>
> (67–8)

The initial inference here is that before Ovid's exile his friends would have gloried in the honour of being named in his poetry, but fear of exposure checks their ambition after the poet's fall. Or could it be that *Tr.* 3.4 is the catalyst for change in his friends, and that the words *ante volebatis* refer to the ambitions which they might have harboured before reading this very elegy? Newly cautioned against consorting with the high and mighty (*nomina magna*, 4) and courting fame (*nomen magnum*) in Ovid's verse, these friends are assumed to have

---

[64] Evans (1983), 58.
[65] See p. 104 *supra*.

learnt the lesson of line 25 (*bene qui latuit bene vixit*):

> nec meus indicio latitantes versus amicos
> protrahit. occulte siquis amabat, amet.
> (71-2)

The term *latitantes* gives Epicurean meaning to the anonymity of Ovid's friends in the *Tristia*, and the point is underscored when the poet urges that he be loved in secret (*occulte*); Horace's *secretum iter* (*Ep.* 1.18.103) is the advised path. Unnamed, Ovid's addressees conform to his injunction in lines 43-4 (*vive sine invidia, mollesque inglorius annos|exige*) by remaining inconspicuous (*inglorii*) and safe from carping detractors – safe even from Augustus.[66] The initiated friend and reader who has understood the message of Ovid's opening discourse will understand the moral significance of his anonymity. It is not just that the alleged Augustan threat enjoins caution; bitter experience has taught Ovid that obscurity is a safe haven, and by concealing the identity of his friends he contributes to what he presents as their general moral well-being.

The art of appeal

The addressee of *P.* 2.9 is Cotys, a Thracian king who receives an appeal for protection in exile (cf. 5-6).[67] In the average appeal of this sort flattery is to be expected, but praise of Cotys' character (cf. *iuvenum mitissime*, 5) and literary talent (47ff.) finds some measure of support in Tacitus' favourable assessment in the *Annals*. After the death in A.D. 12 of Rhoemetalces, Cotys' father,[68] Augustus divided the king-

---

[66] And Ovid heeds his own injunction by no longer seeking *gloria* in his exilic verse (cf. *Tr.* 5.7.28, 5.12.41-2 (*si liceat, nulli cognitus esse velim*) etc.). The life *sine invidia* was a traditional ideal (see Luck (1977), II 89 on 43f.).

[67] Latin references to five Thracian kings of this name are collected in *TLL Suppl. Nom.* 2.677-8 (ours is no. 4). For further background on the Ovidian Cotys see *PIR*² C 1554 with *RE* XI 1554 s.v. Kotys 8 and Jones (1971), 8-10. Syme (1978), 82 identifies Cotys as the unnamed king who, at *P.* 1.8.11ff., is said to have won back Aegisos from the occupying Getae; but cf. p. 29 *supra*.

[68] The date may be as early as A.D. 9 (cf. Marsh (1931), 143); but A.D. 12 is generally accepted because *P.* 2.9, 'hardly later than that year, assumes it' (Goodyear (1981), 400 on *Ann.* 2.64.2).

dom between Cotys and his uncle, Rhescuporis.[69] Tacitus reports that Cotys inherited the cultured part of the kingdom (*arva et urbes et vicina Graecis, Ann.* 2.64.2), Rhescuporis the wilder region (*incultum ferox adnexum hostibus, ibid.*), and that each dominion reflected the character of its ruler; whereas Cotys' *ingenium* was *mite et amoenum* (2.64.2), Rhescuporis' was *atrox avidum et societatis impatiens* (*ibid.*). But Tacitus' portrayal of Cotys' *amoenitas* may not be without qualification. After Tiberius' accession, Rhescuporis conformed to his reported nature by exploiting Cotys' ingenuousness to take control of the whole of Thrace. Tiberius had ordered the two kings to keep the peace, and Cotys immediately responded by disbanding his mobilized force (2.65.1); feigning a treaty, Rhescuporis deceived, imprisoned and eventually murdered Cotys in A.D. 19, rejecting the latter's appeal to the civilized values of *sacra regni, eiusdem familiae deos et hospitalis mensas* (2.65.3). However admirable, Cotys' character would hardly seem to equip him for Thracian *realpolitik* under an emperor who has yet to assert Augustus' hold over Rhescuporis.[70]

Even though Tacitus' portrayal of Cotys may be conditioned by his artistic designs in this Tiberian narrative, the hint of literary sophistication in *amoenum* (2.64.2) supports Ovid's judgement at *P.* 2.9.47ff.[71] The Thracian may also be the addressee of *A.Pl.* 75, an epigram which portrays a certain Cotys as combining the authority of Zeus with Ares' martial prowess and Apollo's beauty (5–6). The epigram, which is generally assigned to Antipater of Thessalonica rather than

[69] Rhescuporis is sometimes rendered Rhascupolis, the form favoured by Woodman (see (1977), 265 on Vell. 2.129.1); I follow Goodyear (1981).
[70] During Augustus' reign Rhescuporis had encroached on Cotys' territory only tentatively for fear of Augustan retribution (cf. *quem* [*Augustum*] ... *vindicem metuebat*, Tac. *Ann.* 2.64.3); Tiberius apparently held no such fear. Velleius overtly praises Tiberius for his subsequent treatment and eventual punishment of Rhescuporis (2.129.1); but cf. Woodman (1977), 264 *ad loc.* If Tiberius tricked Rhescuporis ('he wanted to deceive Rhescuporis, not alarm him', Goodyear (1981), 403 on *Ann.* 2.65.5), such deceit would fit what Tacitus portrays as his dissimulating character (see *Ann.* 4.71.3 with Syme (1958), 422–3). To whom is Tiberius more akin, the agreeable Cotys or the wily Rhescuporis?
[71] For this connotation of *amoenus* see Goodyear (1981), 401 on 2.64.2 with *TLL* 1.1964 s.v. II 2 and III 2.

his Sidonian namesake of the first century B.C.,[72] reveals nothing about Cotys to prove that he is also Ovid's addressee; but if the connection is tentatively accepted,[73] two features of the epigram are of special relevance to *P*. 2.9. First, unless Antipater implies that Cotys resembles Apollo in artistic ability as well as beauty (καλλοσύνην, 5), no reference is made to what Ovid portrays as his outstanding literary talent. It would of course be rash to read too much into Antipater's silence on this point; but if Cotys really was the singularly skilled and committed poet whom Ovid portrays (cf. 47–8), Antipater's failure to develop the inviting Phoeban comparison is at least suggestive about the possible extent of Ovid's hyperbole. Secondly, and to qualify this last remark, Antipater's own hyperbole places Ovid's effusive *laudes* in generic perspective; but even if Ovid pays lip-service to the conventions of βασιλικοὶ λόγοι,[74] the tonal complexities of his Augustan *laudes* in *Metamorphoses* 15 and elsewhere suggest that he may be more subtly ironic in his hyperbole than the seemingly deadpan Antipater.[75]

Take, for example, lines 21–36, which use the conventional idea that animal-sacrifice is offered to the gods with a view to ensuring favours in return.[76] The references to Jupiter (25–6), Ceres (29–30) and Bacchus (31–2) are presented as generalized truisms which nobody would be inclined to question: the gods take our gifts and so must grant the favours asked of them. When Augustus is suddenly introduced in line 33, we immediately think of him in this connection; the established parallel with Jupiter and the constant appeals for a show of favour in return for the poet's humble offerings[77] lead us to

[72] See Gow and Page (1968), II 59.
[73] Gow and Page (1968), *ibid.* term it 'a plausible guess', although various dynasts of the name Cotys are known. Antipater's allusion to Zeus's σκῆπτρον suggests that the epigram could not be earlier than A.D. 12, the probable year of Cotys' accession (but cf. André (1977), xxv for possible delay until A.D. 14). Whether it is earlier than *P*. 2.9 is unclear; but it is not impossible that Ovid is among the poets to whom Antipater refers in terming Cotys ἔργον ἀοιδοπολῶν (4).
[74] On the generic form see Pérez Vega (1989), 213 with Cairns (1972), 105–10.
[75] Tonal ambivalence in Ovid's Augustan *laudes* is discussed in Chapter 4.
[76] The conventional nature of the references to animal-sacrifice here (as at *Tr*. 1.10.43) is confirmed by the absence of the reservations suggested by *F*. 1.383–4, *M*. 15.96–142, Hor. *C*. 3.13 and above all Lucr. 2.352–66.
[77] This appeal is most fully and formally expressed at *Tr*. 2.547–78.

expect that Augustus will be shown here to be fulfilling his mutual obligations as Jupiter, Ceres and Bacchus do, especially in view of the general summing-up along these lines which follows in 35–6:

> utilitas igitur magnos hominesque deosque
> efficit, auxiliis quoque favente suis.

Augustus is here closely tied in with the (other) divine examples of favours being shown to suppliants – but, of course, the embarrassing fact is that Augustus has failed to live up to his obligations in this respect, and the couplet devoted to him (33–4) turns out to be nothing more (for how *could* it be more?) than a rather unimpassioned plea for good government! We are being shown how, if Ovid's appeals to him had been answered, Augustus would feature proudly among the the divine dispensers of benevolence to humanity. The emperor's failure to comply with divine precedent could have been quietly suppressed, but by inserting his name here Ovid ensures that his failure is highlighted by the embarrassingly modified way in which his name has to be introduced.

Our doubts about the current validity of these familiar precedents have been aroused by lines 27–8, where the poet's personal experience is drawn on apparently to reinforce the divine *exempla* which surround it:

> si pacem nullam pontus mihi praestet eunti,
> irrita Neptuno cur ego tura feram?

Ovid's appeal to his experience can only be accepted if it is taken to be referring to his arrival in one piece at Tomis or to some possible future sea-journey. For one of the recurring themes of *Tristia* 1 is that the sea-journey to Tomis was anything but a peaceful affair and that constant supplications to the gods in fact failed to avert every kind of maritime disaster except ultimate destruction.[78] It is difficult to see lines 27–8 as

---

[78] The notion of Ovid's peaceful sea-journey is contradicted by *Tr.* 1.2 (Neptune is *ferox* (9)), 1.4 (cf. the *supplicatio* in lines 25–8), and 1.11. The genre-related nature of much of this material is exposed in Juv. 12.1–92, but this will not explain how Ovid can reconcile one of the most memorable features of his journey to Tomis with the claim that offering sacrifice beforehand ensures him a fair and peaceful voyage.

confirming anything but the merely conventional nature of the references which surround them. These are not precedents in which much faith can now be placed, for Ovid's experience in general tells against the idea that appeals and sacrifices bring much in the way of a positive response.[79]

This does not mean that *P.* 2.9 is an empty rhetorical exercise. I have already shown how it makes its discreet but not too delicate point about Augustus' *clementia* in an open letter to a foreign king. In fact, the reader's mind constantly returns to the image of Augustus, with whom Cotys is compared through much of the poem by the device of transferring to the Thracian ruler forms of address which are most familiar to us from a Roman context. Augustus was famously the *regia progenies* whose noble *origo* had begun with Venus and Aeneas,[80] and central to Ovid's strategy in *P.* 2.9 is the wish to endorse Cotys' claim to a distinguished ancestry which extends back to Eumolpus and Erichthonius (1–2, 19–20). This Erichthonius is not the son of Dardanus and father of Tros;[81] no Eumolpus is connected with this Dardanian Erichthonius in the mythical tradition. Rather, the Erichthonius to whom Ovid refers is the legendary Athenian king who was fathered by Hephaestus and nurtured by Athena.[82] This Erichthonius was the grandfather of the Erechtheus with whom he is sometimes confused;[83] in turn, Erechtheus was the great-grandfather of a Eumolpus produced by Chione and Poseidon.[84] By claiming descent from this Athenian line, Cotys

[79] This is especially the case if the reference to Neptune (28) is taken as a typological reference to Augustus (see Hardie (1986), 204–5).
[80] It is at *F.* 4.19–84 that Augustus' *adoptiva nobilitas* is most elaborately set out.
[81] Cf. *F.* 4.33–4; it is odd that Augustus and Cotys both list a (different) Erichthonius among their ancestors.
[82] Apollodorus reports two traditions, by one of which Erichthonius was the son of Hephaestus and Atthis (3.14.6). By the other (*ibid.*), Hephaestus ejaculated against Athena's thigh in trying to force himself on her; produced from the seed which Athena threw to the ground in disgust, Erichthonius was raised in secret by the goddess (cf. Ov. *M.* 2.553, *Erichthonium, prolem sine matre creatam*). For further testimony see Frazer (1921), II 90 n. 1. For the Dardanian Erichthonius identified with the Athenian king by one tradition (cf. D. H. 1.62.1–2, Str. 13.1.48) see Edwards (1991), 317 on *Il.* 20.219.
[83] At *Il.* 2.547 Erechtheus is named as the child nurtured by Athena. Cf. Frazer (1921), 93 ('Erechtheus and Erichthonius may have been originally identical').
[84] See Apollod. 3.15.4, Paus. 1.38.2–3, Hyg. 157; cf. Isoc. 4.68.

finds mythical support for his godly *nobilitas* (cf. *a superis ortae nobilitatis*, 18) in the divine parentage of both Erichthonius and Eumolpus. But what justification did he have for tracing his Thracian descent to Athenian origins?

The answer is to be found in Eumolpus' Thracian exile after what Apollodorus portrays as his attempt to seduce his wife's sister while living in Ethiopia (3.15.4). According to Apollodorus, Eumolpus sought refuge with Tegyrius, king of Thrace, and eventually succeeded to the kingship (τὴν βασιλείαν παρέλαβε, 3.15.4); this Eumolpus subsequently joined Eleusis in war against Athens under Erechtheus (*ibid.*), but the name Eumolpus is more famously associated with Eleusis for other reasons. In the Homeric *Hymn to Demeter* a certain Eumolpus is depicted as one of the rulers of Eleusis (154) and instructed by the goddess in the Mysteries (cf. 473ff.). 'His name, the "good singer", indicates his function: he had to have a strong, clear voice, for it was he who enunciated (presumably either singing or "intoning") the sacred words of the Mysteries.'[85] No reference is made in the *Hymn* to the parentage of this Eumolpus, but one tradition credited a Thracian Eumolpus, distinct from Poseidon's son, with founding the Mysteries.[86] Euripides seems to have reconciled (but not identified) these two Eumolpi in his *Erechtheus*; Poseidon's son (cf. fr. 39 Austin) is apparently killed in battle against the Athenians, but Athena appears to predict that an eponymous descendant will found the Mysteries (cf. Εὔμολπος γὰρ Εὐμόλπου γεγὼ[ς|τοῦ κατθ[ανόντος, fr. 65.100–1 Austin).[87] For Cotys, however, the significant point of his genealogical connection with Eumolpus is not that the latter either founded the Mysteries or created a line which led to their foundation; Cotys inherits the rich artistic talent traditionally associated with the name Eumolpus.

Various Eumolpi with musical expertise have to be distinguished at this point. One is the Theocritean Eumolpus, son

[85] Richardson (1974), 197.
[86] See Plu. *Mor.* 607b, Lucian *Demon.* 34 with Richardson (1974), 198.
[87] See Carrara (1977), 26–7 and 88 on fr. 18.98–9 (= 65.98–9 Austin).

of Philammon, who teaches Hercules the lyre as part of the latter's bardic training (24.109–10).[88] A second is Neptune's son who, according to Hyginus (273.11), accompanied Olympus' flute to win the prize for singing at the Argive games established by Acastus.[89] A third is the Eumolpus connected with the Thracian singer Musaeus and variously portrayed as the latter's father, son or pupil.[90] As Eumolpus' father and allegedly the author of a poem called the Εὐμολπία and of Ὑποθῆκαι to his son,[91] this Musaeus is himself variously portrayed in mythical tradition as the son or pupil of Orpheus.[92] Ovid has Eumolpus share this Orphic connection by casting him as Orpheus' pupil at *P.* 3.3.41 (*non Chionides Eumolpus in Orphea talis*). In terming Eumolpus *Chionides*, Ovid clearly follows the tradition reported by Apollodorus (3.15.4): Eumolpus, son of Poseidon and Chione is Athenian in origin, and Ovid explicitly portrays him as such when he links Thracian Orpheus *cum Cecropio Eumolpo* as Midas' joint sources of mystical instruction at *M.* 11.92–3. As we have seen, this same Eumolpus prevails in *P.* 2.9 through Athenian descent from Erichthonius (20) – and the further implication in the light of *P.* 3.3.41 is that the Eumolpus from whom Cotys claims descent was the pupil of Orpheus, who is himself introduced, perhaps significantly in this connection, at *P.* 2.9.53.

The extensive range of the genealogical allusions in *P.* 2.9 had to be carefully researched by the poet and cunningly deployed, since they constitute an important part of his *supplicatio*. We can see how this is the case by comparing the appeal to Cotys with Aeneas' appeal to Evander in the *Aeneid*

---

[88] This Eumolpus is nowhere else attested; see Gow (1952), 432 on 24.105 ('Whether T.'s Eumolpus is an invention or drawn from some recondite source cannot be determined.')

[89] This Eumolpus would seem to be the son whom Apollodorus attributes to Poseidon (3.15.4); but Apollodorus makes no reference to Eumolpus' musical talent.

[90] For *testimonia* see Kern (1922), nos. 18, 161 and 166 with Richardson (1974), 79 and 198 and Gow (1952), 432 on 24.105.

[91] On these apocryphal works see Richardson (1974), 78–9.

[92] For *testimonia* see Kern (1922), nos. 97 and 166ff.

(8.127–51).[93] Addressing Evander as a *supplex* (145), Aeneas
begins with a reference to the king's ancestry (*optime Graiuge-
num*, 127) as Ovid does by referring to Cotys' (cf. *P.* 2.9.1–2).
Each suppliant has been guided to his potential saviour by
Fortuna (*cui me Fortuna precari|... voluit, Aen.* 8.127–8; cf.
me Fortuna tibi ...|tradidit, P. 2.9.7–8) to emphasize the op-
portunity which this goddess is now offering for a show of
indulgence.[94] Aeneas also unfolds a long, complicated genealogical table reaching to the remote past (134–42), and it is on
the basis of this (cf. *his fretus*, 143) that he constructs his
appeal, just as Ovid hopes that his invocation of Cotys' ancestry will ensure him a favourable response:

> hoc nitor iste tui generis desiderat, hoc est
> a superis ortae nobilitatis opus.
>
> (17–18)

What the genealogical material is designed to achieve in each
case is to connect the suppliant closely with his source of assis-
tance. In Aeneas' case this link is clear enough: if their ancestors are traced back far enough, Aeneas and Evander are seen
to have *cognati patres* (132), who enable Aeneas to make his
direct appeal (143) and to seek an alliance based on their
distant relationship. Not even Ovid can devise a genealogy
which links him to Cotys in quite this way; but his genealogical researches have uncovered a relation to Cotys which is
potentially of greater significance than the remote kinship
with Evander that Aeneas has been able to establish. It is the
ancestral devotion to the Muses, which Cotys has been shown

[93] The elements which make Aeneas' speech a *rhetorica persuasio* are briefly summarized by Servius *auctus* on 8.127. Also, the opening lines of *P.* 2.9 (1–10) correspond closely to the rhetorical model given for such a *captatio benevolentiae* by
Servius *auctus* on *Aen.* 1.522 (the beginning of Ilioneus' *supplicatio* to Dido). In
fact, Ovid exemplifies the four basic elements required at the start of these appeals
more neatly than Ilioneus does: identification of the addressee, self-identification,
naming of one's adversary (Fortuna, of course, in Ovid's case) and the basis of the
complaint (cf. 7–8) are clearly structured in the opening ten lines. Perhaps it is by
way of allusion to the appeal of Ilioneus and his men that Ovid refers metaphori-
cally to his own condition after four years in Tomis as *naufragium ... nostrum* (9).

[94] I follow Richmond (1990) in reading *Fortuna* at *P.* 2.9.7; Owen (1915) prints
fortuna.

to have inherited from Eumolpus, that constitutes the basis of their *foedus* in Ovid's appeal to him (63–6; *ad vatem vates orantia bracchia tendo*, 65).

The poem's interest in genealogy thus turns out to have a direct bearing on its central theme – that king and suppliant are fellow-travellers along the path of the Muses (cf. 62). Cotys is therefore portrayed as Eumolpus' worthy successor, dividing his time between his regal duties and cultivation of the Muses:

> tempora sic data sunt studiis ubi iusta paternis,
>   atque suis numeris forte quievit opus,
> ne tua marcescant per inertis otia somnos,
>   lucida Pieria tendis in astra via.
>
> (59–62)

Cotys' kingly responsibilities are described in language which foreshadows his literary diversion in lines 61–2. Respite from the task (*opus*) of seeing through his official business in all its parts (*numeri*) comes in the form of retreat to *opus* and *numeri* in different senses,[95] and after devoting himself to the *studia paterna* inherited from Rhoemetalces I, Cotys reverts to the ancestral *studia* of Eumolpus.[96] Instead of wasting his leisure (*otia*) in idle sleep, Cotys applies himself to poetic *ars* in the productive ἀγρυπνία of distinctively literary *otium*.[97] The terms used here are intended to identify Cotys not merely as a king interested in culture but – a compliment never offered to Augustus – as an artist whose intelligence and sensibility were very much akin to Ovid's own. Addressed as *iuvenum mitissime* in line 5, Cotys is praised as much for his commitment to literary pursuits (cf. *mitibus ... studiis*, 50) as for his exemplary character; although he knows the realities of battle (55–6) as one apparently *doctus* (58) in the art of warfare, his

---

[95] *Opus* is of course used of literary activity or its product (see *OLD* s.v. 1b and 9c for examples), *numerus* of poetic metre and (in the plural) of metrical lines (see *OLD* s.v. 14 a and b for examples).

[96] For examples of *paternus* applied to ancestral rather than strictly paternal relationship see *OLD* s.v. 2.

[97] On ἀγρυπνία as the mark of Alexandrian industry see Brink (1971), 307. Cotys' wakeful *ars* is set in contrast to *iners somnus* (cf. 61).

literary *doctrina* is such that Bistonia can pride itself on producing two *vates* of legendary stature – Orpheus and Cotys (cf. 53–4).

High praise indeed; but there is of course another *vates* active in the region, and if Cotys has heard rumour (cf. *fama loquax*, 3) of Ovid's presence in Tomis, he will already know of the *fama* which the latter's voice and work command. Ovid seeks Cotys' protection in a suppliant voice which is potentially beguiling in its deference, for in his own way Ovid is empowered to protect and promote the king's own *fama* through poetic celebration – or perhaps to propagate a different kind of myth should Cotys reject his plea. An implicit warning to this effect is given in lines 41–2:

> quis non Antiphaten Laestrygona devovet? aut quis
> munifici mores improbat Alcinoi?

The reputations transmitted in Homer remain immutable in the popular imagination: Antiphates is universally condemned for his brutal killing of Odysseus' men (cf. *Od.* 10.116ff.), Alcinous regarded with universal favour for his treatment of Odysseus, his suppliant at *Od.* 7.146ff. In courting Cotys' favour, Ovid naturally implies that the king is like Alcinous (cf. 47–8); but we, like Cotys, are left with the discomforting hint in line 41 that, should Ovid's appeals be ignored, literary models for a poem of a very different sort lie readily to hand.

Ovid's overt flattery in lines 43–6 harbours a similar implication. Like father, like son: Rhoemetalces was no tyrant like Apollonius of Cassandrea, Alexander of Pherae or the notorious Phalaris (43–4), but a model ruler, harsh and invincible in war (45) and yet never bloodthirsty once peace was made (46). The negative parallel is obviously connected with the familiar motif in which an inflexible nature is said to derive from a savage or bestial parentage,[98] and the inversion of this motif here effectively associates Rhoemetalces with the exilic por-

[98] For the many examples of the motif see Pease (1935), 315–19 on *Aen.* 4.365–7.

trayal of Augustus as an ardent campaigner but clement victor (cf. *Tr.* 2.43–50, 5.2.35–8, *P.* 1.2.121–6 etc.). Like a Roman *princeps*, a Thracian king is claimed in lines 45–6 to be equally responsive to the injunction *parcere subiectis et debellare superbos* (cf. *Aen.* 6.851–3). The comparison is apt, for Rhoemetalces had come over to Octavian's side at Actium,[99] and he was an active ally in suppressing the Thracian revolt of *c.* 11 B.C. and during the Pannonian revolt of A.D. 6–9. But the historical evidence hardly suggests that he was a total stranger to defeat (cf. *vinci nescius armis*, 45).[100] Dio reports that during the Thracian revolt Rhoemetalces was stripped of his army without a fight by Vologaesus, the rebel leader of the Bessi and himself a Dionysiac priest who laid terrifying claim to divine power (τῇ παρὰ τοῦ θεοῦ δόξῃ, 54.34.5). After this bloodless defeat Rhoemetalces, *Marte ferox* (45), fled to the Chersonese to escape Vologaesus; Vologaesus pursued him and it was left to L. Calpurnius Piso, governor of Pamphylia, to thwart and finally suppress the Bessi (54.34.6–7). According to Velleius, Rhoemetalces' cavalry was also routed in what was very nearly a disaster for the Romans at the Volcaean Marshes in A.D. 7 (2.112.4–5);[101] victory was snatched from the jaws of defeat, but not by Rhoemetalces.

Whether or not Ovid knew of such incidents, his portrayal of Cotys' father is clearly designed to suggest a paternal model in the authentic and best Roman tradition. As well as maintaining the familiar balance between severity and clemency which Virgil and Horace set before Augustus,[102] Cotys is seen in lines 47–8 to be fulfilling the injunction *paci imponere*

---

[99] So Plu. *Mor.* 207a, reporting that Rhoemetalces gave drunken offence by making disparaging remarks about his new alliance. Hence Augustus' riposte as reported by Plutarch (and qualifying Ovid's praise of Rhoemetalces): ἐγὼ προδοσίαν φιλῶ, προδότας δ' οὐκ ἐπαινῶ (cf. *Rom.* 17.3).

[100] This distinctive phrase is here given a positive force, though its source is a tragic context in the final battle between Aeneas and Turnus (*rumpuntur nescia vinci| pectora*, *Aen.* 12.527–8).

[101] For details see Woodman (1977), 167–70 with Wilkes (1969), 72.

[102] With *Aen.* 6.851–3 cf. Hor. *Saec.* 51–2 (... *bellante prior, iacentem|lenis in hostem*). Augustus was careful to claim that he had followed the instruction (cf. *R.G.* 3.1–2, 26.3).

morem (cf. *Aen.* 6.852) as he follows up his victories with a character-refining *studium* for the civilizing arts. He clearly responds *fideliter* (cf. 47) to the Roman literary model of the ideal ruler. Yet, if Cotys is here being promoted as a ruler who outshines even Augustus in the display of authentic Roman virtues, there is also a familiar warning implicit in the eulogy. The three tyrants to whom Ovid alludes in lines 43–4 all figure in the curse-catalogue of the *Ibis* – an ominous coincidence if it reminds Cotys of how Ovid is capable of dealing with his enemies. In the *Ibis* Ovid wishes on his enemy the gruesome deaths of all three tyrants. Apollodorus of Cassandrea was buried alive (461–2 La Penna); Alexander of Pherae was killed by his wife after she discovered his plot to murder her brothers (321–2); Phalaris died in the brazen bull invented – and first tested – by Perillus (439–40; cf. 437–8).[103] If Cotys fails to reply sympathetically to Ovid's appeal, he may lay himself open to an equivalent retribution through Ovidian *ars*.[104]

I have pointed out how suggestive it is that Ovid can appeal to Cotys in a way he cannot appeal to Augustus, as one *vates* to another (65) and as a fellow-worshipper at the same altar of the Muses (64). But just how flattering is Ovid's assessment of Cotys' literary powers? If Cotys' literary sensibility naturally disposes him to recognize the allusions and possible ambivalence in lines 41–6, then he may also detect latent irony in lines 51–2:

> carmina testantur, quae, si tua nomina demas,
> Threicium iuvenem composuisse negem.

The typically Ovidian *lusus* here at first seems to say that if Cotys' poems did not bear his name, Ovid would not believe on the basis of their quality that the young Thracian had

---

[103] Accepting the arguments of Housman (1918), 223–9 = (1972), 970–4, which rest in part on the evidence of *P.* 2.9.43–4, La Penna (1957) rightly brought 439–40 (Phalaris) and 461–2 (Apollodorus) together and placed them before 339, close to Alexander. (Note that Owen's *OCT* numeration for *Ibis* is not standard).

[104] Ovid had already vilified his addressee in *Tr.* 3.11, a faithless friend and malicious persecutor, by casting him as more cruel even than Busiris and Phalaris (39–40).

written them. There is more than a hint of cultural condescension in this, of course, but we immediately recall that the *Threicius vates* in Roman poetry is invariably Orpheus,[105] who is in fact named in the next line, and we find Ovid saying that if it were not for the king's name at the top he would judge the poems to be of inferior quality (i.e. that no Orpheus had written them).

The unsettling effect which comes from discerning the ambivalent message in lines 41–54 should not be taken too seriously, however. While it is possible that Ovid inserted some unflattering insinuations into an apparent eulogy of Augustus without expecting them to be fully appreciated, he is unlikely to have had equally low expectations of Cotys' *ingenium*, which has after all been trained by the *mitia studia* of great poetry (cf. 50) to value the very kind of subtle wit at which Ovid excelled. As there is no compelling reason for Ovid to have written to Cotys in the first place, he is unlikely to have done so simply to subvert the king's self-esteem. Much more probable is that these ludic undertones unite poet and reader in a shared enthusiasm for the Muses by exposing something of the instability of all superficially rigid statements.

Consider in this light the tantalizing subtlety of Ovid's allusive language in lines 57–8:

> ... es excusso iaculum torquere lacerto
> collaque velocis flectere doctus equi.

Compare Phaedra's words to Hippolytus in *Heroides* 4:

> aut [libet] tremulum excusso iaculum vibrare lacerto
> aut in graminea ponere corpus humo.
> saepe iuvat versare leves in pulvere currus
> torquentem frenis ora fugacis equi.
>
> (43–6)

Phaedra is of course taking up hunting in order to identify herself with the favourite occupation of Hippolytus. The idea comes from Euripides (cf. *Hipp.* 215–27) and is not, as one

---

[105] Cf. Prop. 3.2.3–4, Hor. *C.* 1.24.13, Virg. *Ecl.* 4.55, *Aen.* 6.120, Ov. *M.* 11.2, 92, and later Stat. *Silv.* 5.5.54, Sil. 12.398.

might have thought, a typical case of Ovidian extravagance. But Ovid brings about a radical change in tone here: what affects us in Euripides as a tragic, pathetic abandonment of self is transformed in the *Heroides* into the discovery of a new hobby (cf. *ignotas mittor in artes*, 37). Ovid's Phaedra enters into the spirit of the hunt with the youthful relish and fresh enthusiasm of someone recently initiated by reading a didactic poem on the subject, and her description to Hippolytus (37–46) contains echoes of the instructional mode of a *Cynegeticus* which are, given the context, both humorous and ironic. In the case of Cotys, however, Phaedra's words are recalled to very different effect.

Cotys is using his spear and horse in war, not in hunting,[106] as is clear from the contrast in lines 55–62 between the *forte opus* of the battlefield and the *otium* he devotes to the Muses, and the activity which provided Phaedra with a healthy (if hardly innocent) pastime becomes for him a serious matter of life and death (cf. 56). That *should* at least be the impression we are given, but the reference in lines 57–8 to Cotys also acquiring his skills through *doctrina* suggests greater familiarity with a book like Xenophon's *De re equestri* than with the grim experience of real fighting. An allusion to Phaedra's novel pastime and instruction from a manual on horsemanship scarcely provide a solid basis for a tough military reputation, especially in the part of the world in which Cotys had to learn to survive. If the implication of lines 55–8 was that Cotys, with his cultural interests and refined *mores*, really lacked the brutal ruthlessness needed to secure his place in the murderous feuding of Thracian dynastic politics, then Ovid's judgement would be only too quickly confirmed by events.

The emphasis which the poem places on Cotys' literary predilections reaches its climax in the final supplication (65–80), which bears out the arguments of my previous paragraph by

---

[106] For the military application of the manoeuvres described in lines 57–8 cf. Lucan's description of the fighting skills of the Leuci, Remi and Sequani: *optimus excusso Leucus Remusque lacerto,|optima gens flexis in gyrum Sequana frenis* (1.424–5).

showing more faith in the king's cultured sensibility (cf. *ad vatem vates* ... , 65) than in the likelihood of obtaining any particular material advantage or benefit (note the vagueness of lines 79–80). Ovid presents himself as an extraordinary kind of criminal: no law has been broken (71), and yet his *noxa* exceeds that of a murderer, poisoner or forger (72). These crimes of 'lesser guilt' are described in lines 67–70 in sufficient detail to stimulate the memory of any enthusiastic reader of poetry, without the allusions having to be too precise, restrictive or accurate. Murder, poison and the Pontic region (67–8) call Medea to mind with little difficulty, an association which had already been partially exploited in *Tr.* 3.9,[107] while falsifying a document or letter by the malicious use of a seal on the binding threads (69–70) may recall the infamous way in which Phaedra procured the death of Hippolytus *credulitate patris, sceleratae et fraude novercae* (*M.* 15.498).[108] The suggestive hint in these lines that we should remember at this point the wicked excesses of Greek tragic heroines is designed to complicate the perspective in which we see Ovid's own *noxa* (cf. *his gravior*, 72), so that the unveiling of the source of his guilt in line 73 as the writing of the *Ars* is more than simply a witty deflating of our overblown expectations. Ovid's guilt is at once raised to the level of tragic drama, leaving him with the stained hands of a Medea or a Phaedra (cf. 74). And yet, with the *error* suppressed, his guilt is located

---

[107] Jason alludes to Medea's murder of Absyrtus at *Med.* 1334 (cf. in Ovid *Her.* 12.113–16, *Tr.* 3.9.25–32); Glauce/Creusa is of course murdered by poison (*Med.* 1125–6; cf. in Ovid *A.A.* 1.335, *M.* 7.394) before Medea commits infanticide and flees into exile.

[108] The allusion to Phaedra is, I suggest, possible but not inescapable. For *tabella* as 'a page of a letter' cf. *Am.* 1.11.24, *P.* 4.2.27, but the plural is normally used for 'letter' in all poets. There are parallels between the document described at *P.* 2.9.69–70 and Theseus' description of the letter from Phaedra at E. *Hipp.* 862–5, but these do not prove that the Ovidian document is necessarily a letter. Moreover, Phaedra's letter did not bear a false seal, which is the required mark of criminality in lines 69–70, and we must take her imprint to be *mendax* in the extended sense that it seals the ψευδεῖς γραφάς which are so described by Artemis at *Hipp.* 1311. The usual explanation of lines 69–70 is that they refer to the forging of literary documents or wills, for which see the case of Oppianicus at Cic. *Clu.* 41 and also Juv. 1.67–8 and 8.142.

entirely in the area of literary judgement rather than personal morality: cease to ask my misdemeanour, urges Ovid, *ut lateat sola culpa sub Arte mea* (76).

Lateat here repeats the point ostensibly argued in *Tristia* 2, that Ovid's guilt is not obviously present in the *Ars*. Indeed, in the wider area of Ovidian *ars* as displayed in *P*. 2.9, it is very doubtful whether even a discerning reader and critic like Cotys, a student of *ingenuas artes* (47), would be able to discover any *culpa* at all in what is evidently a subtle and carefully contrived poem. Yet it was in the Ovidian *Ars* that Augustus, the angry *vindex* of line 77, found a sufficiently serious *culpa* to merit a sentence of banishment (78). Is Augustus' judgement of the *Ars* likely to be more reliable than the literary judgement which Cotys is able to bring to the poem? I have argued earlier that a comparison between Cotys and Augustus is implicit from the poem's opening lines. Here, at the climax of the poem, that comparison also reaches its climax, as Augustus is shown to be blind to the sophisticated poetic art of which Cotys has been shown to be such a sympathetic admirer. Cotys can thus be relied on to take *stultam* (73) to mean 'foolishly undertaken' rather than 'lacking in wit and intelligence',[109] and so it is with Cotys that Ovid shares *vicinia* in the sense of a similarity in taste and judgement as well as physical proximity.[110]

The Muses

The most complex of all Ovid's relationships with friends and enemies in the exile poetry is that which he shares with the Muses. In many ways they share the qualities of the closest

---

[109] The adjective causes some surprise to the informed reader, for it is here applied for the first time to the *Ars* itself. It is used again in this way at *P*. 3.3.37, but was earlier used to refer to the witless folly of the poet (cf. *Tr*. 3.8.11), his *mens* (cf. *Tr*. 1.2.100) and his *pectora* (cf. *P*. 1.6.20). In the terms of the rather muddled distinctions proposed in the *OLD* (s.v.), Cotys reads *stultam* (73) in sense 2 and not in sense 1a.

[110] For *vicinia* as 'similarity' see *OLD* s.v. 5. Although the earliest examples given there come from the generation after Ovid, this sense of *vicinia* can easily be adduced from the many earlier examples of a parallel extension to the sense of *vicinus* (cf. *OLD* s.v. 5a) and of *vicinitas* (cf. *OLD* s.v. 4).

and most faithful friends he addresses from Tomis, bringing
necessary relief and alleviating his burden of suffering. His
initial addressee in *Tr.* 3.4 alleviates his grief as a loyal friend
should (*mala vix ulla parte levanda levas*, 42); the ideal is set
out at *P.* 2.7.61 (*recta fides comitum poterat mala nostra le-
vare*); and at *P.* 4.6.43–4 he expresses his gratitude to those
friends who have met that ideal (*mala solliciti nostra levatis*,
44). The Muses are similarly anxious friends, but companions
in exile as well (*sollicitae comites ex Helicone fugae*, *Tr.* 4.1.50;
cf. 20) and so an ever present source of alleviation (cf. *iure
deas igitur veneror mala nostra levantes*, *Tr.* 4.1.49).[111] The
consolation which his committed friends bring him (cf. *nec vos
parva datis pauci solacia nobis*, *P.* 2.7.81) is paralleled by the
solacia which he attributes to his single Muse at *Tr.* 4.10.117
(*tu solacia praebes*). And just as the young Ovid looked upon
Tuticanus as *duxque comesque* (*P.* 4.12.23) in his early years as
a poet, so the Muse is addressed as *dux et comes* in his ad-
vanced years as an exile (*Tr.* 4.10.119).[112]

But Ovid's relationship with his Muse has of course its less
serene side. Torn between love and hate, with the Muses both
the partial cause of his exile and his source of exilic comfort,
he gives way to the anguish of conflicting emotions at *Tr.*
4.1.30: *carmen demens carmine laesus amo*. The poems which
he addresses to faithless friends in the *Tristia* (1.8, 3.11, 4.9,
5.8) and in the *Epistulae ex Ponto* (4.3) counterbalance the
typological picture which he draws of his loyal friends, and by
cursing his worst enemy in the *Ibis* Ovid goes to an extreme
matched only in his relationship with the Muses (cf. *carmina
devoveo Pieridasque meas*, *Tr.* 5.7.32). But whereas Ibis is the
victim of an unmitigated assault which takes Callimachean
venom and obscurantist vilification to new extremes, Ovid
cannot help but cherish the Muses whom he curses and who

---

[111] On the consolatory function of the Muses in exile see Schilling (1972), 209–11,
Lieberg (1980), 20–2 and Stroh (1981), 2644–9.
[112] Cf. Claassen (1986), 305: 'In his "Aeneas" or "Odysseus" roles she is the equivalent of Venus or Athene-Minerva. This Minerva-role is subtly evoked by the use
of *duxque comesque* (*T.* 1.10.10) for both the ship named after Minerva's helmet
(vv. 1, 2) and for his Muse (*T.* 4.10.119).'

help him to curse in the *Ibis* (cf. *cum bene devovi, nequeo tamen esse sine illis*, *Tr*. 5.7.33). While the *Ibis* may share an ambivalent relationship with Ovid's exilic poetics by modifying a number of staple programmatic themes in the *Tristia*,[113] Ovid himself shares with his exilic Muse a love/hate relationship which is yet another adaptation of erotic elegiac motif.

Like Catullus (*odi et amo*, 85.1), Ovid is momentarily caught between love and hate at *Am*. 3.11b.1–2:

> luctantur pectusque leve in contraria tendunt
> hac amor, hac odium; sed, puto, vincit amor.

In the exile poetry Ovid's Muse supplants the elegiac mistress as the instigator of this familiar tension between the simultaneous passions of love and hate.[114] This correlation between Muse and elegiac mistress complements the further correlation which has frequently been drawn between Corinna in the *Amores* and Ovid's wife in the exilic corpus.[115] By addressing his wife in such elegies as *Tr*. 1.6, 3.3 and 5.5, Ovid certainly breaks Roman elegiac convention; but the correlation between Muse and elegiac mistress offers further evidence to suggest that Ovid's break with his erotic past is not as complete as he claims at (e.g.) *Tr*. 5.1.7–8. The familiar apparatus of the elegiac woman continues to make its presence felt in the exile poetry, even though Ovid now shares out her role between the Muse and his wife.

Once the connection is made between Ovid's depiction of his loyal friends and his depiction of the Muses, between the elegiac woman and the Muse, the theme of friendship in the exile poetry assumes a new perspective. By communicating with his friends at Rome, Ovid keeps alive the relationships which his relegation has disrupted; but his perseverance with poetry in Tomis also keeps alive a relationship which is more profound than his friendship with any other addressee in the exilic corpus. Ovid fell under the spell of the Muses in his

---

[113] See G. D. Williams (1992a), 171–89.
[114] See Lieberg (1980), 20 n. 138 for extensive references to Ovid's oscillating attitude to the Muses in exile.
[115] For the latter see (e.g.) Nagle (1980), 43.

early youth (cf. *Tr*. 4.10.19–20), and his love-affair with them survives the disastrous consequences of the *Ars Amatoria* to continue into the wretchedness of his exilic period. Just as this relationship is fraught with tension and the mixed emotions of love and hate in the exile poetry, the exilic elegies themselves thrive on equivalent tension – the mixed complexion of Ovid as a poet in decline and as a poet at the height of his powers, as a poet who denies before his closest friends that he is motivated to write for artistic considerations and who simultaneously shows himself to be the consummate artist.

4

OVID'S TREATMENT OF AUGUSTUS IN
TRISTIA 2

If dissimulation is a recurring phenomenon in Ovid's addresses to his friends in the exile poetry, does it also extend to
his treatment of Augustus? We saw earlier that Ovid's praise
of Augustus and the imperial family in *P.* 4.13 can be read in
a way which alerts us to a discordant hint of irreverence in the
poem, but ambiguously so:[1] is it possible, we ask, to reconcile
that most imposing literary form of imperial Roman culture,
a *recitatio* lauding the emperor, with the hostile and culturally
alien wilderness of Tomis? As we saw, the answer hinges on
the reader's own response to the possible dissimulation detectable in Ovid's tone of voice. *Tristia* 2 poses the same problem,
but on a much larger scale: in what tone(s) of voice does Ovid
address Augustus? Ovid's pose of poetic decline makes for
irony at the expense of his own (recognizably persisting) technical mastery; in *Tristia* 2, however, we shall see that Ovid
proves to be equally adept as an ironist at Augustus' expense.

Behind such terms as 'Augustan' and 'anti-Augustan' in
Ovidian criticism lies the presupposition that a consistent attitude to Augustan political ideology is detectable within the
poetry. One danger of this approach is conveniently summarized by Galinsky, who objects that the terms 'Augustan' and
'anti-Augustan' 'implicitly postulate the primacy of ideological and political values over literary and aesthetic values in
Augustan literature'.[2] Too rigid a characterization of Ovid as
either 'pro-' or 'anti-Augustan' in any given instance rules out
the possibility that he could simultaneously be both or neither, according to the perspective from which a particular text
is read. What, then, of the discordant elements in *P.* 4.13?

---

[1] See p. 98 *supra*.
[2] (1975), 217.

Is Ovid 'Augustan' or 'anti-Augustan', defying or deifying? The answer in this instance is surely that Ovid is ambiguously both and completely neither. But while this flexible approach is usually more persuasive than any rigid characterization, it would be a mistake to conclude that Ovid never shows genuine political interest. Even for an Augustan poet there are ways of being political without being 'pro-' or 'anti-Augustan'. A poet to whose *materia* Roman history and politics (indistinguishable in contemporary ideology) contributed so substantially is likely to benefit from a political dimension to the reading of his work. The form that dimension takes should not be too closely aligned with a particular artistic evaluation of Augustus, whether that of Livy or Tacitus. Ovid does not, in this sense, express a political ideology; he treats a variety of ideological attitudes from the perspective of his own poetic *ingenium*.[3]

A conspicuous passage which has aroused divergent opinions on the role of political ideology in Ovid is his treatment of Augustus in *Metamorphoses* 15. One view is that the poet's flattery of the emperor is 'so grotesque and absurd that its implications cannot possibly be unintentional' and must suggest a 'lack of sincerity and seriousness in Ovid's attitude toward Augustan themes'.[4] But is this lack of seriousness to be interpreted as a rigid ideological comment on the Augustan imperial image and its attendant values? Otis states that 'the heroic and Augustan portions of the *Metamorphoses* are ... intentionally anti-Augustan',[5] and Curran is equally forthright in claiming that the epilogue to the work is firmly 'anti-Augustan'.[6]

A more balanced judgement is offered by Little, who argues

---

[3] But gauging 'ideological attitude' presents its own difficulties; see now Kennedy (1992), 26–58.

[4] Galinsky (1967), 181–2. For similar views on various aspects of *Metamorphoses* 15 see Coleman (1971), 476, Holleman (1969), 49 and Moulton (1973), 6 with Claassen (1987), 43 n. 3 for further bibliography.

[5] (1970), viii. Cf. Otis (1966), 339: 'in the way he felt and thought about the world, Ovid was fundamentally anti-Augustan'.

[6] (1972), 71–91, also following Coleman (1971), 477 in raising the possibility that the *Metamorphoses* contributed to Ovid's exile.

TREATMENT OF AUGUSTUS IN *TRISTIA* 2

that the *Metamorphoses* is a 'non-Augustan' poem, by which
he means that Ovid was indifferent both to Augustus and
to conventional Augustanism as a poetic theme.[7] Little's approach offers a welcome alternative to the crude enforce-
ment of such antithetical terms as 'Augustanism' and 'anti-
Augustanism'; in the *Metamorphoses* Ovid treats Augustus as
a theme which he can playfully manipulate, and such treatment need not presuppose an initial ideological position on
Ovid's part. Galinsky sees this point in his discussion of the
possible overtones of the Cipus episode at *M*. 15.565–621,
rightly warning against labelling Ovid as ideologically 'anti-
Augustan': 'It would amount to attributing to Ovid a sense of
political involvement which was alien to him, whereas his true
inclination, that of the *lusor*, the poet of *nequitia*, was to play
on Augustan conventions, to refuse to take them seriously,
and to exploit them for his comic purposes. At times this
procedure could lead to a mockery of the *princeps* himself.'[8]
On this reading, to call Ovid irreverent in his treatment of
Augustus is hardly equivalent to calling him a committed and
active opponent of Augustan ideology.

Galinsky's view offers a useful working hypothesis, but it
needs to be qualified in two respects. First, however exclusively artistic we judge Ovid's intentions to have been, there
can be no certainty that those subtle, ludic ambivalences were
in fact appreciated by Augustus in the spirit in which they
were written. What we know of Augustus' reaction to the *Ars
Amatoria* as portrayed in *Tristia* 2 suggests that the opposite
may have been the case. Secondly, Galinsky restricts his view
to Ovid's attitude to the Augustan question. As we saw
earlier, acceptance of Galinsky's hypothesis does not preclude
the possibility that Ovid expresses a position, which may
fairly be termed 'political', towards the broader spectrum of
Roman history and society which contributed so much to the
material of the *Fasti* and the later books of the *Metamorphoses*. Whatever the emperor may have wished, 'Augustus'

---

[7] (1972), 389–401, especially 400.
[8] (1967), 182.

was never, in Ovid's eyes, symbolically identified with the whole of Rome's institutions, history and *mores*.

It remains to be seen on what criterion we can justifiably claim that Ovid's treatment of Augustus is playfully ambivalent in passages which at first appear to contain nothing but imperial flattery. Ovid does not do the reader's work for him; the audience is left to activate the subtle nuances which complicate the initial impact of his panegyric. In his discussion of *M*. 15.750–8, Hinds offers a fine illustration of the ambivalence which can arise from reading a different nuance in Ovid's phraseology.[9] The particle *scilicet* (752), which can signal either an evidently absurd proposition or an evidently true one,[10] invites a double reading of lines 752–8. If we take *scilicet* in the former sense, the passage reads as follows: it is absurd to believe that Julius Caesar's military exploits are more important than the fathering of Augustus. But the length and impact of Ovid's all-conquering list in lines 752–7 may equally lead us to suspect that Caesar's exploits *are* in fact more significant than his fathering of Augustus. Hinds neatly balances the alternative readings: 'Evident absurdity; or evident truth?'[11] The passage can be viewed as either flattering panegyric or irreverent humour according to the perspective from which it is read. How, then, do we decide between the alternatives? Hinds is right to insist that neither sense can demonstrate its exclusive claim on our attention.[12] The reader's response is thus enriched – if also at first a little disconcerted – when the balanced alternatives are recognized, so that a choice between them would impose unnecessary limits on the text. And yet the superficial impression of effusive eulogy protects Ovid from the emperor's displeasure; although he exploits verbal ambivalence to witty effect, he equips himself with what Hinds terms his 'hermeneutic al-

9 (1987a), 24–6.
10 See *OLD* s.v. 2 ('as particle, in affirming an obvious fact') and 4 ('iron., in suggesting something palpably impossible or absurd') with the examples cited.
11 (1987a), 25.
12 *Ibid.*: 'The real error, into which critics on both sides tend to fall, is to imagine that the matter is susceptible of final proof either way. It is not.'

ibi'[13] to evade the charge of deliberate flippancy. He writes in such a way that the alert reader is invited, while the unsympathetic reader is not forced, to view the text from more than one perspective.

The ambivalence which complicates Ovid's representation of Augustus in *Metamorphoses* 15 also complicates his treatment of the emperor in the exile poetry. It has been argued that Ovid flatters Augustus in the *Tristia* and *Epistulae ex Ponto* simply to win his favour;[14] but the dividing line between Ovidian flattery and impudence is thin, and Ovid treads gingerly on this line in *Tristia* 2.

Establishing an approach

The influence of rhetorical figures on Ovid's compositional technique is commonly recognized and associated with the stylistic tendencies of the age: '[Ovide] modèle et travestit la rhétorique qu'on lui a enseignée. Il ne s'agit plus d'un exercice, mais d'une activité ludique au sens le plus noble du mot. Le poète joue ... lorsqu'il polit son style et renouvelle quelques-unes des figures traditionnelles. Et, dans le temps, la situation d'Ovide apparaît comme exceptionnelle puisque c'est approximativement à l'époque d'Auguste que s'accomplit la fusion entre poétique et rhétorique.'[15] In making this last point, Viarre is following Barthes' well known view of the development of rhetoric into a 'techné poétique', or creative art, under Augustus.[16] We do not have to go along fully with Barthes – surely too little poetry survives from the second half of Augustus' reign to make generalizations of any kind – to accept Viarre's basic point. It is not a point I can explore exhaustively here, but I propose to bring out something of the complexity of Ovid's treatment of Augustus by explaining

---

[13] (1987a), 26.
[14] See, e.g., G. Williams (1978), 97: 'Here is the finished creation of an Augustan poetic mystique of ruler worship.'
[15] Viarre (1976), 55.
[16] Barthes (1970), 172–223, especially 178.

that treatment in part as the skilful application of a rhetorical figure.

In his analysis of the σχήματα λέξεως, the author of the treatise Περὶ ἑρμηνείας, long attributed to Demetrius of Phalerum but now thought to have been written by another Peripatetic possibly during Ovid's lifetime,[17] discusses the figure of ambivalent allusiveness (τὸ ἐσχηματισμένον, *Eloc.* 287). Figured speech enables a writer to make an apparently simple statement which has, with a greater or lesser degree of concealment, other possible meanings placed there by the author for the reader to discover.[18] It was evidently in very common use, being regularly mixed with 'low, and (so to say) suggestive, innuendo' (μετὰ ἐμφάσεως ἀγεννοῦς ἅμα καὶ οἷον ἀναμνηστικῆς),[19] suggesting a tonal fusion which may have appealed to Ovid.

Two different applications of the figure are demonstrated, each of which is also distinguished by Quintilian. Both are in different ways relevant to Ovid, though only one is conspicuously evident in his treatment of Augustus in *Tristia* 2. The first application is the prudent and subtle modification of outspoken criticism directed at tyrants and popular assemblies (cf. *Eloc.* 289, 290, 293, 294). Self-preservation is the priority (hence the figure is sometimes termed λόγος ἀσφαλής, 293), and the examples given illustrate how even the direct censuring of tyrants can be tempered with an irony which averts a punitive response. Quintilian similarly advocates using the figure, *si dicere palam parum tutum est* (*Inst.* 9.2.66–8). Such circumstances require the successful critic to make his reproach with a gentle whiff of irony to prevent natural resentment becoming vindictive (*in illos tyrannos bene dixeris, quia periculum tantum, non etiam offensa vitatur*, 67). The practice of such manipulative skill is *dicere aperte* rather than *dicere palam*.[20]

[17] For this dating see Easterling and Knox (1985), 859, but the precise date is not relevant to my argument.

[18] See Ahl (1984), 174–208, with a brief history of the figure on 187f.

[19] *Eloc.* 287; the rendering is that of Rhys Roberts (1902), 199. For the common use of the figure see also Quint. *Inst.* 9.2.65.

[20] For the distinction see Ahl (1984), 193.

TREATMENT OF AUGUSTUS IN *TRISTIA* 2

The dominant impression left by *Tristia* 2 as well as *Metamorphoses* 15, however, is not one of subtly modified criticism of the emperor, but, notoriously, of scarcely veiled flattery. An examination of the apparent adulation in the eulogy of Augustus' imperial successes or literary sensibility reveals that Ovid is here practising the other application of this figure, ambivalence in meaning (ἐπαμφοτερισμός, cf. *Eloc.* 291). This is the art of making criticism seem the unintentional by-product of something else (ψόγοι εἰκαιόψογοι, *ibid.*),[21] an art which is illustrated by the tone said to have been used in Aeschines Socraticus' dialogue *Telauges*: πᾶσα γὰρ σχεδὸν ἡ περὶ τὸν Τηλαυγῆ διήγησις ἀπορίαν παρέχοι, εἴτε θαυμασμὸς εἴτε χλευασμός ἐστι (*ibid.*). This ambivalence of tone, εἶδος ἀμφίβολον (*ibid.*), can be suitably applied to Ovid's address to Augustus, where a eulogistic intent can sometimes hardly be distinguished from a satirical one. The effect on the reader is to shake his complacent assumptions about the poetry and to put the sophistication of his literary sensibility to the test, while the imperial addressee is also the unwitting object of the poet's equivocal criticism: νουθετεῖται ἀκούων ἅμα καὶ οὐ λοιδορεῖται (292). For Quintilian, the critical potential of the ambivalence lies in a kind of sub-meaning, *aliud latens et auditori quasi inveniendum* (*Inst.* 9.2.65), activating in the recipient a suspicious response through which *quod non dicimus accipi volumus* (*ibid.*). Subtle ambiguity of this sort is usually distinguished from εἰρωνεία,[22] where contrasting meanings are more obviously contradictory.

Also applicable to Ovid may be the additional motive which Quintilian ascribes to the user of the figure. To the two traditional motives of refinement of taste (εὐπρέπεια) and personal security (ἀσφάλεια) which he shares with the *De Elocutione* (cf. 287), Quintilian adds a third. He proposes that the skilled user may have a purely artistic motive for resorting to the figure (*tertius [usus est] qui venustatis modo gratia adhibe-*

---

[21] I follow Rhys Roberts' interpretation of Victorius' boldly contrived emendation εἰκαιόψογοι ('censures which seem unintentional hits', (1902), 201).
[22] As at *Eloc.* 291 and Quint. *Inst.* 9.2.65.

tur et ipsa novitate ac varietate magis quam si relatio sit recta delectat (*Inst.* 9.2.66). The use of the figure to attract a sophisticated readership through subtle ambivalence accords well with Ovid's own depiction of his erotic poems as *deliciae*.[23] Augustus had allegedly viewed these *deliciae* as sexually licentious and socially irresponsible, reading them with a literal eye; but the audience sympathetic to the Ovidian *ingenium* responds to the same *deliciae* as exemplifying the use of such rhetorical figures as ambivalence and searches out the hidden sense. This is also the style with which Ovid will address Augustus in *Tristia* 2. To return briefly to *M*. 15.752–8, the ambivalence of tone which Hinds rightly detects here is dependent on the reader finding an unexpected twist (*aliud latens*), which mischievously counteracts his initial impression of the glory being heaped on Augustus through the portrayal of Julius Caesar's imperial conquests. The offence such a reading might cause to the imperial dynasty would not endanger the poet since the section can also be interpreted as unreserved flattery, so that on Hinds' reading it is difficult to tell εἴτε θαυμασμὸς εἴτε χλευασμός ἐστι. Ovid's artistic motivation is now irrecoverable, but Quintilian makes it at least as likely that his aim was to attract a sophisticated readership as, in any real and urgent way, to save his own skin.

Although *Tristia* 2 contains extended illustrations of Ovid's use of figured speech, recent scholarship has found a tone of undisguised irreverence towards Augustus. Marache, for example, views the poem as directly subversive because of the assertive argumentation which Ovid uses to defend the *Ars Amatoria* against the charge of immorality,[24] while Evans states that that defence is 'a *reductio ad absurdum* designed to amuse its readers and ridicule the emperor's decision to relegate him because of the poem [the *Ars*]'.[25] Vulikh goes further, claiming that Ovid speaks out against the despotism of

---

[23] So *Tr*. 2.78, 349, 5.1.15; cf. 4.1.35, *nos quoque delectant, quamvis nocuere, libelli.* For the wider application of *deliciae* see *TLL* 5.447.6ff.

[24] (1958), 412–19.

[25] (1983), 16, paraphrasing Wilkinson (1955), 311.

Augustus, attacking him not for his statesmanship but for his attitude to literature and poets.[26] Elsewhere Vulikh argues that Ovid revolts against imperial vindictiveness, setting the power of his poetic genius against the inflexible authority of Augustus, so that the poem becomes a battleground between ruler and writer, 'entre le pouvoir despotique et le génie poétique'.[27]

These three positions, the French, American and Russian, illustrate with different emphases the inviolable status accorded the poet in modern, post-revolutionary cultures. Their caricature of Augustus as an artistic tyrant is complemented by the caricature of the poet himself as the lone voice appealing for freedom of expression. But just as this portrait of Ovid is created by the poet himself, so also is the portrait of Augustus. To take sides with the self-caricature of the poet against his caricature of the emperor may be to enter into the spirit of the poem, but it is not criticism. Nevertheless, it is true that Ovid displays a confident assurance in his defence of the *Ars Amatoria*. The tone is matched by a continued confidence in his poetic skill, and the imaginative subtlety with which this skill continues to be practised is the most impressive aspect of *Tristia* 2. As a preliminary to developing this point, the balanced structure which here provides the basis for Ovid's portrayal of his downfall must first be outlined.

Ovid presents his life before his relegation as following the familiar pattern, long advocated by writers of ethical treatises, of a delicate balance between extremes. Every facet of that life seems to exhibit the Roman virtue of *mediocritas*, that 'persistent ideal of the poets',[28] though it is not in Ovid's manner to be dogmatic, as Horace is in the ode to Murena (*C.* 2.10). Both poets treat the physical environment as symbolically indicative of an inner self-restraint. Ovid's house may have been small, but it was not undistinguished (111–12); it could not be singled out for its wealth or its poverty, *unde sit in neutrum*

---

[26] (1968), 160.

[27] (1968a), 382.

[28] Nisbet and Hubbard (1978), 160 on *C.* 2.10.5 (*mediocritatem*), supporting the remark with a range of parallels.

conspiciendus eques (114); of modest means (115), it rears off-spring like itself. Ovid performs his civic duties in such a way that though he fails to win renown for his services, he does not commit any culpable offence (91–2). Without claiming to have acted well in his judicial capacities, his insistence that it was no mistake to entrust cases to him as a member of the centumviral court suggests the competence that brings neither acclaim nor criticism (93–4); as referee in the settlement of private cases, he remains impartial and acts *sine crimine* (95) in dispensing justice. That even unsuccessful defendants acknowledge his fairness (96) may be mentioned to remind Augustus of the standard he must adhere to in judging Ovid's own appeal. In short, *tutus* (98) characterizes Ovid's status at Rome, moderately successful in positions of moderate significance.

What upsets the balanced tenor of this domestic and public *mediocritas* is, of course, the fatal extremity to which Ovid was carried by his poetic *ingenium*. Its excessive display (cf. *nimium*, 117) has won him a *grande ... nomen* (118) which transcends his modest family origins (115). *Certe* (116) is as ironic as it is assertive: the blind following of an inner impulse beyond the familiar path of *mediocritas* (the Actaeon simile of lines 105–6 is suggestive here) leads Ovid, as it led Icarus, to the ruinous consequences of his own irresponsibility.[29] By his fall from grace, Ovid loses the stability that characterized his formerly uncontroversial existence. Now hope comes and goes (*spes mihi magna subit ... spes mihi ... cadit*, 147–8), now his fears come and go with equally unpredictable variation (153), as fickle as the winds when there is no *aequalis rabies continuusque furor* (150). Like the storm, Ovid is deprived of a consistent continuity as he endures extreme hardship (*ultima perpetior*, 187) in the geographical extreme of Tomis (*nec quisquam patria longius exul abest*, 188; cf. 193–4). His plea is for the granting of *mitius exilium ... propiusque* (185), a partial restoration of the stabilizing centre.

---

[29] For the idea cf. *Tr.* 2.2 and *Ibis* 6. Icarus neglects the forceful instruction to keep to the *via media* (cf. *inter utrumque vola!*, *M.* 8.206; cf. *Tr.* 3.4.21–4 and 1.1.87–90).

These familiar themes of moderation and centrality do more than provide the joint structure for Ovid's conception of his life and relegation. They relate this conception to the want of sound and balanced judgement which finds fault with the *Ars*. That there is a kind of conceptual correlation between this lack of judgement and the immoderate extremity he faces in Tomis goes without saying: his structured approach to both is strikingly similar. In Ovid's imagination both are conceived as a radical dislocation of the natural balance, just as they share potentially menacing consequences for the poet himself.

The assessment of the readers' powers of discrimination implicitly given in lines 265–74, where it is thinly disguised by standard clichés, well illustrates this point. Casually using the conventional Stoic term for the faculty of discrimination, Ovid maintains that his poem will harm no one, *recta si mente legatur* (275). The unbalanced reading of texts by those lacking *recta mens* has consequences as potentially hurtful (cf. 266) as the loss of balance which underlies Ovid's conception of his fall from favour and exile. The conventional examples (267–74) which support the advantages of balanced judgement[30] are reinforced by an instance of the opposite: the judgement which concludes that Ovid corrupts his female readers is false (277), the error being ascribed to unbalanced reading (*nimium scriptis adrogat ille meis*, 278). In this way Ovid fashions his picture of the balanced reader, as he would of course ideally like Augustus to be.

The significant point is his claim that the *Ars Amatoria* is morally neutral and harmless if read with 'right understanding'. The contrast between right and wrong understanding is brought out in the contrast between *recta mens* (cf. 275) and the corruptibility of *perversae mentes* (cf. 301). In either case, Ovid's contention is that he is not responsible for the reader's reaction to his work. This same argument underlies his depic-

---

[30] These are standard examples of μέσα used in instruction (e.g. ἰατρική in Chrysippus; see *SVF* 3.741–2) to illustrate ἀδιάφορα (see *SVF* 3.117–23, where ὑγίεια figures prominently). *Recta mens* is the Stoic ὀρθὸς λόγος (called *recta ratio* by Cic. *Leg.* 1.12.33) which distinguishes κατορθώματα from ἁμαρτήματα (see *SVF* 3.500–2). Ovid is not, of course, philosophizing, but offering a kind of παραίνεσις in the Stoic fashion in order to defend the *Ars Amatoria*.

tion of the Circus, the porticoes and the temples (279ff.). Each of these has the potential to corrupt, *semina ... nequitiae* (279–80), though this phrase is used here to contradict the point made in the context where it originally appears. At *Am.* 3.4.9–10 Ovid argues that simply allowing people to do what they want weakens the potential for wrongdoing (*ipsa potestas|semina nequitiae languidiora facit*), where the context – a paraclausithyron – clearly suggests for *semina nequitiae* the more restricted accompanying sense of 'sexual misconduct'. Something of the latter sense carries over to *Tr.* 2.279–80, where the argument is turned on its head: now it is the easy opportunity which excites and even promotes sexual licence in the theatre, the porticoes and the Circus. Yet Ovid stresses the absurdity of suggesting that each does nothing *but* corrupt, or that those who frequent such places are all morally suspect. Such a view would be as unbalanced as the claim that these places were never sullied by any corruption. If, however, the *Ars* is assessed with *balanced* judgement, the penalty he has paid for its composition will in turn be shown to be as extreme as the judgement which imposed it – a judgement which was erratic and based on an unbalanced reading of the text.

Ovid's argument here is not merely designed to suggest a poetic parallel; it claims to make a valid point. Dickinson represents the quandary of many: 'How one reacts to this book of the *Tristia* may well depend on one's reaction to the *Ars Amatoria*.'[31] If, like Owen or Kenney,[32] one takes the view that the *Ars Amatoria* is of dubious moral character, then it is hard to sympathize with Ovid's argument. That argument may be elaborated as follows: the disposition (ἕξις) which makes certain people liable to perform certain actions, 'depraved' or not, is activated by an external stimulus, which may be a place, a book or the like. The variations in the ἕξις activated in this way explain why certain people react differently to the same external stimulus. As the author (or man-

[31] (1973), 173.
[32] Owen (1924), 55; Kenney (1958), 208: 'it was an immoral and subversive work, and not all the specious pleading of the Second Book of the *Tristia* can disguise that it would tend to foster adultery'.

ager of the circuses or the architect of the porticoes) is responsible for the stimulus but not for the individual ἕξις, he cannot
be held responsible for the outcome which is a combination of
both, unless it is his declared intention to achieve precisely
that outcome. As long as his declared intention is different,
and that intention is actually realized in a substantial body of
people, he cannot be held culpable for the perverse reaction of
a certain proportion of people, even if he could reasonably
have foreseen such a reaction among this group.

So far, Ovid's position may seem defensible, if not fully
persuasive. But it is shaky on two counts, and it may not be
unreasonable to suppose that a mind of Ovid's sophistication
could not fail to be alert to these points. First, the *Ars* is of
course a parody of the didactic genre. It is customary for a
didactic poem to contain a προτροπή/*exhortatio* to take up
and excel in the activity in question (hunting, star-gazing etc.).
Whatever Ovid may claim, a protreptic intention may fairly
be deduced from a didactic format.[33] If this is the case here,
then we are beginning to cross the grey area between the illustration of depravity and incitement to commit it. True, only a
parody may be intended, but Ovid may be assumed to realize
that the distinction between *seria* and *lusus* is even less keenly
perceived in the minds of the majority than that between
fact and fiction. Secondly, the situations described in the *Ars
Amatoria*, themselves evidently the product of a sharply ob-
servant imagination, can easily extend to provide a situational
framework for self-indulgent fantasy. But as this latter feature
is also to be found in most Roman love elegy, it is difficult to
see why the *Ars Amatoria* should be singled out for criticism
unless the protreptic mode, which is so much more strongly in
evidence here, was decisive in weighing the scales against the
poem. In this light Ovid's defence is in fact much weaker than
it might at first appear.

[33] This is not, of course, to suggest that poets like Virgil or Ovid had a serious
didactic purpose (see now Thomas (1988), I 4); but might such a purpose be
assumed by those unfamiliar with the sophistication of Roman poets' treatment
of the genre?

But if, like Hollis,[34] we regard the *Ars Amatoria* more favourably, Ovid's argument in defence of the poem can be read in another, more favourable light. Compare D. H. Lawrence's defence of the supposed indecency of his work in his essay 'Pornography and Obscenity'. Pornography is a relative term, debased by popular prejudice and rash presuppositions. Lawrence terms such popular prejudice 'mob-reaction', and commenting on 'the so-called obscene words', he illustrates the irresponsibility of mob-reaction in a way which has direct bearing on Ovid's defence of the *Ars Amatoria*: 'When it comes to the so-called obscene words, I should say that hardly one person in a million escapes mob-reaction. The first reaction is almost sure to be mob-reaction, mob-indignation, mob-condemnation. And the mob gets no further. But the real individual has second thoughts and says: Am I really shocked? Do I *really* feel outraged and indignant? And the answer of any individual is bound to be: No, I am not shocked, not outraged, nor indignant. I know the word, and take it for what it is, and I am not going to be jockeyed into making a mountain out of a molehill, not for all the law in the world.'[35] The crucial words are 'making a mountain out of a molehill'; Lawrence's appeal for a sense of perspective, liberated from the strict constraints of official censorship or the puritanical prejudices of mob-reaction, closely resembles a central aspect of Ovid's defence of the *Ars* in *Tristia* 2.[36] Ovid's appeal for balanced judgement is echoed in Lawrence's preference for 'second thoughts' and the rejection of extreme reactions such as outrage and indignation. Both writers also know the 'menacing constraint of official censorship', and one

---

[34] (1973), 84–6: 'no Roman could well have considered it [the *Ars Amatoria*] obscene; their tradition, both in oratory and in verse, was for considerable frankness in sexual matters ... The most one can fairly say is that the general atmosphere of the *Ars* was unhelpful to Augustus' policy of moral reform.'

[35] Lawrence (1961), 63–4.

[36] Cf. 301–2, *omnia perversas possunt corrumpere mentes:|stant tamen illa suis omnia tuta locis*, where the first *omnia* need not denote only the places which Ovid has just mentioned as possible agencies of moral corruption (279–300). His point is more general, taking up the point made at 267–76: all things have the power to corrupt, the *Ars* included, depending on how they are perceived or applied.

of the readers of his work whose sensibility Ovid sets out to refine is of course Augustus himself. He challenges the emperor in *Tristia* 2 with a poem as richly allusive as the *Ars*, while Lawrence writes for his discriminating audience of 'real individuals', and not to win over the repressive authoritarians lurking in the background.

Different critics, then, react to the *Ars Amatoria* in different ways. Ovid's argument that reading the poem with balanced judgement (275) prevents it from being taken as a stimulus to moral corruption has important implications for our reading of *Tristia* 2 and Ovid's treatment of Augustus. Is there, on the analogy of the *Ars*, a correct perspective or balanced approach which we should bring to reading its apologia? I suggest that a key argument in Ovid's defence of the *Ars* (265–76) is directly relevant to our understanding of *Tristia* 2: according to the different perspectives from which the poem is read, Ovid can be regarded as either flattering or irreverent in his portrayal of the emperor. The functional ambivalence ascribed to fire in lines 267–8 equally applies to Hinds' analysis of *M*. 15.752–8: in each case the reader/user is left to resolve for himself the ambivalence inherent in the poem/material. The reader, then, and not the poet, must take responsibility for the view of Augustus he carries away from *M*. 15.752–8, and just as Ovid claims (*Tr.* 2.275–6) that the *Ars* will not corrupt those who read with *recta mens*, so those who read *Metamorphoses* 15 with suitable reverence need see no more than a display of obsequious flattery. The implicit ambiguities in Ovid's apparent devotion to the imperial cause will attract only *perversas mentes* (to borrow Ovid's own words) with a capacity for relishing irreverent wit. Such playful manipulation of the εἶδος ἀμφίβολον, whose critical pedigree was considered earlier, continues actively to characterize the Ovidian *ingenium* in *Tristia* 2.

Ovid's mischievous Muse

At *Tr.* 2.353–8 Ovid bases his claim to moral probity on a distinction which is itself a specious poetic ploy, namely the

distinction between the 'unreality' of the projected persona of
the poet in his poetry and the 'reality' of the alleged private
life of the poet outside his poetry. The speciousness of this
distinction is emphasized by our finding this 'real', extra-
poetical persona unveiled to us in the very kind of poetical
construction where the *Musa iocosa* is a dominant influence
and where, on the poet's own admission (355), his assertions
should not be confused with statements of fact. Thus Ovid's
position in these lines is like that of the man who says, 'To be
frank, I regularly tell lies. Do believe me, I regularly tell lies.'
When poetry disclaims (as Ovid does in lines 354–5) any close
relation with 'objective' truth, we are reluctant to give credence to *any* supposed assertions of fact which the poet makes
in his verse. Nor was Ovid the first to play this trick with the
poetic ego. Indeed, the fact that Catullus had made exactly
the same claim before him (cf. 16.5–6) helps us to appreciate
that Ovid not only asserts the self-contradiction of an extra-
poetical persona in these lines, but works partly within established literary precedent as well.[37]

Another implication may be usefully drawn from lines 353–
8. *Magna ... pars mendax operum est et ficta meorum* (355):
although these words are taken by Owen and Luck to refer to
the situational episodes of the *Amores*,[38] I see little justification for this limited point of reference, for Ovid is anxious to
state that it is the material of the *Ars Amatoria* in particular
which is beyond the ambit of his experience (cf. 345–8). But
the relevance of line 355 need hardly be restricted just to the
situational episodes of the *Ars Amatoria*, since a generaliza-
tion of this kind suggests that there are no clear boundaries to
the range and complexity of the fiction within an Ovidian
poem. If, however, we momentarily accept the limitation on
the range of reference in line 355, a line which could apply
with equal validity to the *Heroides*, *Metamorphoses* and much
of the *Fasti* (and possibly even the *Tristia*), another question

[37] Ovid draws the same distinction between his 'real' and 'poetic' personalities at *Tr.*
1.9.59–60 and *P.* 2.7.47–50. Cf. Plin. *Ep.* 4.14.4–5, Mart. 1.4.8, 11.15.13, Apul.
Apol. 11.
[38] Owen (1924), 198; Luck (1977), II 132 *ad loc.*

arises. When the *Ars Amatoria* is not to be considered a true reflection of the poet's own character (cf. *nec liber indicium est animi*, 357), but a fictitious invention written to offer a respectable kind of entertainment (*honesta voluptas*, 357)[39] and to please the ears of his audience (358), what implication does this have for his treatment of Augustus?

As soon as Ovid argues that the material of the *Ars* is not a valid depiction of his personal character, the extent to which *any* of his material can be taken as truly reflecting a real inner self is immediately open to question. Since, then, the *Ars Amatoria* seems to have taken on a life of its own (cf. *plus sibi permisit*, 356), morally different from and independent of its *compositor* (356), Ovid's disavowal of its contents as largely deceitful fiction (355) does not leave him with a position from which he can convincingly discriminate between some parts of his poetic material and others. In lines 65–6, for example, he claims that Augustus will find his name glorified in the *Metamorphoses* (*vestri praeconia nominis*), along with many pledges of the poet's devotion to him (*invenies animi pignora multa mei*); again, in lines 561–2 he states that on perusal of the same work Augustus will see *quo ... favore animi teque tuosque canam*. What confidence can we have in Ovid's supposedly sincere statements of loyalty to the *princeps* in view of the self-revealing (or self-betraying?) qualification which is introduced in line 355 with no evident limit set to its possible range of application? Indeed, what confidence can we have in the very claim that the *Ars* is not representative of his true disposition (353) when he states in the next couplet that much of what he writes is fiction?

Despite the ostensible argument which they present in Ovid's defence, then, lines 353–8 are disconcerting in their possible implications. Their basic complexity lies in the diffi-

---

[39] Though most editors accept *voluntas* in 357, I am inclined to read *voluptas* with Burman's text of 1727 (drawn from Heinsius and supported by at least two important mss), taking Ovid's point to be one of twofold defence: the *Ars* is not a reflection of his own character (*indicium animi*), but a form of entertainment (*voluptas*) which is ludic – without being lewd (cf. *honesta*). Diggle (1980), 417–18 offers further arguments in favour of *voluptas*.

culty of sustaining in verse the credibility of an extra-poetical persona which is the antithesis of the poem's ego. Ovid *needs* this new dimension to the meaning of his text in order to avert the condemnation which a superficial and unsophisticated reading of the *Ars Amatoria* would, by implication, inevitably produce. But Ovid's defence leaves him with a new problem. He defends the *Ars* by appealing to the benefits of a reading which is alive to the disjunction between poet and poetic persona; but he invites us to believe that in lines 353–8 poet and poetic persona are as one. His defence can only stand if it is read without the kind of literary sophistication which that defence calls for to vindicate the *Ars*.

The dangers (or delusions) of reading *Tristia* 2 in this simplistic way are evident as early as lines 29–76, part of the *probatio* of Ovid's formal plea to the *princeps*.[40] Dickinson comments that in this section of the poem 'the poet is meek and repentant: awe of Augustus' power and large slices of flattery are mingled with firm legal arguments'.[41] Such a claim gives Ovid what Hinds would call his 'hermeneutic alibi', the impression of subservient reverence which disguises his less complimentary insinuations. Take, for example, the familiar association which Ovid draws between Augustus and Jupiter, the ruler on earth and the ruler of the gods (Jupiter is termed *genitorque deum rectorque*, 37; cf. Augustus, *patriae rector . . . paterque*, 39). In lines 40–1 Ovid writes *utere more dei nomen habentis idem.|idque facis*. High praise, indeed; in managing his domain, Augustus acts in the manner appropriate to a god. But does the injunction in line 40 initially imply that Augustus does not in fact act in the manner proper to his station? And are the words *idque facis* in line 41 added as a hasty corrective, to remove that implication? Remove the im-

---

[40] On the rhetorical divisions of *Tristia* 2 (*exordium*, 1–26; *propositio*, 27–8; *tractatio* with various subdivisions, 29–578) see Owen (1924), 48–54, Dickinson (1973),172 and Focardi (1975), 87–105; the *probatio* (29–154) presents (in Owen's words) 'the proof by evidence that the poet deserves mercy' (p. 49).
[41] (1973), 172. Cf. Evans (1983), 15: 'Ovid at first presents standard panegyric'.

plication they do – but only *after* it has been raised, however fleetingly.[42]

In lines 61ff. Ovid invites Augustus to peruse his writings in order to see just how many times the poet mentions his name; the supposition is that such personal references offer proof of Ovid's devotion to the *princeps*. As Ford observes,[43] however, a hint of insincerity underlies Ovid's suggestion that Augustus should consult the *Ars Amatoria* for regular references to himself; he is rarely mentioned in the work (cf. 1.77,197, 203, 3.116, 389–92, 614). Could it be that this anomaly is designed to suggest to the informed reader (who would of course know the *Ars* well) that Augustus is still unfamiliar with the content of a work which formed the basis of his sentence on Ovid? I would see here an early reference by implication to the emperor's ignorance of the *Ars*, anticipating a point which is developed explicitly in lines 219ff. and to which we will return. When Ovid subsequently directs Augustus to the *Metamorphoses* (63–4), his obsequious tone again harbours a less than favourable implication. *Inspice maius opus, ... in non credendos corpora versa modos*: is Augustus' apotheosis, anticipated at *M.* 15.868–70 (cf. *Tr.* 2.57), to be included among those bodily transformations of the *Metamorphoses* which take place *in non credendos ... modos*, in astonishing and fantastic ways – or, perhaps more pertinently, in ways which are simply *not* to be believed?[44]

After claiming that he has shown his devotion to Augustus by celebrating him in his poetry, Ovid goes on to suggest that this should win him the emperor's favour: even Jupiter, despite all his superior advantages, derives pleasure from hearing his achievements being celebrated in verse (69–72). Again,

---

[42] Cf. Davisson (1979), 54 on 143–6: 'the speaker reminds Augustus that, since Jove often allows stricken victims to recover, he too will hope for mercy even if Augustus forbids hope. Thus the speaker distinguishes between Jove and Augustus, holding up the former as an example to the latter and implying that Augustus' mercy is not yet perfect.'

[43] (1977), 22.

[44] Cf. Davisson (1979), 101 on 64: 'One might wonder if the praises of Augustus supposedly contained in the *Met.* (*Trist.* 2.65) are also not intended to be credible.' For the construction *in ... modos* as equivalent to *non credendis modis* see Owen (1924), 133 *ad loc.*

Ovid's tone appears to be polite and deferential in anticipation of winning Augustus' compliance; if Jupiter enjoys having his deeds celebrated in verse, then so should Augustus. But several qualifications must be entered here. First, the *facta Iovis* celebrated in verse invariably include reference to the defeat of the Giants, and there is strong literary evidence to suggest that this was made a significant point in the mythical elaboration of the Augustus–Jupiter comparison.[45] Ovid, however, explicitly dissociates his praise of Augustus from an epic celebration of the emperor's heroic *facta* (529–32), just as he is drawn away from a Gigantomachy in his treatment of Jupiter in *Am.* 2.1; moreover, the style and brevity of the treatment of the gigantomachic theme at *M.* 1.151ff. hardly support Buchheit's view that Ovid here treated the theme and its implied comparison with heroic seriousness.[46] Ovid's reluctance to develop the heroic aspect of the Augustus–Jupiter comparison is a really disabling, self-imposed limitation (especially for those who think that Ovid undertook such a comparison in full earnest), for he thus debars himself from treating, except by implication, a major feature of the Augustan myth – and very few would now go along with Owen in listing a Gigantomachy among Ovid's lost works.[47]

Another qualification concerns the celebration of imperial/divine *fama*. Is Ovid exploiting the solemn Pindaric point that rulers depend for their *fama* upon poetry, and that by celebrating Augustus he deserves the latter's recognition of his faithful service? If the point were pressed, it could even be claimed that Ovid tacitly warns the *princeps* not to bite the hand that feeds the imperial ego, or that he exploits the irony implicit in the way he, Augustus' subject, makes Augustus the celebrated subject of his poetry. More striking, however, is the ironic insinuation in *iuvat* (70) and *laetum laudibus ... suis* (72). In stating that Jupiter derives pleasure from having his deeds celebrated in verse, Ovid implicitly refers to the gratification of a ruler whose vanity is satisfied by the poet; the

---

[45] Cf. Fraenkel (1957), 281–3 and p. 190 and n. 69 *infra*.
[46] Buchheit (1966), 80–108.
[47] Owen (1924), 65.

further implication is that the celebration of Augustus in poetry appeals just as much to the emperor's own form of Jovian
vanity.

In these various ways Ovid's mischievous Muse allows his
Augustan text to be viewed from more than one perspective.
But in *Tristia* 2 as a whole, and most obviously and succinctly
in line 354, Ovid juxtaposes what he portrays as his playful
Muse with what appear to be sincere, self-revealing references
to his personal life and history. A famous example of Ovidian
self-revelation is his reference to the mysterious *error* which
contributed to his downfall (103–10), but even here – and
despite the overt tone of painful reminiscence – Ovid's playful
Muse proves to be surreptitiously active. As in the case of
Actaeon, whose unpremeditated sighting of Diana led to his
downfall, Ovid claims that his *error* took place in innocence
(cf. *cur imprudenti cognita culpa mihi?*, 104). The exact nature
of Ovid's *error* is of course notoriously problematic and now
irrecoverable, despite the growth of a whole industry devoted
to cracking the mystery.[48] A basic misconception, however, is
to assume that because Ovid writes *cur aliquid vidi?* (103), he
literally means that the accidental witnessing of some compromising scene was the cause of his downfall. This assumption
has led to absurd fictions being invented to explain the *error*;[49] it has also led to a defective understanding of the association between Ovid and Actaeon. The words *cur aliquid vidi?*
are carefully chosen to facilitate the association which is made
two lines later (105), and the significance of the association
relies in part on Ovid's depiction of the Actaeon myth in
Metamorphoses 3, where he follows the same version of the
story as that referred to in *Tristia* 2.

---

[48] See Thibault (1964), *passim* for stock-taking of the industry; Della Corte (1973),
63–9 offers an abbreviated catalogue of conjectures. Green (1982), 202–20 up-
dates the question, arguing that only a political solution is feasible; but the mystery remains.

[49] A token example: Alexander (1957), 321–2 suggests that while Ovid was away
from Rome, he entrusted his home to a friend who promptly held a party there;
unexpectedly returning to Rome, Ovid walked into the party and (oops!) saw the
younger Julia cavorting naked. Hence the poet's anguished cry *cur aliquid vidi?*.

At *M*. 3.186–97 Diana's reaction to Actaeon's presence at the pool where she bathes is depicted as a fit of pique, a wilful and spontaneous response to her sense of personal outrage; her immediate reaction is to wish that she had her arrows at the ready (188) to punish Actaeon without hearing any plea in mitigation of his action.[50] This is unlikely to be a slavish imitation of some Hellenistic exemplar. The portrayal of the goddess' response may well be an original Ovidian contribution, since the parallel story in Callimachus' fifth *Hymn* has Athena attribute her punishment of Teiresias to Κρόνιοι νόμοι (100); her reaction is not personally vindictive. If Diana's personal pique and vindictiveness are genuinely an Ovidian emphasis, then we have a good reason why Ovid should want us to know that it is his version of the Actaeon myth in *Metamorphoses* 3 which is recalled at *Tr.* 2.105ff.[51] In both cases Actaeon's innocence is stressed, and his innocence intensifies our sense of outrage at his treatment.

Ovid's verdict at *M*. 3.141–2, before he actually recounts the myth, is sympathetic to Actaeon:

> at bene si quaeras, Fortunae crimen in illo,
> non scelus invenies: quod enim scelus error habebat?

In line 142 *error* has, of course, the dual connotation of losing one's way and of making an accidental mistake. Despite his own comment on the case, however, Ovid later portrays a divergence of opinion on Diana's treatment of Actaeon:

> rumor in ambiguo est. aliis violentior aequo
> visa dea est; alii laudant dignamque severa
> virginitate vocant.
>
> (253–5)

---

[50] Cf. Galinsky (1975), 66: 'It is really the pique of Diana that is Actaeon's downfall. There is no great outburst of moral outrage on her part, because the offence would not warrant it'.

[51] The connection between these lines of *Tristia* 2 and the emphasis on Actaeon's innocence in *Metamorphoses* 3 is made by Bömer (1969), 488–9, who concludes, without sufficient justification, that *M*. 3.141–2 is a post-exilic addition made to facilitate the connection. In fact, the structure of Ovid's Actaeon narrative has a consistent emphasis which the presence of 141–2 is necessary to explain.

What implication does this portrayal of Actaeon have for Ovid's depiction of his own *error*? If Ovid is to be associated with Actaeon, then Diana, the affronted goddess, is to be associated with the affronted emperor/god. Does Ovid suggest, like those who support Diana's action (cf. *M*. 3.254–5), that Augustus was right to preserve his dignity by meting out a harsh punishment? Or, despite his earlier assertion that Augustus' anger was justified (*illa* [*ira*] *quidem iusta est*, 29) and despite his later praise of the emperor's restraint (125–8), does he insinuate that in the case of his *error* he has been the victim of an excessively harsh reaction to an accidental misdemeanour – the victim, in effect, of a fit of pique on Augustus' part? Ovid has just described the fair and impartial way in which he himself dispensed justice when the *fortuna reorum* was entrusted to him (93). Does he imply that Augustus has not judged him with the same impartiality? Like the 'jury' which reaches a split decision on Diana's treatment of Actaeon in *Metamorphoses* 3, the reader who explores the full implications of the cross-reference is left to draw his own conclusion about the fairness of Augustus' treatment of Ovid.

The ambivalent tone of *scilicet* (107) complicates Augustus' role in the implied comparison between Ovid and Actaeon. The double-edged effect which Ovid achieves through his use of the term here closely resembles that which Hinds detects at *M*. 15.752. From one perspective, the tone is uncritical: 'naturally (*scilicet*), where the gods are concerned even accidents of fortune demand retribution, and mischance is no excuse when a deity is slighted'. But what if *scilicet* is interpreted in its *other* sense as an expression of palpable absurdity? 'I ask you! Where the gods are concerned even accidents of fortune demand retribution!' Given the latent ambivalence of *scilicet*, does Ovid point innocently to the justification, however hard, of Augustus' reaction to his misdemeanour – a harsh but necessary, and therefore acceptable, consequence of his actions? Or does he point more cynically to the overreaction of a powerful deity to a simple human failing? Or is the preferred reading to depend on the reader's own sophistication and approach to Augustus? As at *M*. 15.752, the term *scilicet* caters simultaneously for different kinds of reader.[52]

The language in which Ovid refers to his *error* in lines 103–4 and 109–10 carries its own form of ambivalent suggestiveness. Ovid's catalogue of disaster is portrayed in three stages: his initial act of vision (*cur aliquid vidi?*, 103), his insistence that he made an accidental mistake (*me malus abstulit error*, 109), and the bitter consequence which nevertheless follows (*periit ... domus*, 110). The words *me malus abstulit error* are borrowed from *Ecl.* 8.41, where Virgil's Damon recalls how he first fell in love when he saw Nysa collecting apples with her mother: *ut vidi, ut perii, ut me malus abstulit error.* Ovid's Virgilian echo is unusually full and clear, but the quotation belies the novel sense it is adapted to carry in the Ovidian context. At *Ecl.* 8.41 *error* refers to the madness of infatuated love,[53] *perii* to the hyperbolical sense in which Damon 'dies' with passion.[54] Now that he has experienced the agony of burgeoning passion, now that Nysa is united with Mopsus, Damon learns what sort of being Love really is (*nunc scio quid sit Amor*, 43), a pitiless savage (cf. *saevus Amor*, 47) who induced Medea to slay her own children (47–8). Doubtless alert to Medea's presence in *Eclogue* 8, Ovid depicts her initial sighting of Jason at *Her.* 12.31ff. in language which closely echoes Damon's despairing cry:

> tunc ego te vidi, tunc coepi scire quid esses;
>   illa fuit mentis prima ruina meae.
> ut vidi, ut perii! nec notis ignibus arsi.

The terms in which both Damon and Medea portray the di-

---

[52] Drucker (1977), 157 who partially explores the wider implications of *Tr.* 2.105ff. (p. 153; cf. Ford (1977), 27), briefly discusses *scilicet* (107) as a term which indicates Ovid's dismay at the harsh severity of divine/Augustan justice, but without addressing the possible ambivalence of the word.
[53] For *error* in this sense cf. Prop. 1.13.35, Ov. *Am.* 1.2.35, 1.10.9.
[54] For *pereo* in this sense cf. Catul. 45.5, Prop. 2.15.13, Hor. *C.* 1.25.7. The usage seems to have come into elegy from comedy; cf. Plaut. *Poen.* 142, *nunc ego amore pereo.* For background on the *ut ... ut* construction see Gow (1952), 51–2 on 2.82 with Timpanaro (1978), 219–87.

sastrous consequences of their initial acts of seeing provide a suggestive parallel for Ovid's own choice of language in lines 103–10. With *vidi* (103) and *periit* ... *domus* (110), he reapplies the cause and effect of erotic infatuation to his own downfall, and the suggestive erotic analogy is underpinned by direct allusion to Damon's words in line 109. But how are these erotic associations to be understood in their non-erotic context?[55]

One possibility is that Ovid's objective is ironic pathos. Damon and Medea both 'die' with passion (*perire*) on seeing Nysa and Jason respectively; because of what Ovid accidentally sees, however, he and his house are ruined (*periit* ... *domus*, 110) in a more profound, more personally destructive sense. The ruin of lovers as evoked in a pastoral landscape or a mock amatory epistle counts for little when set beside a much more realistically conceived and portrayed ruination like that of Ovid himself. The allusions which at first seem to give Ovid's predicament the distinction of a literary pedigree finally help us to distinguish the 'realism' of his exilic suffering from the mythical world they evoke.

But there is another possibility. Could the amatory overtones of lines 103–10 mischievously implant in Ovid's apologia for the *Ars Amatoria* a hint of the eroticism for which he has been punished? Or, alternatively, does Ovid deliberately commit an 'accidental' *error* in the portrayal of his initial *error* by using diction so redolent of poetic eroticism? Of course, the merest hint of innocent passion need hardly be read as another instance of Ovidian salaciousness to which the emperor would inevitably react with stern disapproval. The point to be stressed is rather that while the literary allusions in lines 103–10 are clear enough, the erotic nuances of these allusions are only implicitly present, and the reader is left to elaborate the collective significance which such nuances may suggest. This procedure is not as whimsical as it may at first appear,

---

[55] Della Corte (1973), 79–80 and Baligan (1959), 49–54 both note the amatory associations of lines 103–10, but apply them to dubious theories about the nature of Ovid's *error*.

for the resulting interpretation must be coherent and demonstrably related to the texts to carry conviction. Given these implicit nuances, then, does Ovid show tact in the account of his *error* which he sets before Augustus, combining appropriate vagueness as regards the facts of the case with an abject show of guilt and sorrow, or does he tactlessly clothe his penitential declarations to the emperor in erotically allusive phraseology? Again, Ovid's mischievous Muse defies strict characterization by not inclining exclusively to one extreme or the other, and the reader is left to weigh up the different implications of an ambivalent passage.

Augustus, *otium* and the Ovidian *recusatio*

As Ovid's address to Augustus progresses, the kind of ambivalence which is present in the early stages of the poem proves to be a recurring phenomenon, but its various manifestations range in complexity and the scale of their ironic effect. Two conspicuous passages in which initial certainties are gently undermined by closer examination of Ovid's ambivalent Muse are 213–38 and 313–42. In both cases, the subtle undercurrents which complicate Ovid's superficial show of candour and obsequiousness prove to be devastatingly ironic.

i

In lines 213–38 Ovid prepares the way for his defence of the *Ars Amatoria* by claiming that the burden of Augustus' workload is such that the offending poem is scarcely worth his attention: what time does the emperor have to give to such a frivolous performance (cf. 237–8)? There is no need to detect in these lines an implicit criticism that Augustus has wasted precious time by concerning himself with the trivial issue of an Ovidian poem when he is pressed by much more important affairs of state. Ovid's ostensible point is simply that the emperor's commitments deprive him of the time to read the *Ars Amatoria* for himself with a thoroughness that would vindicate its propriety. Were Augustus free to read the work at leisure, claims the poet, he would not find fault with it (239–40).

Seen from one perspective, Ovid's tone in lines 213–38 may appear excessively obsequious to us and doubtless would have done so to some of his contemporaries, especially those familiar with a parallel passage in Horace. At the start of *Ep.* 2.1 Horace tactfully approaches Augustus, aware that 'he is trespassing upon the time of a man whose obligations are so numerous and great'.[56] To take up his time is to interfere with the *publica commoda* (3), the interests of the public and state both at home and abroad (cf. *res Italas armis tuteris, moribus ornes,*|*legibus emendes*, 2–3). Following Horace, Ovid draws attention yet more effusively to the enormity of Augustus' responsibilities both at home (in his *legum* ... *tutela* ... *et morum*, 233–4) and abroad (in bringing order to the far reaches of Roman dominion, 225–30); the emperor is depicted as not only responsible for, but essential to, the management of the state and Rome's universal supremacy (cf. *de te pendentem* ... *circumspicis orbem*, 217).

Seen from another perspective, however, Ovid's description of Augustus' immense responsibilities differs greatly from that of Horace. The many similarities in theme and language which reinforce the notion of close Ovidian dependence on *Ep.* 2.1 in fact disguise the crucial differences which should make us see Ovid's 'imitation' as an ironic comment on Horatian *laudes*, not as a verbose expansion of them. For one thing there is the matter of location. At *Ep.* 2.1.1–4 Horace views Augustus and his responsibilities not merely from a Roman standpoint, but from the impregnable security of Rome itself, from where *tanta negotia* can be seen as a convenient way to summarize the tedious business of foreign wars and frontier campaigns. Ovid is more explicit (225–30) about the details of the burden imposed upon the emperor (cf. 221–2), but this ceases to seem mere elaboration of detail and becomes a telling, ironic point when we remember that Ovid is in close prox-

[56] Fraenkel (1957), 383–4, comparing (384 n. 1) Cic. *Att.* 9.11.A.3 (to Caesar); but for blunt speaking before the emperor by Ovid's contemporaries cf. Suet. *Aug.* 54–6.

imity to what he describes; positioned at the very edge of the Roman frontier, he faces the barbarian enemies of Rome in the front line, as he has just been reminding us with great passion and in some detail (189–206).

With his listing of campaigns and locations, Ovid's elaboration of Horace's brief generalizations does not look now like mere verbosity. To the exiled Ovid, the success or failure of Roman campaigns in Thrace, Dalmatia and Armenia can be said to mean something in terms of increasing or diminishing his personal security (which is, of course, an all-pervading theme of the exilic poems), and the intensely felt insecurity portrayed in lines 189–206 points to what is personally relevant in the panegyric about to come. Horace, by contrast, must inevitably see these troubles as an indistinguishable mass of distant distractions. Horace's Roman viewpoint is reversed by Ovid, who begins with the provinces to the north and east (225–30) and comes eventually (*denique*, 231) to Rome (233–4), which is presented as adding even more to Augustus' pile of troubles (cf. *lassat*, 233). The force of these lines becomes more urgent and personally relevant when we remember that Tomis, not Rome, is the location from which the events are viewed.

On the matter of Augustus' literary tastes Ovid and Horace would seem to agree. Horace praises the emperor's judgement of poets at *Ep.* 2.1.245–7: *at neque dedecorant tua de se iudicia ...|dilecti tibi Vergilius Variusque poetae.* Ovid himself implies that Augustus showed a marked preference for poetry which displayed a *frons severa* (cf. 241), exemplified by the epics of Virgil and Varus,[57] and that he had little time for pieces like the *Ars Amatoria.* I take the imperial preference to be clearly implied in, for example, 241–2, and we shall find Ovid returning to the point later in the poem. In lines 213–38, however, there is an underlying suggestion that what Augustus lacks is not merely or even primarily the time to give to poetic *ioci* like the *Ars Amatoria*, but rather the literary sensibility

---

[57] For L. Varius Rufus, epicist and tragedian, see now Courtney (1993), 271–5. The older literature is recorded by Nisbet and Hubbard (1970), 81.

needed for their real appreciation. What prompts this suggestion in lines 225–30 is Ovid's selective treatment of Augustus' military achievements.

The references to Augustus' military exploits here pose a number of problems, at least if we assume that the passage is intended to convey praise and to solicit imperial favour. It is conventionally agreed that *Tristia* 2 was written in A.D. 8–9,[58] and we are to envisage Ovid writing in Tomis in the first year or so of exile. The campaigns referred to in lines 225–30 can now be seen to share one curious but largely consistent feature: they constitute much earlier successes whose impact had recently been severely impaired by fresh outbreaks of hostilities. Thrace and Raetia (226) are something of an exception to the general pattern. Twenty years before (11 B.C.), L. Calpurnius Piso, the legate of Galatia, had suppressed a widespread rebellion among the Thracian tribes (Vell. 2.98.1), but on the eve of Ovid's exile the Thracian king Rhoemetalces was actively supporting Rome, leading his army to join the Roman counter-offensive against the insurrection in Pannonia and Dalmatia (Vell. 2.112.4). The province of Raetia had also been consolidated by Drusus and Tiberius a quarter of a century earlier (Dio 54.22).

Elsewhere, however, the picture is somewhat different. Illyricum (225) had been the scene of one of the young Octavian's greatest victories over forty years before, celebrated as part of the famous triple triumph of 29 B.C. (cf. App. *Ill.* 28). The province had been reorganized after 11 B.C., but in A.D. 6 came the revolt of two Illyrian tribes, the Breuci and Daesitiates, provoking wider discontent in the province (Dio 55.29), and the process of re-conquest by Tiberius was still under way as Ovid was writing (cf. Suet. *Tib.* 16.2). While neither Thrace nor Raetia seem to have constituted in themselves a serious threat at this time, the case of Illyricum is rather different, and that of Germany (229) even more so. Tiberius had been appointed to a command in Germany in 8

---

[58] For this date see Wilkinson (1955), 302; Luck (1977), II 8; Syme (1978), 38; Claassen (1986), 32 etc.

B.C., and his victories caused special satisfaction in view of his defeat of the Sugambri, who had conquered the *legatus* M. Lollius (cf. Tac. *Ann.* 2.26.3, Vell. 2.97.4). Tiberius' decisive victory earned him a triumph (Suet. *Tib.* 9.2). This operation was so thorough that three years later L. Domitius Aheno-barbus was able to penetrate further into Germany across the Elbe (Tac. *Ann.* 4.44.3). But after twelve years of comparative peace there was further trouble in Germany, and Tiberius, now back from Rhodes and adopted by Augustus, launched another campaign across the Weser in A.D. 5 (Suet. *Tib.* 16.1, Vell. 2.105ff.). On this occasion success was denied Tiberius by the outbreak of the calamitous revolts in Dalmatia and Pannonia in A.D. 6. At the time when *Tristia* 2 was written, the situation in Germany was still unclear, an outcome very different to the triumphant pacification of seventeen years be-fore. As in the case of Illyricum, earlier successes and military consolidation had come undone only a couple of years before Ovid's exile.

A similar story emerges in Pannonia (225). A Roman army under P. Silius had forced the Pannonians to come to terms in 16 B.C. after they had invaded Istria (Dio 54.20.2), and two years later they were again subjugated after a rebellion (Dio 54.24.3). It seems that nearly two decades followed which were mainly free of hostilities until the Pannonians broke into open revolt along with the Dalmatians in A.D. 6. This was a rebellion of major proportions which was thought to pose a threat even to Italy itself (Vell. 2.111.1). Tiberius was immedi-ately sent to fight the Pannonians, and Germanicus followed in A.D. 7. At Rome money and food were both running low, and Dio records growing popular discontent over the war (55.31.3–4). In the year of Ovid's exile, Augustus had been forced to make the journey north to Ariminum to discuss strategy with Tiberius and Germanicus (Dio 55.34.3), and the crisis in Pannonia dominated Roman policy throughout the year. It is important to remember that Ovid may well have written *Tristia* 2 before news of Tiberius' victory reached him.

Another source of trouble is identified in lines 227–8, the problems of Armenia and Parthia. Anyone might gather from

Ovid's description that both areas were subjugated and at peace, but the reverse was the case. True, nearly thirty years before Augustus had himself directed from Syria the reduction of Armenia by Tiberius (cf. Tac. *Ann.* 2.3) and the much vaunted return of the *capta signa* from the Parthians (Suet. *Aug.* 21.3). These successes produced stability for nearly twenty years, until the murder of the pro-Roman king in Parthia also brought back to power the anti-Roman faction in Armenia. Augustus sent his adopted son Gaius, aged nineteen, on an expedition to the east in 1 B.C., the results of which were an uneasy truce with Parthia by negotiation (Dio 55.10a.4), the loss of Roman influence in Armenia until the reign of Tiberius (despite the claim of *R.G.* 27.2), and Gaius' eventual death on the return journey in A.D. 4. The expedition could hardly be called a success. Once again, an early achievement which looked set to last had gone badly wrong, leaving an uncertain and intractable situation.

If we now look again at *Tr.* 2.225–34, the following facts present themselves to complement Ovid's picture. In so far as the passage is read as a panegyric of Augustan military achievements, it must be taken as referring to successes achieved between about twenty and forty years before. In the early part of his reign Augustus had stabilized and pacified Thrace, Raetia, Pannonia, Illyricum, Germany, Armenia and Parthia. Within about half a dozen years before Ovid's exile all but the first two of these were in active revolt against Roman authority, and in none of them had a satisfactory outcome been achieved in Augustus' favour by the time *Tristia* 2 was written. Pannonia, mentioned first in Ovid's list, was at a crucial stage when he left Rome, and the crisis was rumoured to have brought Augustus to the verge of suicide (cf. Plin. *Nat.* 7.149).[59] Germany, Illyricum, Armenia and Parthia were all to a greater or lesser degree unsettled, and Ovid may be hinting in line 226 of further trouble to come in Raetia and Thrace. Moreover, the fact that Rome now seems to add to

---

[59] As noted by Wiedemann (1975), 265. Does Ovid work mischief by reminding Augustus, via Pannonia, of his personal crisis?

Augustus' troubles (233–4) may be an oblique reference to the disturbance which Dio independently records as taking place over food-shortages and taxes caused by the prolonging of the Pannonian war: τὸ πλῆθος ἄλλως τε καὶ διὰ τοὺς πολέμους τόν τε λιμόν, ὃς καὶ τότε αὖθις συνέβη, δεινῶς ἐταράττετο (55.31.3). This was hardly a time to be suggesting that Augustus should be reading the *Ars Amatoria*!

Now an intelligent reader of Ovid like S. G. Owen interpreted *Tr.* 2.225–32 as flattering panegyric: 'In these lines Ovid reviews the wars by which under Augustus the frontiers of the empire were secured. The dates range from 20 B.C. to A.D.10, a considerable period, during which the emperor had felt the anxiety of war, and successfully confronted its shocks (232 *pars nulla est, quae labet, imperii*).'[60] '*Frontiers ... secured*' when Germany, Armenia and Parthia were so unsettled? '*Successfully confronted its shocks*' when Augustus was reduced to panic and despair by the crisis in Pannonia? And is it not the case that line 232 must in the circumstances be devastatingly ironic? Owen supports his reading by giving in his notes a number of historical references which cover up the crisis facing Augustus on so many fronts in A.D. 8. Yet Owen honestly read the lines in this way. How might have Augustus read them? More importantly, perhaps, how did Ovid suppose that Augustus might read them? Would Augustus, like Owen, have read these lines as a superficial record of imperial successes? Would he have been shocked by the powerfully suggestive implications of a listing of current Roman troublespots? We are left to ask whether Augustus' reading would have penetrated beneath the most superficial impression conveyed by the words, and the suspicion arises (strongly supported by lines 317–26 and 529–30) that the Augustus Ovid portrays feels much more at home with the *frons severa* (cf. 241) of epic than with the ironic playfulness of Ovidian elegy.

Ovid's foreshadowing of Augustus' literary tastes and sensibility is perhaps confirmed by an extraordinary fact. We

[60] (1924), 158. Note that Owen assumes that *Tristia* 2 was not earlier than A.D. 10; but cf. n. 58 *supra* for A.D. 8–9.

have seen that in lines 227–8 Ovid refers back nearly thirty years to the pacification of Armenia and Parthia by Augustus and Tiberius, and that there is a remarkable omission of any reference to the great expedition mounted against Parthia and Armenia by Gaius Caesar a few years before. Why the omission? Why did Ovid choose not to dress up the indecisive outcome of Gaius' campaign as a victory of sorts? I suggest that the answer is this: had Augustus read the *Ars Amatoria*, he could hardly have failed to notice the section in the first book (177–228) which celebrated Gaius' eastern mission with a grandiloquent propempticon and anticipated his triumph on his return. If taken literally and viewed from a *post eventum* standpoint, the whole episode must appear as a most unfortunate lapse of taste. Not only did Gaius' mission fail in its most modest aims, let alone the hyperbolical aims set for it by Ovid (cf. 177–8), but the projected triumph never materialized because of Gaius' early death in Lycia. Moreover, the triumph-scene is explicitly presented as an opportunity for lovers' assignations on the route (cf. 217ff.). There is thus every reason to suppose that at *Tr.* 2.227–8 Ovid aims to divert Augustus' attention away from this potentially damaging section of *Ars Amatoria* 1 only four years after his adopted son's premature death. The poet's obvious fear is that if Augustus recalls this section of the *Ars Amatoria*, he will at once be confronted by the apprehension, grief and eventual heartbreak which Gaius' expedition caused him.

But Ovid need not have been so tactful if he had had more confidence in Augustus' literary sensibility, since *A.A.* 1.177–228 is shot through with the kind of humour which makes a 'literal' reading seem superficial and difficult to sustain. The humour of the passage rests on the striking contrast between Gaius' youthful immaturity and inexperience on the one hand[61] and his divinely favoured, heroic stature on the other as he turns the Parthians to flight like a second Mars (199–204). A superficially 'literal' reading of the whole section

---

[61] Cf. especially 188, *in cunis iam Iove dignus erat*, where the subject is Hercules/ Gaius and Jupiter is, as usual, Augustus.

would prove after the event to be highly embarrassing both
for the poet who got his predictions wrong and for the emperor who can see his expectations dashed: no military victories, no heroic vengeance, no triumph. I suggest that by
omitting to refer to Gaius' expedition to Armenia and Parthia
at *Tr.* 2.227–8, Ovid implies that Augustus was predisposed
to read the *Ars* in this 'literal' way. The further implication
follows that the emperor's literary sensibility is such that he
cannot share the values and conceptions out of which a poem
like the *Ars Amatoria* has grown.

A close examination of some vocabulary which Ovid uses in
lines 213–38 helps to widen the gap between Augustus and the
world of Ovidian elegy. Take, for example, *non vacat* (216)
and *otia* (224, 235). The price which Augustus has to pay for
bringing peace (*pax*; cf. 227) and tranquillity (*otia*, 235) to
distant regions under Roman dominion is the denial of free
time (*otium*) to himself. But his workload also deprives him
of *otium* in the more technical sense of literary leisure. Such
otium is of course a necessity for the poet (cf. *carmina se-
cessum scribentis et otia quaerunt*, *Tr.* 1.1.41) and also describes the products of his creative leisure, as when Ovid
writes that Augustus is not free to scrutinize *otia nostra* (224),
his *Ars Amatoria*. A conspicuous point of comparison for
otium in the sense of time given to the appreciation rather
than the production of literary work is offered by *M.* 5.333–6.
Before recounting to Minerva Calliope's song in the contest
against the Pierides, the Muse asks

> sed forsitan otia non sint,
> nec nostris praebere vacet tibi cantibus aures?

Minerva is in no hurry: *ne dubita*, she replies, *vestrumque mihi
refer ordine carmen* (335). In these lines *otia* and *vacare* are key
terms which strike a programmatic note, suggesting the circumstances appropriate for studying sophisticated compositions
produced under the Muses' guidance.[62] Augustus' image is

---

[62] On the literary/programmatic implications of this passage and its surrounding
context see Hofmann (1986), 228–32.

not characterized by *otium* either in this literary sense or in its non-literary sense, but by *curae* (218), by which is meant his concern for the administration of the Roman dominion, not the technical sense of literary study (cf. *Tr.* 1.11.12) or the products of literary study (cf. *P.* 4.16.39).

Ovid's use of such terms as *otium* and *cura* in non-literary senses serves to illustrate the distinction between the world of the statesman on the one hand and that of the erotic elegist on the other. *Otium* and *cura* have one meaning for Augustus, another for Ovid. It is not simply time that the *princeps* lacks; Ovid implicitly raises the question of whether the emperor, leading a life of *negotium* and administrative *curae*, is so far removed in both ideology and in the nature of his activity from the leisurely *otium* of the love-poet that he can hardly be expected to read the *Ars Amatoria* with a literary sensibility attuned to that which produced the work.

The words *minora* (214), *exiguis rebus* (216) and *inferiora* (218) also contribute to the picture of Augustus' alienation from the world of the love-elegist. The *Ars Amatoria*, Ovid argues, need not detain Augustus since (to adapt line 216) it is also an *exigua res*, or too insignificant and small a matter (*minor, inferior*) for his attention. But the poem is also *exigua res* in the generic sense of being small-scale elegy as opposed to large-scale epic,[63] and because of its humble literary status the *Ars* is 'beneath' Augustus for a variety of reasons. Not only is the work an insignificant triviality which does not deserve a place on the busy imperial agenda (cf. 221–4); the poem's lowly generic affiliations are also incompatible with the 'Augustan phenomenon'. The emperor shoulders a heavy burden of responsibilities, military and civic (cf. *tantarum pondere rerum*, 237), and epic is the appropriately 'weighty' medium in which to celebrate a figure of such *gravitas*.[64] So,

---

[63] For *exiguus* in this lowly generic sense see Hor. *Ars* 77, Prop. 3.9.35–6, 4.1.59–60, Ov. *Tr.* 2.329–30, 531–2, *P.* 3.3.33–4. *Parvus* (cf. *minora*, 214) also distinguishes elegy and lyric from the more elevated genres; see Hor. *C.* 4.2.31, 4.15.3, *Ep.* 2.1.257–8, Prop. 3.3.18, 4.1.58, Ov. *Tr.* 2.331–2, *P.* 2.5.25–6 with Bramble (1974), 156–73 and Cairns (1979), 21.

[64] For the generic connotation of *gravis* see p. 62 n. 24.

at *F.* 2.125–6, Ovid is fully aware of the difficulties he faces in
attempting an elegiac celebration of Augustus:

> quid volui demens elegis imponere tantum
> ponderis? heroi res erat ista pedis.

In the elegists' *recusationes* of epic, the Augustan theme is of
course synonymous with the mode of composition which is
rejected;[65] at *Tr.* 2.529–32 Ovid distinguishes his own limited
powers of song from those needed to celebrate Augustus in a
suitably powerful medium, and in doing so he reiterates the
point made in his own *recusatio* at 327–42. Lines 221–3 present the inevitable poetic outcome:

> non ea te moles Romani nominis urget,
> inque tuis umeris tam leve fertur onus,
> lusibus ut possis advertere numen ineptis.

Since he shoulders a burden of epic proportions (*non ... leve*),
Augustus' natural affinities lie not with the *numeri leves* of
amatory elegy,[66] but with epic *gravitas*.

Both as a statesman, then, and as a literary phenomenon
most appropriately celebrated in the epic mode, the *princeps*
would hardly seem to be naturally attuned to the ludic subtlety of Ovidian elegy. As the rival readings of lines 225–36
illustrate, Augustus' sensibility is portrayed as one which is
potentially blind to the variety of conflicting implications
which the initiated reader detects. This interpretation helps to
clarify a number of curious features about the historical content of this passage. Moreover, the basic distinction which
these lines invite us to make between poet and statesman is
sustained by Ovid's ambivalent use of some key terms of Roman literary vocabulary.

ii

Equally disconcerting in its implications is Ovid's description
in lines 313–42 of his incompetence as an epicist and his dis-

---

[65] Cf. Prop. 2.1.25–6, Hor. *Ep.* 2.1.250ff., *C.* 4.2.33ff.
[66] For this generic connotation of *levis* see p. 65 n. 38.

carded attempt at an epic celebration of Augustus. This passage has obvious affinities with the elegists' traditional *recusationes* of epic, but it also contains idiosyncratic features which add depth to Ovid's superficial tone of fawning deference.

The projected epic on Augustus which Ovid mentions in lines 337–42 is best considered in connection with the Gigantomachy portrayed in *Am.* 2.1, though this association is as purely notional as I consider both epics themselves to be. Though Jupiter, and not Augustus, is Ovid's theme in his alleged Gigantomachy, the familiar link between the two makes the god's victory an obvious paradigm for the Augustan supremacy. This parallel is already implied at *Tr.* 2.67–72, and in lines 333–6 the *inmania acta* of Augustus are again set alongside those of Jupiter:

> at si me iubeas domitos Iovis igne Gigantas
> dicere, conantem debilitabit onus.
> divitis ingenii est inmania Caesaris acta
> condere, materia ne superetur opus.

As Owen states on these lines, 'it is noticeable that ... there is no particle indicating comparison [between the achievements of Jupiter and Augustus]; the two subjects are treated as identical'.[67] There is much evidence elsewhere to suggest that the Gigantomachy was employed as an allegorical representation of Augustus' achievements. At the outset of Augustus' reign nearly forty years before, and with clear relevance to the battle of Actium, Horace's lesson in *C.* 3.4 that crude and rebellious violence is crushed by the disciplined force of rule directed by intelligence (65–8) is symbolized by the defeat of the Giants (42ff.).[68] There are many other examples of this same correlation,[69] and Augustus is explicitly associated with Jupiter on a number of occasions in the exile poetry.[70]

---

[67] (1924), 65. Cf. Innes (1979), 167: 'In *Tristia* 2.61ff. and 331ff. Ovid couples Gigantomachy with the deeds of Augustus in obvious flattery to the emperor.'

[68] Fraenkel (1957), 273 n. 3 locates the poem in 27 B.C.

[69] See Owen (1924), 74–5, adding the opening invocation to Apollo in Tib. 2.5, where the defeat of the Giants may be an allegory for Augustan order (see K. F. Smith (1964), 446 on 2.5.5); on the possible Augustan overtones of the Gigantomachy at *M.* 1.151ff. see Buchheit (1966), 86ff. Hardie (1986), 85–90 surveys the tradition of political gigantomachic imagery.

[70] See Warde Fowler (1915), 46–7 for extensive references with Scott (1930), 52–8.

Such evidence consolidates the identification of *Caesaris acta* with *Iovis acta* at *Tr.* 2.333–6 and forges the notional connection between Ovid's previous attempt at writing an Augustan epic (337) and the Gigantomachy described at *Am.* 2.1.11ff.[71] Are we, then, to believe that Ovid did in fact attempt a Gigantomachy, despite my earlier reservations on the point? Owen argues that he did, but the fragmentary evidence he adduces is unconvincing and he mistranslates lines 337–8 to give the illusion of support in the text.[72] The better course is surely to suppose that Ovid follows Propertius (cf. 2.1.19–20, 39–40) in choosing the Gigantomachy as the most epic of epic themes for him to discard in the *recusatio* expected of him as an elegist; there is certainly no evidence to suggest that Ovid's Gigantomachy ever existed as anything other than a programmatic device.[73] My immediate concern, however, is to assess the significance which Ovid's depiction of his failed epic project in *Am.* 2.1 has for his depiction of what I take to be the same project at *Tr.* 2.333–6.

According to *Am.* 2.1.11ff. Ovid was courageously embarking on his great enterprise, getting together the necessary materials and resources (cf. *cum Iove fulmen habebam*, 15), when all of a sudden *clausit amica fores* (17): both Jupiter and his bolt are unceremoniously dropped and Ovid's project is suspended. The door has a *fulmen* of its own (20; cf. *Am.* 1.6.16 for the same idea), a bolt which holds greater power over the poet than even that of Jupiter himself. The Jovian weaponry is of no use to Ovid, who must revert to weapons of his own (*blanditias elegosque levis, mea tela*, 21) in order to break down the girl's resistance. The poetic narrative here is a fairly

---

[71] So Nagle (1980), 123.

[72] (1924), 65ff., translating 337–8 thus (p. 109): 'Yet I had indeed attempted this, but was judged to belittle and disparage your achievements, which is treason.' This is self-justification masquerading as objective translation. In fact, *audere* need only mean 'to have the courage or daring for a task' (*TLL* 2.1255.64ff.), with the added idea of 'showing originality' in literary contexts (cf. Macleod (1977), 362 n. 14); and *videbar* refers not to other people's judgement, but to the poet's own view of himself (see *OLD* s.v. *video* 21). I understand lines 337–8 thus: 'Even so, I had the daring and the originality for the task, but I thought I was disparaging you and detracting from your political authority.' *Vires* cannot mean 'achievements' as Owen has it.

[73] For scepticism about the existence of Ovid's alleged Gigantomachy see Pfister (1915), 472–4, Reitzenstein (1935), 87–8 and Innes (1979), 167.

obvious comic dramatization of the *recusatio* of epic material in favour of love-elegy. The dismissal of Jupiter is flippant and casual as Ovid rises to the greater challenge.

This flippancy is absent at *Tr.* 2.337–40 – or, at least, so it seems. The task of relating Augustus' achievements requires an exceptionally rich *ingenium* (cf. 335) which Ovid claims to lack. He seemed to belittle his theme (*detractare*, 337) by failing to do justice to Augustus' power (*videbar ... damno viribus esse tuis*, 337–8), just as he lacks the strength for a Gigantomachy (333). The tone with which he gives his reason here for reverting to elegy appears to be respectful and apologetic. But if we look back to *Am.* 2.1.11ff. once more, it was not a lack of ability or strength which led Ovid to reject his epic theme, or fear of belittling his subject-matter; indeed, he indicates that it was sufficiently inflated in diction to meet the generic requirement (cf. *et satis oris erat*, 12). The *exclusus amator* is there forced to give up his epic project for a reason which has nothing to do with generic weakness; he must take up the urgent challenge of breaking down the girl's resistance. In reverting to elegy Ovid shows scant respect for Jupiter, disparaging him (cf. *detractare*, *Tr.* 2.337) in the way he simply drops *cum Iove fulmen* (17), and belittling the god's power (cf. *Tr.* 2.338) by rejecting his *tela* in favour of his own weapons (*mea tela*, 21). Although the tone of *Tr.* 2.333–42 appears at first to be tactfully apologetic, this initial impression of polite self-depreciation is immediately qualified when the association is made with *Am.* 2.1 and Ovid's *other* motive for abandoning that same epic project becomes apparent. The fact is that Ovid is as easily sidetracked from his epic exaltation of Jupiter/Augustus by the challenge of winning Corinna as he is by the difficulty of the task itself.

In the light of *Am.* 2.1, then, Ovid's use of the gigantomachic *recusatio* motif at *Tr.* 2.333ff. proves to be double-edged in its interpretational possibilities. The reader (Augustus?) who accepts Ovid's seemingly candid account of why he turned away from Augustan epic will find no cause for complaint; but the reader who makes the connection with *Am.* 2.1 will find that Ovid's tact in *Tristia* 2 thinly disguises a cavalier attitude to the poetic treatment – and flippant rejection – of Jupiter/Augustus.

Ovid on literature

One of the most emphatic arguments which Ovid makes in defence of the *Ars Amatoria* is that though he is not the only poet to have written on the theme of 'tender' love, he alone has been punished for embarking on the theme (361–2). This argument perhaps shows Ovid at his boldest in *Tristia* 2, for it involves what looks like an Ovidian revaluation of Greco-Roman poetry, an assertion of his own place in the tradition (cf. *his ego successi*, 467), and a demand for imperial recognition of the poet's sincerity. What is at stake here is nothing less than Ovid's status as a poet, and the recognition due to the quality and authority, supported by tradition, of his poetic *ingenium*. The historical section (363–470) becomes, in effect, a virtuoso display of the powers of that *ingenium*, ranging from a rewriting of Tibullus 1.6 – the recent poet with whose independent voice Ovid seems to have felt closest sympathy – to an amatory elegist's (incredible) view of the central themes of the *Iliad* and *Odyssey*.

By portraying both epics as if they were Hellenistic love-romances (371–80), Ovid makes his inevitable point: if Augustus takes action against the *Ars Amatoria*, why does he not also take action against any literature or vulgar show which contains supposedly salacious material? The implications for literary censorship which result from the incrimination of his *Ars* are carried to their logical extreme; but equally extreme in its own way is Ovid's characterization of the *Iliad* as nothing more than a poem about adulterous love (371–2) and of the *Odyssey* as a poem concerned only with a woman surrounded by a host of suitors while her husband is away on his travels (375–6). These odd judgements, which reduce the fount of epic to a pair of typical scenes from Roman erotic elegy, can be seen as the poet's act of literary distortion set up in response to the emperor's judicial caprice. If Augustus has been critically naive and one-sided in his evaluation of the *Ars*

Amatoria, then Ovid can be equally one-sided and simplistic in his assessment of the Homeric poems, as well as of Greek tragedy and the poets he mentions in lines 363–470.

In effect, Ovid's response is to challenge Augustus with the provocative claim that the *Ars Amatoria* springs naturally from, and even perhaps forms a climax to, a central tradition in Greco-Roman poetry. The claim is, of course, misleading, since the *Ars* is a highly original poem, and the distortion employed in *Tristia* 2 to substantiate the claim is comically perverse. Yet this historical defence, far from lessening or qualifying Ovid's audacity as a poet in the presence of the emperor, actually raises that audacity to new heights. The examples he cites far exceed what is required to make his point. He could conceivably have limited himself to a far smaller selection of poets to show that he alone of authors writing on the theme of love has been punished. Indeed, if he were genuinely or solely interested in presenting such a case, he might have concentrated much more on Hellenistic elegy and epigram and far less on Greek tragedy. Why, then, does Ovid choose to give in *this* form and with *these* emphases a summary of the literary tradition which precedes him?

The bond which unites the writers listed by Ovid is claimed to be their common commitment to the theme of love. Though Ennius and Lucretius are kept aside here (423–6), Ovid has already used both to suggest how Roman *matronae* may be corrupted by the most unlikely sources (259–62). Virgil, omitted in the present list, is held back, a trump card which Ovid finally plays in lines 533–8. But though his list of writers is primarily designed to excuse the *Ars Amatoria*, their presence in lines 363–470 also serves to remind Augustus of the immortality which literature confers on its best practitioners – and, by implication, on Ovid himself, despite the fact that during his lifetime he is a poet oppressed, censored and banished from the public eye. Poetic immortality is Ovid's declared theme in *Am.* 1.15, an elegy which offers an instructive parallel for his similar but more covert procedure at *Tr.* 2.363–470.

Eschewing the life of the military or civic careerist at the start of *Am.* 1.15, Ovid seeks immortal fame through his writings (cf. *mihi fama perennis\quaeritur, in toto semper ut orbe canar*, 7–8), fame equivalent to that which the writers he enumerates in lines 9–34 have won. Here, as in *Tristia* 2, Ovid lists both Greek and Latin poets from Homer (9–10), Hesiod (11–12), Callimachus (13–14), Sophocles (15), Aratus (16) and Menander (17–18) to Ennius and Accius (19), Varro Atacinus (21–2), Lucretius (23–4), Virgil (25–6) and Tibullus and Gallus (27–30). Poetry lives on (*carmina morte carent*, 32), and armed with that knowledge Ovid confidently predicts his own immortality (*vivam, parsque mei multa superstes erit*, 42). The claim is of course common among the Roman poets, repeated by Ovid at *Am.* 3.15.20 and, rather differently, at *M.* 15.877–9. After the Horatian manner in *C.* 3.30, the claim is made in *Metamorphoses* 15 for the unique and original achievement of one poet,[74] but in *Am.* 1.15 Ovid claims that he is the last in a long line which secures his fame. In the latter case the listing of poetic predecessors has a double function: it both secures the fame of the poet by linking him with the tradition to which he aspires to belong, and it fulfils the promise of that tradition by ensuring that the poet's predecessors continue to be immortalized in verse. The poem which claims to add a new name to a tradition also helps to create and perpetuate a sense of continuity which has no legitimacy outside the poem itself. The immediate context of *Tr.* 2.423–66 is not self-congratulatory, but the catalogue of Ovid's predecessors has much the same purpose as it does in the *Amores*: Ovid is not merely attaching himself to a tradition, but recreating and vindicating the fame of the poetic predecessors he celebrates, perhaps most obviously in the case of Tibullus.

Ovid's numerous reminiscences of Tibullus in lines 447–62 provide proof of how a poet can remain 'alive' after his death, in this case for another poet to imitate him.[75] But poetic *imitatio* is not a matter of copying or simply adapting earlier

---

[74] Cf. Hor. *C.* 2.20, Prop. 3.1.35–8, 3.2.17ff. etc. Curran (1972), 84–5 detects irreverence in the epilogue to the *Metamorphoses* because Ovid couples his own immortality with that of Augustus: not even Jupiter(/Augustus) will be able to destroy the work (871–2). Cf. Anderson (1963), 27 (Ovid predicts for himself 'a permanence that he implicitly denies to *Romana potentia*').

[75] This section (447–62) is an adaptation of Tib. 1.6.7–32, though line 449 combines 1.6.9 and 1.2.15, and lines 459 and 460 are based on 1.5.74.

poetry, as Owen's note on 447–62 suggests it is.[76] The skilled poet does not merely record or anthologize his predecessor, but recreates his achievement by giving it a novel context or sense of direction – as Ovid does here with Tibullus 1.6. Tibullus fears that Delia is deceiving him, playing him off against her husband. If so, Tibullus has been caught in his own trap, since it is he who has taught Delia such tricks. Ovid records the Tibullan narrative in a way which brings out the basic similarity between Tibullus' case and his own, though the two situations are so different in tone and context: line 450, *se ... sua miserum nunc ait [Tibullus] arte premi*, deftly evokes Tibullus 1.6.10. Tibullus taught Delia the tricks with which she now deceives him. This is also precisely the form of self-reproach which dominates the earlier part of the exilic period. At *Ibis* 5–6, for example, Ovid states

> nec quemquam nostri, nisi me, laesere libelli,
> artificis periit cum caput Arte sua,

and the same idea is repeated on a number of occasions (cf. *Tr.* 1.1.56, 2.2, 3.3.74, 3.14.6). Ovid's retelling of Tibullus' predicament (*Tr.* 2.447–62) therefore contains a paradigm of its own. It is not too fanciful to believe that Tibullus' telling complaint *heu heu nunc premor arte mea* (1.6.10) is what first led Ovid to select the poem as eminently suitable for reproduction in *Tristia* 2. His ostensible point is, of course, that Tibullus' case is different to his own (cf. *non fuit hoc illi fraudi*, 463), but Ovid's choice of Tibullus 1.6 leads the reader to infer the fundamental similarity between the two poets' basic conditions; the differences are confined to the narrative situations and to the *fatum poetae* in each context.

The practice of creative poetic *imitatio* illustrated here is of great importance in securing Ovid's *fama* against imperial vengeance. While he cites example after example to support his case, he makes an implicit but telling point: whatever measures Augustus takes against him, he is secure in a tradition of poets whom posterity will, partly through him, keep alive.

---

[76] (1924), 244–5.

The emperor imposes on Ovid such restrictive measures as relegation to Tomis and censorship of his work (cf. *P.* 1.1.5–6); but just as he has no jurisdiction over Ovid's *ingenium* (cf. *Tr.* 3.7.47–8), so he has no power to control or restrict the renown which the products of that *ingenium* can win for the poet (and for his predecessors) both during his lifetime and after his death (cf. *Tr.* 3.7.49–52).[77]

In one sense, of course, Ovid is already dead: *ingenio perii ... miser ipse meo* (*Tr.* 2.2). The verb here equates his downfall with death just as it does at *Ibis* 6 and in the epitaph which he writes for himself at *Tr.* 3.3.73–4:

> hic ego qui iaceo tenerorum lusor amorum
> ingenio perii Naso poeta meo.

Ovid has met his 'death' as a poet, providing a new context for the familiar motif of the elegist's 'dying' from the extremity of his experiences. The more familiar cause of the elegist's 'death' is, of course, all-consuming love, and Ovid's exilic 'death' gives a new dimension to the amatory 'deaths' recorded in Catullus (45.5), Virgil (*Ecl.* 8.41, 10.10), Propertius (2.15.13), Horace (*C.* 1.25.7) and Ovid himself (*Am.* 2.14.21). In either context the motif is obviously self-dramatizing, and in the new context of exilic/artistic 'death' the motif once again develops its own hyperbole: Ovid's 'death' immediately locates him securely in his own catalogue of the great and famous among Roman poets (cf. *his ego successi*, 467). Such 'death', in both love and exile, is a sure sign of the extreme intensity of the experience.

A poet, however, can win not only renown after his death but an extended dimension to his *fama* which is unattainable in his own lifetime. Such is Propertius' forecast at 3.1.21–4:

> at mihi quod vivo detraxerit invida turba,
> post obitum duplici faenore reddet Honos;
> omnia post obitum fingit maiora vetustas:
> maius ab exsequiis nomen in ora venit.

---

[77] Cf. *R.A.* 361ff., where Ovid recalls that the *Ars Amatoria* has been criticized because of his *Musa proterva*; but Ovid can afford to disregard the carping criticism since he already enjoys universal fame and popularity (cf. 363–4, 389–90). His defiant tone here is implicit at *Tr.* 2.363–470.

Ovid echoes Propertius at *Am.* 1.15.39–40:

> pascitur in vivis Livor; post fata quiescit,
> cum suus ex merito quemque tuetur honos.[78]

Things were simpler when Ovid was a love-elegist, since his expectations were more easily definable from the available precedents. In the exilic wilderness, however, Ovid establishes both the outlines of an elegiac tradition and a monument for himself within it. He ensures that by consigning him to his 'death' in Tomis partly in punishment for the *Ars Amatoria*, the emperor inadvertently and ironically contributes to the enhancement of the poet's fame, principally as a love-elegist. *Pascitur in vivis Livor*: if *Livor* can damage a poet while he is alive, then so can Augustus. But just as a poet's posthumous fame defies the carping detraction of *Livor*, Augustus is powerless to restrict the 'posthumous' renown which awaits Ovid after his 'death' as a love-elegist. In effect, the function of the catalogue, assessed in connection with the more conventional example in *Am.* 1.15, is to present Augustus with evidence of the poet's future renown and of the famous company he will keep.

The mythical characters listed in lines 383–406 offer Augustus a timely reminder that poetry can immortalize persons other than the poet himself. Ovid's long, familiar catalogue of tragic passion and personal disaster is designed to support the idea of an author's moral blamelessness. The priority given to Hippolytus may arise, I suggest, from the fact that his famous dictum ἡ γλῶσσ' ὀμώμοχ', ἡ δὲ φρὴν ἀνώμοτος (E. *Hipp.* 612) illustrates so clearly the very kind of dichotomy between performance and moral responsibility which *Tristia* 2 sets out to promote. This could be Ovid speaking of the *Ars Amatoria*. Greek tragedy is a source from which Ovid often takes examples to parallel his predicament in exile, giving them a new poetic life in the process. At *Tr.* 2.383–406 Ovid collects on a larger scale the type of tragic example regularly used in parallels and similes in his amatory as well as exilic elegy. There is,

---

[78] On the envy motif (*livor, invidia*, φθόνος) see Henderson (1979), 91 on *R.A.* 389.

however, a paradox here: the point made in *Tristia* 2 is that epic and tragedy, despite their content (cf. *haec* [*tragoedia*] *quoque materiam semper amoris habet*, 382), are fictional entertainments with no bearing on 'real' life (cf. 353–8), and Ovid aligns himself with their blameless authors (cf. 357) in the paradoxical attempt to create *in* his verse a persona which is wholly distinct in character *from* his verse. It seems that this will be done by forcing a radical disjunction between literary art and 'real' experience, but the relevance of literature to life is a theme which is regularly developed throughout the exilic corpus, as Ovid gives his plight an epic/tragic dimension. Some illustrations will clarify the point.

In *Tristia* 2 the *Odyssey* is simply a love-romance (375–6); but at *Tr.* 1.5.57–84 the *Odyssey* provides a point of comparison which helps to define Ovid's sufferings, albeit in a hyperbolical manner. The contrast between fiction and reality in this latter poem serves not just to polarize them, but to intensify the so-called Ovidian 'reality' on the model of Homeric fiction. Elsewhere, Ovid readily mythologizes his situation with reference to Ulysses (cf. *Tr.* 3.11.61, 4.1.31–4 etc.), and famous tragic characters are regularly used to define the nature of Ovid's fall from grace (e.g. Phaethon, *Tr.* 1.1.79–80), his sufferings (e.g. Philoctetes, *Tr.* 5.1.61–2, 5.2.13–14) and his longing to escape (e.g. Medea, *Tr.* 3.8.3–4). At *Tr.* 2.395 Orestes is an example of a tragic character whose passions are confined to plays; but elsewhere he serves as a model for the relationship between Ovid and his faithful friends.[79] Ovid's wife is also characterized by comparison with literary models such as Penelope, Evadne, Alcestis and Laodameia (cf. *Tr.* 1.6.19–22, 5.5.51–8, 5.14.35–40). This is not a simple matter of the relevance of literature to life; rather, Ovid is dramatizing the emotions and conditions of his exilic life out of models found in tragedy and epic. The reader familiar with this procedure, already in evidence in *Tristia* 1, is unlikely to be impressed by Ovid's claim in *Tristia* 2 that poetry is merely *honesta voluptas* and has no bearing on the way real lives are

[79] Cf. *Tr.* 1.5.21–2, 1.9.27–8, 4.4.69ff., *P.* 2.3.45, 3.2.33–4, 69ff.

shaped and lived. Augustus had only to read *Tristia* 1 in the right way to be aware of the weakness of Ovid's case.

Augustus himself is of course partly dependent on literature for his *fama* both in life and after-life. Or, from a more cynical standpoint, the difference between the likes of Hippolytus, Medea and Theseus (cf. 383ff.) on the one hand and Augustus on the other is that the emperor's is a *new* myth supported, propagated and immortalized through literary elaboration. Although the *princeps* has the power to relegate Ovid and to regulate his status (cf. *relegatus, non exul, dicor*, 137) and finances (cf. *insuper accedunt ... paternae ... opes*, 129–30), the fact remains that the poet retains manipulative powers of his own even in relation to Augustus: he can immortalize him, celebrating his achievements in the perspective of history and mythology (and no doubt blurring the distinction). It is, for example, to the *Metamorphoses* that the emperor is directed to find his praises sung (*vestri praeconia nominis*, 65). The poem is said to be incomplete (*sine fine*, 63), but more significantly the work is *sine fine* in the sense that it has the potential to last endlessly through time – as Ovid confidently anticipates in the last lines of the poem, which culminate in *vivam* (*M*. 15.879). At *Tr*. 2.559–60 Ovid writes of the poem

> surgens ab origine mundi
> in tua deduxi tempora, Caesar, opus.

The word *tempora* is personalized here and defined as the era of Augustan supremacy. But the era of Ovidian supremacy cannot be as closely defined; the *Metamorphoses* defies simple temporal restriction, and Ovid's Augustan *laudes* thereby acquire their own form of timelessness. Again, Ovid is implicitly defiant in the way that he turns the tables on the *princeps*, pointing to the limitations of Augustus' authority over future generations; the poet, by contrast, wields limitless power to fashion and inform the tastes of future generations.

As in various other passages, the question of how Augustus might have read lines 363–470 is raised in the mind of the reader who recognizes the discordant implications of Ovid's argument only too clearly. The most striking irony, perhaps,

THE *ARS AMATORIA* IN *TRISTIA* 2

is that Ovid's confidence in the fact that Augustus has taken the *Ars Amatoria* too seriously emboldens him to assume that the emperor will read *Tristia* 2 in the same way. If so, Ovid can exploit this Augustan reading by mischievously communicating to a sophisticated audience much more than the prima-facie sense of the words he uses, and can do so in the comforting knowledge that Augustus is unlikely to detect the implicit tone of imperial criticism and satire.

The presence of the *Ars Amatoria* in *Tristia* 2

A further argument which Ovid makes in defence of the *Ars Amatoria* is that the poem is no more corrupting than many other institutions of Roman society (277–302), including the theatres (280), the gladiatorial arena (281–2), the Circus (283–4), colonnades (285–6) and the temples (287ff.).[80] Each of these, claims Ovid, has the potential to corrupt the innocent (cf. *ludi quoque semina praebent\nequitiae*, 279–80); if the *Ars* is subject to censorship, then these places should be subject to restrictions of their own as well.

Implicit in these lines is the insinuation that Augustus is responsible for sowing the seeds of moral permissiveness (*semina nequitiae*) by encouraging public spectacles and constructing colonnades and temples. He built the temple and portico of Apollo on the Palatine (*R.G.* 19.1), the portico of Octavius (*R.G.* 19.1) and that of Livia (Suet. *Aug.* 29.4). Of the gods mentioned in lines 289–300, Augustus built temples to Jupiter Feretrius, Tonans and Libertas (*R.G.* 19.2), Juno Regina and Minerva (*R.G.* 19.2), Mars Ultor (*R.G.* 21.1) and Cybele (*R.G.* 19.2). Ovid does not, in this instance, remind the *princeps* of his part in the promotion of these institutions; but the implication of his active involvement is too strong to be overlooked – except, that is, by Augustus himself.[81] In A.D.

---

[80] The Circus, colonnades and temples are conventional places of erotic assignation in pre-Ovidian elegy; see Owen (1924), 172–3 on 283, 285 and 289–300.

[81] Cf. 509–14, where Ovid draws Augustus' attention to the dubious entertainments which the emperor himself has funded – and witnessed (*scaenica vidisti lentus adulteria*, 514). If Augustus can tolerate such scenes, how can he fail to tolerate the *Ars*?

13, four years after *Tristia* 2 was written, Augustus deposited his *Res Gestae* with the Vestal Virgins (Suet. *Aug.* 101.4), and his final text does not offer the slightest hint that Ovid's innuendoes had caused him to qualify his enthusiastic endorsement of his building programmes and gladiatorial and athletic shows. Is this yet another example, like the imperial panegyric of lines 225–36, of Ovid counting on Augustus not seeing the fuller possibilities of the poem's meaning? And yet if Ovid exaggerates the social dangers here, the more immediate implication is that Augustus has himself judged the sexual licence of the *Ars Amatoria* in an exaggerated manner which is out of all proportion to any potential harm the poem may do.

It is no coincidence, however, that in the *Ars Amatoria* Ovid recommends a number of the places listed at *Tr.* 2.277ff. as venues for meeting girls. At *A.A.* 1.67–262 he provides a full account of the hunting-grounds where young men should concentrate their efforts. Among these are the colonnades (67ff.; cf. *Tr.* 2.285–6), the temple of Isis (77; cf. *Tr.* 2.297), the theatres (89ff.; cf. *Tr.* 2.280), the Circus (135–6; cf. *Tr.* 2.283–4) and the gladiatorial contests (163–4; cf. *Tr.* 2.281–2). The places of assignation recommended to women at *A.A.* 3.387–96 are the colonnades, the temple of Isis, the theatres, gladiatorial contests and the Circus. An irony at *Tr.* 2.277ff. is of course that Ovid should try to defend the *Ars Amatoria* by pointing out that moral depravity thrives in the very places which he twice recommends as hunting-grounds in the incriminating poem. The elegiac motif of the amatory *locus* is turned on its head as Ovid's recommendations in the *Ars* are countered by a seemingly frank exposé in *Tristia* 2.[82]

But this irony can be taken further. Ovid states of the temples in lines 287–8

> haec quoque vitet,
> in culpam siqua est ingeniosa suam.

The words *in culpam* ... *ingeniosa suam* have the sense of

---

[82] Cf. Wiedemann (1975), 270: 'it does seem peculiar that he [Ovid] should repeat many of the points he had made as witticisms in the *Ars* in a work in which he is supposedly asking Augustus to pardon him for writing this *crimen*'.

'being capable of bringing a moral defect upon herself'. Ovid later uses a similar phrase in reference to his own part in bringing about his exile: in writing love-elegy, *in ... meas poenas ingeniosus eram* (*Tr.* 2.342). In the very section where he describes the places that should be avoided by any girl who is *in culpam ... ingeniosa suam*, Ovid proves to be incorrigibly *ingeniosus in suam culpam*. Consider his argument: any girl who is potentially open to moral corruption should not even visit the most exalted and venerable places of all, the temples (*quis locus est templis augustior?*, 287). In issuing this warning, Ovid recalls a poetic *locus* which he himself would be better advised to avoid – his enthusiastic commendation of such places as the theatre, Circus and the colonnades at *A.A.* 1.67–262 as well as 3.387–96. The '*in*' phrase which accompanies *ingeniosus* at *Tr.* 2.288 and 342 points to the end-product of the *ingenium*.[83] In the girl's case the result is sexual misbehaviour in Rome's holiest shrines (*culpam*, 288); the result of Ovid's *ingenium* is the *poena* of relegation (cf. 342). This parallel phraseology suggests an association which is not immediately apparent. The product of Ovid's *ingenium* is an affront to Augustus; the product of the girl's is an affront to the place than which none is *augustior* (287). We are also led to associate *culpa* (288) with *poena* (342), the severity of the latter being in a very real sense the result of the sexual licentiousness of the former. The reader does not have to be very astute to realize that the *culpa* of 288 is not entirely the girl's; it is also Ovid's, who recommends the *templa* for this purpose (cf. *A.A.* 1.77) in a way which it can hardly be to his advantage to have remembered here. It surely follows that Ovid's plea is scarcely calculated to win Augustus' sympathy; but the effect achieved by his allusiveness is once again implicit, and the full significance of the associations which Ovid creates with the *Ars Amatoria* remains dormant until activated by the reader. We

---

[83] *Ingeniosus* is found with various other constructions. Some Ovidian examples are collected by Owen (1924), 172 on line 288; add *Am.* 1.11.4 and 3.8.46 (with dative), and another example with *in* at *R.A.* 620 where *hoc* is surely accusative, not ablative as Henderson (1979), 117 takes it in his note *ad loc.* It is correctly understood at *TLL* 7(1).1521.31.

are left to wonder whether Augustus, had he actually read *Tristia* 2, would have made these associations for himself.

Equally dependent on the *Ars Amatoria* is Ovid's depiction of works written on the art of gambling in lines 471–84.[84] Why, he argues, should the *Ars Amatoria* be considered incriminating when other writings on gambling have escaped with impunity? Games of chance were considered disreputable,[85] and were forbidden by law;[86] hence the suggestion that in reminding Augustus of the *crimen* attached to gambling (472), Ovid may be alluding to the emperor's alleged enjoyment of dice-games.[87] The games enumerated in lines 473–82 – *tali* (knuckle-bones, 473–4), *tesserae* (numbered dice, 475–6), *ludus latrunculorum* (a form of draughts, 477–80) and *terni lapilli* (possibly an early form of noughts and crosses, 481–2) – reproduce those listed at *A.A.* 3.353–66, with two omissions – spillikins (*A.A.* 3.361–2) and *duodecim scripta* (probably a kind of backgammon, 363–4).[88] The context in which Ovid lists these games at *A.A.* 3.353–66 describes the attributes which a girl needs to win herself a man (cf. *turpe est nescire puellam|ludere: ludendo saepe paratur amor*, 367–8). Again, Ovid resorts to material from the *Ars Amatoria* to put forward an argument in its defence: of all the authors who have written on these games (and other pursuits listed in lines 485–92), there is no one *quem sua perdiderit Musa* (496). It is difficult not to suspect that Ovid shows a degree of tactlessness, even defiance, in drawing attention to his own enthusiastic advocacy of such games as an essential part of a young lady's

[84] The writers on gambling are unknown. Suetonius was to state that Claudius wrote a book on the subject (*Cl.* 33.2); in Seneca's *Apocolocyntosis* Claudius is condemned to playing dice in the underworld with a perforated dice-box (14–15).

[85] Cf. Juv. 11.176 (*alea turpis*) and Cic. *Catil.* 2.23 (*in his gregibus omnes aleatores, omnes adulteri, omnes impuri impudicique versantur*).

[86] Cf. Hor. *C.* 3.24.58 (*vetita legibus alea*). Plautus mentions a law against gambling (*Mil.* 164). See also Luck (1977), II 147 on 471 with Courtney (1980), 103 on Juv. 1.88.

[87] See Scott (1931), 293–6 with Gómez Pallarès (1993), 355–7.

[88] For a description of some of the games mentioned by Ovid see Austin (1934), 24–34 and (1934a), 76–82. With *neque enim nunc persequar omnes* (*Tr.* 2.483), does Ovid self-consciously announce that he has not reproduced all the games which he enumerates at *A.A.* 3.353–66?

preparation for life. But would Augustus have detected the mischievous implication implanted here?

Ovid's debt to the *Ars Amatoria* in lines 473–84 carries an additional inference. In bringing his list of games to a close, he passes over *qui ... alii lusus ... perdere, rem caram, tempora nostra solent* (483–4). Compared to the games (*lusus*) which waste valuable time, the *Ars Amatoria* – only too well remembered here – represents a form of poetic *lusus* which has a much more devastating effect on Ovid's life.[89] At *Tr.* 1.1.40 the words *tempora nostra* appear in the same metrical *sedes* as at *Tr.* 2.484 (*nubila sunt subitis tempora nostra malis*) and denote the new stage of Ovid's life in Tomitan exile. To adapt his words at *Tr.* 2.483–4, *lusus ... perdit, rem caram, tempora nostra*: Ovid's poetic *lusus* has contributed to his downfall, reducing to ruins (cf. *perdit*) that precious stage in his life when he flourished at Rome and transforming good times to bad in Pontic isolation. True, there is no compulsion to interpret Ovid's language in lines 483–4 as self-referential; but the allusive presence of the *Ars Amatoria* in the immediate context at least suggests that the time-wasting effects of conventional *lusus* are as nothing compared to the much more disastrous, personally harmful connotation which the words *perdere ... tempora nostra* have for Ovid himself. On the analogy of these parallel *lusus*, Ovid 'wasted' his own creative time on a poetic triviality (*lusus*) – and, by implication, it reflects less than well on Augustus that he should have accorded this mere *lusus* a significance quite out of proportion to its true literary status and made it the cause of Ovid's ruin.

In the light of the retrospective glance which lines 277ff. and 471ff. make towards the *Ars Amatoria*, the opening lines of *Tristia* 2 now reveal an important insight. As early as line 21 Ovid subtly foretells the part which borrowings from the *Ars* will play in its self-defence: *Musa ... quam movit, motam quoque leniet iram*. Like the beaten gladiator who returns to the arena (cf. 17), like the shipwrecked vessel which returns to

---

[89] For the *Ars* as a poetic *lusus* cf. 3.809 (*lusus habet finem*). For *ludere/lusus* as terms used to characterize love-elegy see Wagenvoort (1956), 30–42.

stormy waters (cf. 18), Ovid will defend the *Ars* in *Tristia* 2 by resorting to the very Muse which caused his downfall, and by launching arguments which ironically derive their material from the incriminating poem (277ff., 471ff.). The words *mihi res eadem vulnus opemque feret* (20) ominously foreshadow the presence of the *Ars* in *Tristia* 2, though *forsitan* (19) adds a hint of uncertainty to the unqualified force of *leniet* in 21: Ovid may not prove to be a second Telephus, his reassuring *exemplum* of homeopathic recovery in 19–20. The danger inherent in the venture may explain what we have seen in several instances to be the covert nature of the potentially mischievous Muse's presence in *Tristia* 2. When the *Musa ludens* has proved to be the *Musa nocens* (cf. *Tr.* 3.7.9), her future performances have to be more subtly managed.

Although evocation of the *Ars Amatoria* adds deft nuances to the interpretation of lines 277ff. and 471ff., its presence is at its most obvious in lines 247–50. How can Ovid be charged with corrupting married women when he specifically excludes them from his readership? Lines 247–50 reproduce *A.A.* 1.31–4, but with one slight modification: for *nos Venerem tutam* (*A.A.* 1.33), Ovid writes *nil nisi legitimum* (249). Owen's explanation of the change is partially correct: 'Ovid's purpose ... is to show that he had not transgressed the law' (cf. 243).[90] But this emphasis also draws our attention to the phrase which has been suppressed. It would hardly be appropriate to make claims for the innocence of *Venus tuta* here, when only ten lines later (261–2) it is suggested that Roman *matronae* may be morally corrupted by reading of how Venus became *Aeneadum genetrix* by lying her way into a covert and deceitful marriage with Anchises (cf. also 299–300).[91] And Ovid is saving until 377–8 the *Odyssey*'s story of her adulterous intrigue with Mars (8.266–366), which had earlier featured in the *Ars* itself (2.561–90). If, moreover, the *Ars* had been written *solis meretricibus*, as Ovid now maintains (*Tr.* 2.303; cf. *P.* 3.3.51–

[90] (1924), 162. Ovid makes the same point in the *Ars Amatoria* itself (cf. *nihil hic nisi lege remissum|luditur*, 2.599–600).
[91] For the deception see *H.Hom.* 5.75–190.

2), it would be difficult to argue for *Venus tuta* at 1.33 being other than salacious, appetite-whetting irony.

Accompanying the verbal adjustment between *A.A.* 1.31–4 and *Tr.* 2.247–50 is an adjustment in tone from subtle humour to seemingly deadpan seriousness. Consider *A.A.* 1.31–4: quite apart from the fact that Ovid may be mocking the supposed purity of Roman *matronae* by excluding them from his readership, the ritual formula is turned on its head. After Venus is invoked (cf. 30), the words *este procul* (31) introduce the familiar ritual cry in what amounts to a parody of the solemn prelude to a religious festival.[92] Such literary parody is familiar from the quasi-vatic openings of Propertius 4.6 and Horace *C.* 3.1. Ovid, the self-styled *vates peritus* (cf. *A.A.* 1.29), possibly recalls these here, but his formal parody more directly exploits the terminology used by Callimachus in the *Hymn to Apollo* (cf. ἑκάς, ἑκὰς ὅστις ἀλιτρός, 2) and Virgil (cf. *procul, o procul este profani*, *Aen.* 6.258). But whereas Callimachus and Virgil dismiss the uninitiated and ceremonially unclean (ἀλιτρός/*profani*), Ovid reverses the motif by dismissing Roman *matronae* in the same way as he dismisses readers of puritan taste at *Am.* 2.1.3 (*procul hinc, procul este, severi*). By excluding these *matronae*, Ovid wittily applies the traditional formula to ironic effect: the *profani* are his initiates. And they are not likely to be taken in by the assurance *in ... meo nullum carmine crimen erit* (*A.A.* 1.34); for it is only in the ablative *CaRMINE* that *crimen* is, in fact, to be found.

When Ovid reproduces these lines at *Tr.* 2.247–50, the wit and irony associated with their use in *Ars Amatoria* 1 go wholly unrecognized. Ovid cites them not as a clever poetic conceit but as a serious prohibition aimed at Roman *matronae*, his intention being clearly set out at 303–4 (cf. 251–2). This change of tone is more revealing about Ovid's motives in *Tristia* 2 than it is about the supposedly 'real' function of the lines in the *Ars Amatoria*. The reader of *Tristia* 2 is confronted with the poet's apparent failure to read his own poetry as the reader himself has been taught by the poet to read it. The

---

[92] Cf. Norden (1957), 204 on *Aen.* 6.255ff.

witty adaptation of religious formula and of literary allusion, the comic effect achieved at the expense of Roman *matronae*, everything which goes to form the meaning of these lines in *Ars Amatoria* 1 – all this is stripped away in *Tristia* 2 to expose the bare literalism which is not, of course, any part of their meaning in *Ars* 1, except to the reader who is ignorant of poetic allusion and indifferent to the witty application of the poetic *ingenium*. Ovid reads his own lines from within, as it were, the narrow limits of such a reader's (mis-)reading, presupposing that the reader at whom *Tristia* 2 is aimed, Augustus, will find this (mis-)reading of *Ars* 1 fitting well with his general approach to an Ovidian poem.

We have already seen various examples in this chapter which show crucial sections of *Tristia* 2 to be potentially ambivalent; they are capable of a meaning which is both literal and (often achieving the opposite effect) sophisticated in the manipulation of allusion and language. It is now possible to see more clearly that these two different kinds of meaning correspond to two different kinds of readership. One intended readership must be the addressee, Augustus, against whom Ovid makes the basic point that his condemnation of the poet is based in part on a distorted, literal reading of the *Ars*. It is to reinforce this point that at *Tr.* 2.247–50 Ovid offers what I take to be his own 'Augustan' reading of one of the funnier allusive tricks in the prologue to *Ars Amatoria* 1. The substitution of the authoritarian *nil nisi legitimum* for the witty original, *nos Venerem tutam*, itself draws attention to the kind of reading which the lines must now receive.

Ovid's other readership, however, will not only relish the fuller appreciation of the original lines in their context in *Ars* 1. They will also understand more generally the nature of Ovidian literary allusion and of the *Ars* itself as a poetic *lusus*, as well as the poet's habit of self-referential parody. Such readers will be attracted to the more sophisticated interpretation of passages which the emperor will, experience tells us, take more literally. They will also see that lines 247–50 are such a self-referential parody, the function of which is momentarily to exclude them and their sophisticated reading

from the poet–reader relationship which Ovid is constructing
here between himself and Augustus. Though in one way excluded, their presence as observers is always assumed; they are
observers both of the poet's manipulative skill and of Augustus' possible failure to appreciate it. What is more, they
are presented with Ovid's own evaluation of the emperor as
a reader of his poetry. Had Augustus actually detected and
taken offence at this Ovidian evaluation, one wonders what
kind of apologia Ovid would have offered for *Tristia 2*.

CONCLUSION

The challenge which the *Tristia* and *Epistulae ex Ponto* set before the reader is to respond to Ovid's subtle deployment of linguistic nuances which, once detected, can place the superficial certainties of the text in a different, and potentially disconcerting, light. Close scrutiny of Ovidian diction holds the key to detecting these nuances, as we have seen in the various examples examined in the previous chapters. Some brief remarks on *P*. 2.5.39–56 will serve to clarify further the nature of Ovid's verbal dexterity and the self-conscious awareness with which it is employed throughout the exilic corpus.

P. 2.5 is addressed to Salanus,[1] whom Ovid portrays as a friend of Germanicus and the latter's coach in oratory. Reacting to Salanus' instructive lead (*te dicente prius*, 45), Germanicus wins his spurs, displaying the oratorical grandeur (*nobilitas*, 56) which matches his family pedigree (cf. 55). But while Ovid pays tribute to Germanicus' eloquence, it is his own masterly use of diction that commands attention in lines 39–56. One function of this poem is evidently to advertise the distinctive artistry of Salanus' eloquence (40), but Ovid's *artes eloquiumque* are shown in the process to be equally impressive when he describes Germanicus' performance.

The hushed silence which precedes Germanicus' speech (47–8) immediately recalls the scene set for Aeneas' address to Dido and her court in *Aeneid* 2, where Ovid's *ora* (47) and *conticuere* (48) are clearly anticipated (cf. *conticuere omnes intentique ora tenebant*, *Aen*. 2.1). This connection with Aeneas is consolidated by the description of Germanicus as *Iuleo iuvenis cognomine dignus* (49), marking his descent from

---

[1] For Salanus (possibly Cassius Salanus, mentioned by Plin. *Nat*. 34.47), see Syme (1978), 88.

Iulus.[2] But a very different speech is recalled here as well. The phrase *mortaliaque ora quierunt* (47) reminds us in this context of Virgil's *et trepida ora quierunt* (*Aen.* 11.300), the words which describe the silence when King Latinus rises to make his fateful speech warning the Latins that they cannot hope to sustain the fight against the Trojans.[3] Virgil explicitly connects this speech with Aeneas',[4] and Ovid combines them both in lines 47–8 to present Germanicus as uniting in himself and his family both the Trojans and the Latins, the two warring peoples of early Italy. When Germanicus rises to speak (49–50), Ovid's simile comparing him to Lucifer is derived directly from *Aen.* 8.589–91, Virgil's gallant image of the young Pallas as he rides out to battle. At *Aen.* 8.591 Lucifer raises his 'holy countenance' (*os sacrum*) in the sky; at *P.* 2.5.49–50 Germanicus rises like Lucifer to display his *os caeleste* (53) in the sense of his 'god-like eloquence'. In his allusion to Virgil's Lucifer simile Ovid subtly modifies the Virgilian sense of *os* in an act of typically creative *imitatio*.

In the light of these Virgilian echoes, Ovid 'speaks' in these lines with the *docta vox* which he anticipates in Germanicus (cf. 52). And the Ovidian 'voice' illustrates for Salanus the very kind of subtle, allusive speech which Salanus is passing on to his pupil. It is therefore no surprise that Salanus considers Ovid's work worthy of his close attention (58), for as highly skilled practitioners of language in their different spheres they have much in common and much to offer each other in the way of mutual advice and influence (cf. 69–70). Ovid supports and illustrates the implicit comparison which he draws between poetic and rhetorical eloquence by enriching the poetic texture with a subtle display of his own eloquence at work.

[2] Cf. *Aen.* 1.286–8: *nascetur pulchra Troianus origine Caesar,|... Iulius, a magno demissum nomen Iulo.* Virgil's use of the name Iulus 'plainly reflects his wish to connect the *gens Iulia* and the imperial house of Rome with its Trojan past' (Austin (1964), 216 on *Aen.* 2.563).

[3] A similar phrase, *et rabida ora quierunt*, is used earlier when the Sybil falls silent (6.102), but it is in a shared context of the hushed expectancy before a major oration which makes the phrase at *Aen.* 11.300 relevant to that at *P.* 2.5.47.

[4] Cf. *Aen.* 2.2 and 11.301; 2.10 and 11.323; 2.13 and 11.315; 2.21ff. and 11.316.

Ovid's procedure at *P.* 2.5.39–56 is typical of his procedure throughout the exile poetry. It cannot be stressed enough that Ovid caters for a reader who is alive to the potential which poetic vocabulary has to be polysemic in its suggestiveness and interpretative possibilities. Ovid's portrayal of the Pontic environment, his insistence on his poetic decline, his claim that he writes in exile for purely utilitarian reasons, his address to Augustus in *Tristia* 2: all these exilic themes can yield a more complex, and sometimes less consistent, set of meanings, giving the appropriately initiated reader access to a literary world of paradox, ambivalence and artful ingenuity.

BIBLIOGRAPHY

(i) Standard works of reference

FGrH   *Die Fragmente der griechischen Historiker*. F. Jacoby, ed. Berlin–Leiden, 1923–58.

LSJ   H. J. Liddell and R. Scott, rev. H. Stuart Jones, *A Greek–English Lexicon*. 9th edn. Oxford, 1925–40.

OLD   *Oxford Latin Dictionary*. Oxford, 1968–82.

PIR²   *Prosopographia Imperii Romani*. 2nd edn. Berlin and Leipzig, 1933–.

RE   *Real-Encyclopädie der classischen Altertumswissenschaft*. Stuttgart, 1893–.

SIG³   *Sylloge Inscriptionum Graecarum*. W. Dittenberger, ed. 3rd edn. Leipzig, 1915–24.

SVF   *Stoicorum Veterum Fragmenta*. J. von Arnim, ed. Leipzig, 1903–24.

TLL   *Thesaurus Linguae Latinae*. Leipzig, 1900–.

(ii) Conference proceedings cited by abbreviation

Atti   *Atti del convegno internazionale ovidiano, Sulmona, maggio 1958*. 2 vols. Rome: Instituto di Studi Romani, 1959.

Ovidiana   N. I. Herescu *et al.*, edd., *Ovidiana: Recherches sur Ovide, publiées à l'occasion du bimillénaire de la naissance du poète*. Les Belles Lettres. Paris, 1958.

Ovidianum   N. Barbu, E. Dobroiu, M. Nasta, edd., *Ovidianum. Acta conventus omnium gentium Ovidianis studiis fovendis*. Bucharest, 1976.

(iii) Books and articles cited

Adamesteanu, D. (1958). 'Sopra il "geticum libellum"', *Ovidiana*: 391–5.

Ahl, F. (1984). 'The art of safe criticism in Greece and Rome', *AJPh* 105: 174–208.

Alexander, W. H. (1957). 'The *culpa* of Ovid', *CJ* 53: 319–25.

Anderson, W. S. (1963). 'Multiple change in the *Metamorphoses*', *TAPhA* 94: 1–27.

André, J. (1968), ed. *Ovide: Tristes*. Collection Budé. Paris.

    (1977), ed. *Ovide: Pontiques*. Collection Budé. Paris.

Aricescu, A. (1976). 'Le mur d'enceinte de Tomi à l'époque d'Ovide', *Ovidianum*: 85–90.

Austin, R. G. (1934). 'Roman board games I', *G&R* 4: 24–34.

(1934a). 'Roman board games II', *G&R* 4: 76–82.

(1964), ed. *P. Vergili Maronis: Aeneidos liber secundus*. Oxford.

Baca, A. R. (1971). 'The themes of *querela* and *lacrimae* in Ovid's *Heroides*', *Emerita* 39: 195–201.

Bakker, J. T. H. (1946). *Publii Ovidii Nasonis Tristium Liber V Commentario Exegetico Instructus*. Diss. Groningen.

Baligan, G. (1959). 'L'esilio di Ovidio', *Atti* II: 49–54.

Balsdon, J. P. V. D. (1979). *Romans and Aliens*. London.

Bardon, H. (1956). *La littérature latine inconnue II*. Paris.

Barthes, R. (1970). 'L'ancienne rhétorique', *Communications* 16: 172–223.

Berciu, D. (1978). *Daco-Romania*. *Archaeologia Mundi* 25. Geneva.

Besslich, S. (1972). 'Ovids Winter in Tomis. Zu *trist*. III 10', *Gymnasium* 79: 177–91.

Blaensdorf, J. (1980). 'Enstehung und Kontamination der Doppelfassung Ovid, *Metam*. 1, 544–547a', *RhM* 123: 138–51.

Block, E. (1982). 'Poetics in exile: an analysis of *Epistolae ex Ponto* 3.9', *ClAnt* 1: 18–27.

Bömer, F. (1969–86). *P. Ovidius Naso, Metamorphosen*. Wissenschaftliche Kommentare zu griechischen und lateinischen Schriftstellern. 7 vols. Heidelberg.

Borzsak, I. (1952). 'Stygius detrusus in oras', *AAntHung* 1: 459–69.

Bouynot, Y. (1957). *Ovide, livre III des Tristes, étude rythmique et stylistique*. Diss. Paris.

Bramble, J. C. (1974). *Persius and the Programmatic Satire: A Study in Form and Imagery*. Cambridge Classical Studies. Cambridge.

(1982). 'Minor Figures'. E. J. Kenney and W. V. Clausen, edd., *The Cambridge History of Classical Literature*. Vol. II. *Latin Literature*. 467–94. Cambridge.

Brink, C. O. (1971), ed. *Horace on Poetry 2. The Ars Poetica*. Cambridge.

(1982), ed. *Horace on Poetry 3. Epistles Book II: the letters to Augustus and Florus*. Cambridge.

Buchheit, V. (1966). 'Mythos und Geschichte in Ovids *Metamorphosen* I', *Hermes* 94: 80–108.

Butler, H. E. and Barber, E. A. (1933), edd. *The Elegies of Propertius*. Oxford.

Cairns, F. (1972). *Generic Composition in Greek and Roman Poetry*. Edinburgh.

(1979). *Tibullus: a Hellenistic poet at Rome*. Cambridge.

Canter, H. V. (1930). 'The figure ADYNATON in Greek and Latin poetry', *AJPh* 51: 32–41.

(1938). 'Praise of Italy in classical authors I', *CJ* 33: 457–70.

BIBLIOGRAPHY

Carrara, P. (1977), ed. *Euripide: Eretteo. Papyrologica Florentina III.* Florence.

Casson, S. (1927). 'Thracian tribes in Asia Minor', *JRS* 17: 97–101.

Castiglioni, L. (1948). 'Ulisse esemplare di virtù. Tardi echi della tradizione cinica e stoica', *Acme* 1: 31–43.

Claassen, J.-M. (1986). *Poeta, Exsul, Vates: A Stylistic and Literary Analysis of Ovid's Tristia and Epistolae ex Ponto.* Diss. Stellenbosch.

(1987). 'Error and the imperial household: an angry god and the exiled poet's fate', *AClass* 30: 31–47.

(1990). 'Ovid's poetic Pontus', F. Cairns, ed., *Papers of the Leeds International Latin Seminar* 6: 65–94. Leeds.

Clausen, W. (1987). *Virgil's Aeneid and the Tradition of Hellenistic Poetry.* Sather Classical Lectures 51. Berkeley and Los Angeles.

Coleman, R. G. G. (1971). 'Structure and intention in the *Metamorphoses*', *CQ* n.s. 21: 461–77.

(1977), ed. *Vergil: Eclogues.* Cambridge Greek and Latin Classics. Cambridge.

Conington, J. and Nettleship, H., rev. Haverfield, F. (1898). *The Works of Virgil, with a commentary.* 5th edn. 3 vols. London.

Coon, R. H. (1928). 'The reversal of nature as a rhetorical figure', *Indiana University Studies* 15: 3–20.

Courtney, E. (1980). *A Commentary on the Satires of Juvenal.* London.

(1993). *The Fragmentary Latin Poets.* Oxford.

Cunningham, M. P. (1957). 'Ovid's poetics', *CJ* 53: 253–9.

Curran, L. C. (1972). 'Transformation and anti-Augustanism in Ovid's *Metamorphoses*', *Arethusa* 5: 71–91.

Curtius, E. R. (1953). *European Literature and the Latin Middle Ages.* Bollingen Series 36. New York. Trans. of *Europäische Literatur und lateinisches Mittelalter.* Bern, 1948.

Dahlmann, H. (1975). 'Cornelius Severus', *AAWM* 6: 5–127.

Dauge, Y. A. (1981). *Le Barbare. Recherches sur la conception romaine de la barbarie et de la civilisation.* Coll. Latomus 176. Brussels.

Davisson, M. H. (Thomson) (1979). *Detachment and Manipulation in the Exile Poems of Ovid.* Diss. University of California, Berkeley.

(1980). '*Omnia naturae praepostera legibus ibunt.* ADYNATA in Ovid's exile poems', *CJ* 76: 124–8.

(1981). 'The functions of openings in Ovid's exile epistles', *CB* 58: 17–22.

(1982). '*Duritia* and creativity in exile: *Epistolae ex Ponto* 4.10', *ClAnt* 1: 28–42.

(1985). '*Tristia* 5.13 and Ovid's use of epistolary form and content', *CJ* 80: 238–46.

De Jonge, T. H. J. (1951). *Publii Ovidii Nasonis Tristium Liber IV Commentario Exegetico Instructus.* Diss. Groningen.

Della Corte, F. (1973). *I Tristi.* 2 vols. Genoa.

215

(1976). 'Ovidio e i barbari danubiani', *RomBarb* 1: 57–69.

(1976a). 'Il "Geticus sermo" di Ovidio', *Scritti in Onore di Giuliano Bonfante*, Vol. I. 205–16. Brescia.

Dickinson, R. J. (1973). 'The *Tristia*: poetry in exile', J. W. Binns, ed., *Ovid. Greek and Latin Studies: Classical Literature and its Influence*. 154–90. London.

Diggle, J. (1980). 'Notes on Ovid's *Tristia*, Books I–II', *CQ* n.s. 30: 401–19.

Doblhofer, E. (1986). 'Die Sprachnot des Verbannten am Beispiel Ovids', U. J. Stache, W. Maaz, F. Wagner, edd., *Kontinuität und Wandel: Lateinische Poesie von Naevius bis Baudelaire; Franco Munari zum 65. Geburtstag*. 100–16. Hildesheim.

(1987). *Exil und Emigration: zum Erlebnis der Heimatferne in der römischen Literatur. Impulse der Forschung* 51. Wissenschaftliche Buchgesellschaft. Darmstadt.

Dobson, B. (1974). 'The significance of the centurion and "primipilaris" in the Roman army and administration', *ANRW* II.1: 392–434. Berlin.

Dodds, E. R. (1951). *The Greeks and the Irrational*. Sather Classical Lectures 25. Berkeley and Los Angeles.

Drucker, M. (1977). *Der Verbannte Dichter und der Kaiser-Gott: Studien zu Ovids Späten Elegien*. Diss. Leipzig.

Due, O. S. (1974). *Changing Forms: Studies in the Metamorphoses of Ovid*. Copenhagen.

Dutoit, E. (1936). *Le thème de l'adynaton dans la poésie antique*. Les Belles Lettres. Paris.

Easterling, P. E. (1982), ed. *Sophocles: Trachiniae*. Cambridge Greek and Latin Classics. Cambridge.

Easterling, P. E. and Knox, B. M. W. (1985), edd. *The Cambridge History of Classical Literature*. Vol. I. *Greek Literature*. Cambridge.

Edwards, M. W. (1991). *The Iliad: A Commentary. Volume V: Books 17–20*. Cambridge.

Ehwald, R. (1884). 'Jahresbericht über Ovid Juli 1881 bis Juli 1883', *JAW* 31: 157–205.

(1887). 'Jahresbericht über Ovid Juli 1883 bis Juli 1886', *JAW* 43: 125–282.

Ehwald, R. and Levy, F. W. (1922), edd. *P. Ovidius Naso Tristium libri V, Ibis, Ex Ponto libri IV*. Leipzig.

Enk, P. (1958). 'Metamorphoses Ovidii duplici recensione servatae sint necne quaeritur', *Ovidiana*: 324–46.

Evans, H. B. (1975). 'Winter and warfare in Ovid's Tomis (*Tr.* 3.10)', *CJ* 70: 1–9.

(1983). *Publica Carmina: Ovid's Books from Exile*. Lincoln and London.

Fitton Brown, A. D. (1985). 'The unreality of Ovid's Tomitan exile', *LCM* 10.2: 18–22.

Focardi, G. (1975). 'Difesa, preghiera, ironia nel II libro dei *Tristia* di Ovidio', *SIFC* 47: 86–129.

Ford, B. B. (1977). *Tristia II: Ovid's Opposition to Augustus*. Diss. Rutgers University.

Fordyce, C. J. (1961). *Catullus: A Commentary*. Oxford.

Fraenkel, E. (1957). *Horace*. Oxford.

Frazer, J. G. (1921), ed. *Apollodorus: The Library*. 2 vols. The Loeb Classical Library. London and Cambridge, Mass.

Froesch, H. H. (1967). *Ovids Epistulae ex Ponto I-III als Gedichtsammlung*. Diss. Bonn.

(1976). *Ovid als Dichter des Exils*. Bonn.

Gahan, J. J. (1978). 'Ovid, the poet in winter', *CJ* 73: 198–202.

Galinsky, G. K. (1967). 'The Cipus episode in Ovid's *Metamorphoses* (15.565–621)', *TAPhA* 98: 181–91.

(1972). *The Herakles Theme: The Adaptations of the Hero in Literature from Homer to the Twentieth Century*. Oxford.

(1975). *Ovid's Metamorphoses: An Introduction to the Basic Aspects*. Berkeley and Los Angeles.

Gandeva, R. (1968). 'Ovide et la population de la Dobroudja antique', *Godisnik na Sofijskija Universitet Fakultet po Filologie* 62: 3–108.

Gilbert, H. (1896). 'Zu Ovidius Ex Ponto', *JKPh* 153: 62.

Goldhill, S. (1991). *The Poet's Voice: Essays on Poetics and Greek Literature*. Cambridge.

Gómez Pallarès, J. (1993). 'Sobre Ovidio, *Tristia* II, 471–92', *Latomus* 52: 372–85.

Goodyear, F. R. D. (1981). *The Annals of Tacitus. Vol. II. Annals 1.55–81 and Annals 2*. Cambridge.

Gow, A. S. F. (1952), ed. *Theocritus*. 2nd edn. Cambridge.

Gow, A. S. F. and Page, D. L. (1965), edd. *The Greek Anthology I: Hellenistic Epigrams*. 2 vols. Cambridge.

(1968), edd. *The Greek Anthology II: The Garland of Philip and some contemporary epigrams*. 2 vols. Cambridge.

Graeber, G. (1881). *Quaestiones Ovidianae. Pars I*. Elberfeld.

(1884). *Untersuchungen über Ovids Briefe aus der Verbannung*. Elberfeld.

Gransden, K. W. (1976). *Virgil: Aeneid, Book VIII*. Cambridge Greek and Latin Classics. Cambridge.

Green, P. (1982). '*Carmen et error*: πρόφασις and αἰτία in the matter of Ovid's exile', *ClAnt* 1: 202–20.

Haarhoff, T. J. (1948). *Stranger at the Gate*. Oxford.

Hardie, P. H. (1986). *Virgil's Aeneid: Cosmos and Imperium*. Oxford.

Harries, B. (1989). 'Causation and the authority of the poet in Ovid's *Fasti*', *CQ* n.s. 38: 164–85.

Hartog, F. (1988). *The Mirror of Herodotus. The representation of the other in the writing of history*. Berkeley. Trans. of *Le Miroir d'Herodote. Essai sur la représentation de l'autre*. Paris, 1980.

Hauben, F. (1975). '*Adnuo* and *abnuo* in Ovid, *Tristia* 5.10.41–2', *AJPh* 96: 61–3.

Helzle, M. (1988). 'Ovid's poetics of exile', *ICS* 13.1: 73–83.

(1988a). '*Conveniens operi tempus utrumque suo est*: Ovids *Epistula ex Ponto* III 9 und Horaz', *GB* 15: 127–38.

(1989). *P. Ovidii Nasonis Epistularum ex Ponto Liber IV: A Commentary on Poems 1–7 and 16.* Spudasmata XLIII. Hildesheim.

Henderson, A. A. R. (1979), ed. *P. Ovidi Nasonis Remedia Amoris.* Edinburgh.

Herescu, N. I. (1958). 'Poeta getes', *Ovidiana*: 404–5.

(1958a). 'Ovide, le premier poète roumain', *Fasti Pontici Ovidio poetae dicati: Acta Philologica* 1: 93–6.

(1959). 'Ovide, le getique (*Pont.* IV.13.18 *paene poeta getes*)', *Atti*: 55–80.

(1960). 'Les constantes de l'humanitas Romana', *RCCM* 2: 258–77.

(1961). 'Civis humanus. Ethnos et ius', *A&R* 6: 65–82.

Herrmann, K. (1924). *De Ovidii Tristium Liber V.* Diss. Leipzig.

Heubeck, A., West, S. and Hainsworth, J. B. (1988). *A Commentary on Homer's Odyssey. Vol. I. Introduction and Books I–VIII.* Oxford.

Hinds, S. E. (1985). 'Booking the return trip: Ovid and *Tristia* 1', *PCPhS* n.s. 31: 13–32.

(1987). *The Metamorphosis of Persephone: Ovid and the self-conscious Muse.* Cambridge Classical Studies. Cambridge.

(1987a). 'Generalising about Ovid', A. J. Boyle, ed., *Ramus: Critical Studies in Greek and Roman Literature 16. Imperial Roman Literature* I. 4–31.

(1989). Review of Knox (1986). *CPh* 84: 266–71.

Hirst, G. (1926). 'The significance of *augustior* as applied to Hercules and to Romulus: a note on Livy 1.7.9 and 1.8.9', *AJPh* 47: 347–57.

Hofmann, H. (1986). 'Ovid's *Metamorphoses: carmen perpetuum, carmen deductum*', F. Cairns, ed., *Papers of the Liverpool Latin Seminar* 5: 223–41. Liverpool.

Holleman, A. W. J. (1969). 'Ovidii Metamorphoseon liber XV 622–870 (*carmen et error?*)', *Latomus* 28: 42–60.

Hollis, A. S. (1973). 'The *Ars Amatoria* and *Remedia Amoris*', J. W. Binns, ed., *Ovid.* Greek and Latin Studies: Classical Literature and its Influence. 84–115. London.

(1977), ed. *Ovid: Ars Amatoria, Book I.* Oxford.

Hornstein, F. (1957). 'ISTROS AMAXEUOMENOS: zur Geschichte eines literarischen Topos', *Gymnasium* 64: 154–61.

Horsfall, N. (1971). 'Numanus Remulus: ethnography and propaganda in *Aen.* ix, 598ff.', *Latomus* 30: 1108–16.

Housman, A. E. (1890). 'Notes on Latin poets [II]', *CR* 4: 340–2.

(1918). 'Transpositions in the *Ibis* of Ovid', *JPh* 34: 222–38.

(1937). *M. Manilii Astronomicon Liber Quartus.* 2nd edn. Cambridge.

(1972). J. Diggle and F. R. D. Goodyear, edd., *The Classical Papers of A. E. Housman.* 3 vols. Cambridge.

Hutchinson, G. O. (1988). *Hellenistic Poetry.* Oxford.

Innes, D. C. (1979). 'Gigantomachy and natural philosophy', *CQ* n.s. 29: 165–71.

Jackson, C. N. (1914). '*Molle atque facetum*: Horace, *Satires* 1,10,44', *HSPh* 25: 117–37.

Jacobson, H. (1974). *Ovid's Heroides*. Princeton.

Johnson, J. W. (1960). 'Of differing ages and climes', *JHI* 21: 465–80.

Jones, A. H. M. (1971). *The Cities of the Eastern Roman Provinces*. 2nd edn. Oxford.

Kennedy, D. F. (1992). '"Augustan" and "Anti-Augustan": reflections on terms of reference', A. Powell, ed., *Roman Poetry and Propaganda in the Age of Augustus*. 26–58. Bristol.

Kenney, E. J. (1958). 'Nequitia poetae', *Ovidiana*: 201–9.

    (1970). '*Novavit opus*'. Review of Kirfel (1969). *CR* n.s. 20: 195–7.

    (1973). 'The style of the *Metamorphoses*', J. W. Binns, ed., *Ovid*. Greek and Latin Studies: Classical Literature and its Influence. 116–53. London.

    (1976). '*Ovidius Prooemians*', *PCPhS* n.s. 22: 46–53.

    (1982). 'Ovid', E. J. Kenney, ed., *The Cambridge History of Classical Literature*. Vol. II. *Latin Literature*. 420–57. Cambridge.

Kern, O. (1922). *Orphicorum Fragmenta*. Berlin.

Kimball Armayor, O. (1978). 'Did Herodotus ever go to the Black Sea?', *HSPh* 82: 45–62.

Kirfel, E. A. (1969). *Untersuchungen zur Briefform der Heroides Ovids*. *Noctes Romanae* 11. Bern and Stuttgart.

Kirk, G. S. (1985). *The Iliad: A Commentary. Volume I: Books 1–4*. Cambridge.

Knox, P. E. (1986). *Ovid's Metamorphoses and the Traditions of Augustan Poetry*. *PCPhS* Suppl. Vol. 11. Cambridge.

Koch, M. (1865). *Prosopographiae Ovidianae Elementa*. Diss. Bratislavia.

Kovacs, D. (1987). 'Ovid, *Metamorphoses* 1.2', *CQ* n.s. 37: 458–65.

La Penna, A. (1957), ed. *Publi Ovidi Nasonis Ibis*. Florence.

Lambrino, S. (1958). 'Tomis, cité gréco-gète, chez Ovide', *Ovidiana*: 379–90.

Lanham, C. D. (1975). *Salutatio Formulas in Latin Letters to 1200: Syntax, Style, and Theory*. Münchener Beiträge zur Mediävistik und Renaissance-Forschung 22. Munich.

Lateiner, D. (1978). 'Ovid's homage to Callimachus and Alexandrian poetic theory (*Am.* 2,19)', *Hermes* 106: 188–96.

Lawrence, D. H. (1961). '*A Propos of Lady Chatterley's Lover' and Other Essays*. Harmondsworth.

Lieberg, G. (1980). 'Ovide et les Muses', *LEC* 48: 3–22.

Little, D. (1972). 'The non-Augustanism of Ovid's *Metamorphoses*', *Mnemosyne* 25: 389–401.

Lozovan, E. (1958). 'Ovide et le bilinguisme', *Ovidiana*: 396–403.

Luck, G. (1961). 'Notes on the language and text of Ovid's *Tristia*', *HSPh* 65: 243–61.

(1967 and 1977), ed. *P. Ovidius Naso, Tristia*. Wissenschaftliche Kommentare zu griechischen und lateinischen Schriftstellern. 2 vols. Heidelberg.

Lyne, R. O. A. M. (1978), ed. *Ciris. A Poem Attributed to Virgil*. Cambridge.

(1980). *The Latin Love Poets from Catullus to Horace*. Oxford.

(1987). *Further Voices in Vergil's Aeneid*. Oxford.

Macleod, C. W. (1977). 'The poet, the critic, and the moralist: Horace, *Epistles* 1.19', *CQ* n.s. 27: 359–76.

(1979). 'The poetry of ethics: Horace, *Epistles* I', *JRS* 69: 16–27.

Marache, R. (1958). 'La révolte d'Ovide exilé contre Auguste', *Ovidiana*: 412–19.

Marg, W. (1959). 'Zur Behandlung des Augustus in den *Tristien*', *Atti* 2: 345–54.

Marsh, F. B. (1931). *The Reign of Tiberius*. Oxford and London.

Marshall, A. J. (1976). 'Literary resources and creative writing at Rome', *Phoenix* 30: 252–64.

Martin, R. (1966). 'Virgile et la "Scythie" (*Georgiques*, III, 349–383)', *REL* 44: 286–304.

McKeown, J. C. (1989). *Ovid: Amores. Vol. II. A Commentary on Book One*. Liverpool.

Merkel, R. (1837), ed. *Ovid. Tristia, Ibis*. Berlin.

Morgan, K. (1977). *Ovid's Art of Imitation: Propertius in the Amores. Mnemosyne* Suppl. Vol. 47. Leiden.

Moulton, C. (1973). 'Ovid as anti-Augustan: *Met*. 15.843–79', *CW* 67: 4–7.

Murgia, C. E. (1984). 'Ovid *Met*. 1.544–47 and the theory of double recension', *ClAnt* 3: 205–35.

Nagle, B. R. (1980). *The Poetics of Exile: Program and Polemic in the Tristia and Epistulae ex Ponto of Ovid, Coll. Latomus* 170. Brussels.

Némethy, G. (1913). *Commentarius Exegeticus ad Ovidii Tristia*. Budapest.

Nisbet, R. G. M. and Hubbard, M. (1970). *A Commentary on Horace, Odes Book I*. Oxford.

(1978). *A Commentary on Horace, Odes Book II*. Oxford.

Norden, E. (1957). *P. Vergilius Maro: Aeneis Buch VI*. 4th edn. Stuttgart.

Otis, B. (1966). *Ovid as an Epic Poet*. Cambridge.

(1970). *Ovid as an Epic Poet*. 2nd edn. Cambridge.

Otto, A. (1890). *Die Sprichwörter und sprichwörtlichen Redensarten der Römer*. Leipzig.

Owen, S. G. (1889), ed. *P. Ovidi Nasonis: Tristium Libri V*. Oxford.

(1915), ed. *P. Ovidi Nasonis Tristium Libri Quinque, Ibis, Ex Ponto Libri Quattuor, Halieutica, Fragmenta*. Oxford.

(1924). *P. Ovidi Nasonis Tristium Liber Secundus*. Oxford.

Paratore, E. (1970). 'L'influenza della Heroides sull'episodio di Biblide e Cauno nel l. IX delle Metamorfosi ovidiane', *Studia Florentina A. Ronconi sexagenario oblata*. 291–309. Florence.

Parvan, V. (1921). 'I primordi della civiltà Romana alla foci del Danubio', *Ausonia* 10: 187–209.

Pease, A. S. (1935), ed. *P. Vergili Maronis Aeneidos Liber Quartus*. Harvard.

Pemberton, R. E. K. (1931). 'Literary criticism in Ovid', *CJ* 26: 525–34.

Pérez Vega, A. (1989), ed. *Ovidio: Epistulae ex Ponto II*. Seville.

Pfister, F. (1915). 'Hat Ovid eine Gigantomachie geschrieben?', *RhM* 70: 472–4.

Pippidi, D. M. (1971). *I Grèci nel Basso Danubio dall' età arcaica alla conquista romana*. *La Cultura: Biblioteca Storica dell' Antichità* 8. Milan.

   (1977). 'Tomis, cité géto-grecque à l'époque d'Ovide?', *Athenaeum* 55: 250–6.

Podosinov, A. V. (1981). 'Ovid as a source for the history of West Pontus', *VDI* 156: 174–94.

   (1987). *Ovids Dichtung als Quelle für die Geschichte des Scharzmeergebiets. Xenia: Konstanzer Althistorische Vorträge und Forschungen* 19. Constanza.

Quinn, K. (1973), ed. *Catullus: the Poems*. 2nd edn. London.

Rahn, H. (1958). 'Ovids elegische Epistel', *A&A* 7: 105–20.

Reitzenstein, E. (1935). 'Das neue Kunstwollen in den *Amores* Ovids', *RhM* 84: 62–88.

Rhys Roberts, W. (1902), ed. *Demetrius on Style*. Cambridge.

Richardson, N. J. (1974), ed. *The Homeric Hymn to Demeter*. Oxford.

Richmond, J. A. (1990), ed. *P. Ovidi Nasonis Ex Ponto Libri Quattuor*. Leipzig.

Richter, W. (1957), ed. *P. Vergilii Maronis Georgica. Das Wort der Antike* 5. Munich.

Rosati, G. (1979). 'L'esistenza letteraria. Ovidio e l'autocoscienza della poesia', *MD* 2: 101–36.

Rosenmeyer, T. G. (1969). *The Green Cabinet*. Berkeley and Los Angeles.

Ross, D. O. (1975). *Backgrounds to Augustan Poetry: Gallus, Elegy and Rome*. Cambridge.

Sabot, A. F. (1976). *Ovide poète de l'amour dans ses œuvres de jeunesse*. Paris.

Saddington, D. B. (1961). 'Roman attitudes to the *externae gentes* of the North', *AClass* 4: 90–102.

Saylor, C. F. (1967). '*Querelae*. Propertius' distinctive technical name for his elegy', *Agon* 1: 142–9.

Schilling, R. (1972). 'Ovide et sa Muse ou les leçons d'un exil', *REL* 50: 205–11.

Scholte, A. (1933). *Publii Ovidii Nasonis Ex Ponto Liber Primus Commentario Exegetico Instructus*. Diss. Amersfurt.

Schoonhoven, H. (1992), ed. *The Pseudo-Ovidian Ad Liviam de Morte Drusi*. Groningen.

Schultz, H. (1883). *Quaestiones Ovidianae*. Diss. Greifswald.

Schwartz, J. (1951). 'Pompeius Macer et la jeuness d'Ovide', *RPh* 25: 182–94.

Scorpan, C. (1973). 'La continuité de la population et des traditions Gètes dans les conditions de la Romanisation de la Scythia Minor', *Pontica* 6: 137–50.

Scott, K. (1930). 'Emperor worship in Ovid', *TAPhA* 61: 43–69.

(1931). 'Another of Ovid's errors?', *CJ* 26: 293–6.

Segal, C. P. (1970). 'Catullan *otiosi*. The lover and the poet', *G&R* 17: 25–31.

(1981). *Poetry and Myth in Ancient Pastoral: Essays on Theocritus and Virgil*. Princeton.

Sinor, D. (1957). 'The barbarians', *Diogenes* 18: 47–60.

Skutsch, O. (1985), ed. *The Annals of Quintus Ennius*. Oxford.

Smith, K. F. (1964), ed. *The Elegies of Albius Tibullus*. New York, 1913; repr. Darmstadt, 1964.

Smith, L. (1968). 'Poetic tensions in the Horatian *recusatio*', *AJPh* 89: 56–65.

Soutzo, M. (1881). 'Coup d'œil sur les monuments antiques de la Dobroudja', *RA* n.s. 42: 287–304.

Stanford, W. B. (1963). *The Ulysses Theme: A Study in the Adaptability of a Traditional Hero*. 2nd edn. Oxford.

Stephens, W. C. (1958). 'Two Stoic heroes in the *Metamorphoses*: Hercules and Ulysses', *Ovidiana*: 273–82.

Stroh, W. (1981). 'Tröstende Musen. Zur literarhistorischen Stellung und Bedeutung von Ovids Exilgedichten', *ANRW* II.31.4: 2638–84.

Syme, R. (1934). 'Lentulus and the origin of Moesia', *JRS* 24: 113–37.

(1958). *Tacitus*. 2 vols. Oxford.

(1978). *History in Ovid*. Oxford.

(1987). 'Exotic names in Seneca's tragedies', *AClass* 30: 49–64.

Talbot Rice, T. (1957). *The Scythians. Ancient Peoples and Places*. London.

Tarrant, R. J. (1976), ed. *Seneca: Agamemnon*. Cambridge.

Taylor, J. H. (1970). '*Amores* 3.9: a farewell to elegy', *Latomus* 29: 474–7.

Thibault, J. C. (1964). *The Mystery of Ovid's Exile*. Berkeley and Los Angeles.

Thomas, R. F. (1982). *Lands and People in Roman Poetry. The Ethnographical Tradition. PCPhS* Suppl. Vol. 7. Cambridge.

(1988), ed. *Virgil: Georgics*. Cambridge Greek and Latin Classics. 2 vols. Cambridge.

Thomson, J. O. (1951). 'Place names in Latin poetry', *Latomus* 10: 433–8.

Thraede, K. (1970). *Grundzüge griechisch-römischer Brieftopik*. Munich.

Timpanaro, S. (1978). 'Ut vidi, ut perii', *Contributi di filologia e di storia della lingua latina. Richerche di Storia della Lingua Latina* 13. 219–87. Rome.

Tränkle, H. (1963). 'Elegisches in Ovids Metamorphosen', *Hermes* 91: 459–76.

Verdière, R. (1983). 'Sur deux destinataires dans les *Tristia* d'Ovide', *Latomus* 42: 139–42.

Viarre, S. (1976). *Ovide, Essai de Lecture Poétique. Collection d'Etudes Latines, Série Scientifique, Fascicule* XXXIII. Paris.

Videau-Delibes, A. (1991). *Les Tristes d'Ovide et l'Elégie Romaine: Une Poétique de la Rupture*. Paris.

Vlastos, G. (1987). 'Socratic irony', *CQ* n.s. 37: 79–96.

Vulikh, N. V. (1968). 'Ovid and Augustus', *VDI* 103: 151–60.

(1968a). 'La révolte d'Ovide contre Auguste', *LEC* 36: 370–82.

(1974). 'Ovid's Tristia and Letters from Pontus as historical source material', *VDI* 127: 64–79.

Wagenvoort, H. (1956). 'Ludus poeticus', *Studies in Roman Literature, Culture and Religion*. 30–42. Leiden.

Warde Fowler, W. (1915). 'Note on Ovid, *Tr.* III.6.8 (*Augustus et Iuppiter*)', *CR* 29: 46–7.

Wheeler, A. L. (1924), ed. *Ovid: Tristia, Ex Ponto*. The Loeb Classical Library. London and Cambridge, Mass.

White, P. (1992). '"Pompeius Macer" and Ovid', *CQ* n.s. 42: 210–18.

Wiedemann, T. (1975). 'The political background to Ovid's *Tristia* 2', *CQ* n.s. 25: 264–71.

Wilkes, J. J. (1969). *Dalmatia*. Cambridge, Mass.

Wilkinson, L. P. (1955). *Ovid Recalled*. Cambridge.

Williams, F. (1978), ed. *Callimachus: Hymn to Apollo. A Commentary*. Oxford.

Williams, G. (1968). *Tradition and Originality in Roman Poetry*. Oxford.

(1978). *Change and Decline: Roman Literature in the Early Empire*. Sather Classical Lectures 45. Berkeley and Los Angeles.

Williams, G. D. (1991). 'Conversing after sunset: a Callimachean echo in Ovid's exile poetry', *CQ* 41: 169–77.

(1992). 'Representations of the book-roll in Latin poetry: *Tr.* 1,1,3–14 and related texts', *Mnemosyne* 45: 178–89.

(1992a). 'On Ovid's *Ibis*: a poem in context', *PCPhS* n.s. 38: 171–89.

Wimmel, W. (1960). *Kallimachos in Rom: die Nachfolge seines apologetischen Dichtens in der Augusteerzeit. Hermes Einzelschriften* 16. Wiesbaden.

Wistrand, E. (1968). *Sallust on Judicial Murders in Rome. A Philological and Historical Study. Studia Graeca et Latina Gothoburgensia* XXIV. Gothenburg.

Woestyne (van de), P. (1929). 'Un ami d'Ovide, C. Julius Hyginus', *MB* 33: 31–45.

Woodman, A. J. (1977). *Velleius Paterculus: The Tiberian Narrative (2.94–131)*. Cambridge.

INDEX OF MODERN AUTHORS

INDEX OF PASSAGES CITED

228

INDEX OF WORDS AND THEMES

INDEX OF WORDS AND THEMES